Mankind United

A Cult Text

By

Arthur Bell

First published in 1936

Published by Left of Brain Books

Copyright © 2023 Left of Brain Books

ISBN 978-1-397-66561-4

First Edition

All rights reserved. No part of this publication may be reproduced, distributed, or transmitted in any form or by any means, including photocopying, recording, or other electronic or mechanical methods, without the prior written permission of the publisher, except in the case of brief quotations permitted by copyright law. Left of Brain Books is a division of Left Of Brain Onboarding Pty Ltd.

PUBLISHER'S PREFACE

About the Book

"20th century California was a prolific hotbed of new religions. One of the lesser-known of these was the 'Mankind United' cult. The primary reason this group is of interest is because of a sociological study by a scholar from Harvard, California Cult, The Story of 'Mankind United' by H.T. Dohrman, (Beacon Press, Boston, 1958), which was one of the first such studies to examine a new religion.

Founded by Arthur Bell in the depths of the Great Depression, Mankind United claimed that a huge malevolent conspiracy ran the world, (the "Hidden Rulers" and "Money Changers") responsible for war, poverty and injustice. Opposing them were the "Sponsors", founded in 1875. The Sponsors were shortly going to announce their presence, and put in place a world-wide utopia, based on universal employment, a financial system of credits, and an artificial language. The work day would be four hours a day, four days a week. However, in order to do so, they had to get massive support for their plan, promoted by the 'Pacific Coast Division of North America, International Registration Bureau.' When 200 million people accepted the Mankind United plan, the Sponsors would make their move, and within 30 days utopia would ensue.

Of course, there were no Sponsors, no International Bureau: the group was founded by Arthur Bell, never got much further than the Oregon border and never numbered more than a few thousand adherents, if that. The only true beneficiary of the group was Bell, who had several luxurious apartments and mansions, including a swinging pad in Hollywood on the Sunset Strip with an indoor swimming pool, a pipe organ and a secret cocktail bar (alcohol was forbidden to the rank and file) [Dohrman, pp. 89-90]. Bell was seen in the swankest nightclubs and was a good tipper. He received $50,000 a year in tax-free income, which adjusted for inflation would be the equivalent of nearly a million today. His devotees, on the other hand, worked in various cult businesses full time, including hotels, ranches and shops. They were paid less than $40 a month, and worked up to 16 hours a day, seven days a week, year round [Dorhman p. 59]--quite a bit more than four hours a day, four days a week as promised in this book.

The group came under surveillance during World War II. They incorporated as a church ('The Church of the Golden Rule') to obtain tax exemption. Bell made bizarre claims, including that he could be in several different places at once, and that the Sponsors had advanced technology which would allow the dead to be resurrected on a distant planet [Dohrman p. 72]. In 1951 Bell abdicated and the cult withered away completely. Unlike other groups of that time such as 'I AM' there were no successors.

This book, Mankind United, was the primary text of the cult. It was undoubtedly written by Arthur Bell. The date of publication is uncertain; the copy used here has '1937' pasted on the verso, and library entries vary from 1936 to 1938. Much of the cult income was derived from sales of this book. It is written in a turgid, repetitive style, with overuse of bold type and large blocks of capitalized text. Of interest is the description of the ant-hill dystopia that the Hidden Rulers had in store for humanity (Chapter VI), which could be straight out of a Golden Age science fiction yarn."

(Quote from sacred-texts.com)

CONTENTS

PUBLISHER'S PREFACE
FRONT MATTER 1
PREFACE 2
   OUR EARLY HISTORY AND SIXTY SUCCESSFUL YEARS OF SECRET SERVICE 7
   THE WORLD'S HIDDEN RULERS 25
   THE INTERNATIONAL LEGION OF VIGILANTES AND THE LEADERSHIP OF ETERNAL RIGHT IDEAS 39
   UNIVERSAL SECURITY, PEACE AND HAPPINESS VERSUS POVERTY, FEAR AND WAR 49
   THE GOLDEN RULE—OR—THE RULE OF GOLD WHICH SHALL IT BE? 58
   40,000 PRINCIPALITIES ONE THOUSAND MILLION SLAVES AND DEATH FOR ALL OF THE WORLD'S EDUCATED AND RELIGIOUS PEOPLES. SUCH ARE THE RESULTS WHICH WILL CONSTITUTE THE SUCCESSFUL CULMINATION OF THE CENTURY-OLD PLANS OF MANKIND'S HIDDEN RULERS 73
   SHALL JESUS—OR—JUDAS PREVAIL? 79
   CHRISTIANS WANTED! 85
   MANKIND'S SELF-APPOINTED GODS AND THE MONSTER CALLED "GREED". 91
   THE PRICELESS GIFT OF LIFE AND WHAT WE DO WITH IT 104
   SHALL WE BE MASTER BUILDERS OR MASTER MURDERERS "EXTERMINATION" OR "ECONOMIC EQUALITY"? MANKIND MUST CHOOSE 109
   LIMITLESS FIELDS OF INTEREST A "UNIVERSE" TO EXPLORE 116
   DOES OUR WORLD BELONG ANY MORE TO ONE THAN TO ANOTHER? 123
   EARNINGS—HOURS—EDUCATION GENEROUS BENEFITS AND AMPLE VACATIONS 128
   THE UNIVERSAL SERVICE CORPORATION EQUALLY OWNED—EQUALLY CONTROLLED EQUALLY BENEFICIAL 136
   BIGOTED SKEPTICISM AND INEVITABLE EXTERMINATION OR INTELLIGENT CO-OPERATION AND "ECONOMIC EQUALITY" WHICH SHALL IT BE? 161
   MANKIND UNITED-&-THE INTERNATIONAL 4-4-8-3-4 CLUB 170
   NOT A MAD DREAM 174
   CHRISTIANS OF THE WORLD! HAVE YOU THE COURAGE TO ACCEPT OUR INVITATION ? 181
   A CALL TO ARMS! AND A BRIEF SUMMARY OF THE INSTITUTE'S PROGRAM WHAT YOU CAN DO TO HELP 193

FRONT MATTER

MANKIND UNITED

.... PURPOSE ....

TO END ILLITERACY, POVERTY AND WAR. AND TO

BRING THE ASSURANCE OF LASTING PEACE

AND GUARANTEED SECURITY TO THE

PEOPLE OF EVERY NATION

Please return this book to the party from whom it was borrowed—as soon as you have finished reading it—in order that it may be lent out again and thereby be immediately placed in the hands of as many readers as possible.

Copies of "Mankind United" are now being lent—as rapidly as public cooperation permits—to 200,000,000 educated and clear-thinking men ant women throughout the civilized nations of our world. It is most important that the vital information it contains, be promulgated without delay. Due to the urgent necessity of keeping this book in constant circulation it should not be lent, to any one person, for a period of mare than three days' time.

If, after reading "Mankind United," you believe, that its mes. sage should also be brought to the attention of your friends and acquaintances, your compliance with the recommendations contained on the last two pages thereof, will be most deeply appreciated.

PREFACE

THIS book has been published by The Pacific Coast Division of The International Registration Bureau, as a means of answering the public's many questions regarding the startling discoveries and ambitious plans of the Research Department of The International Institute of Universal Research and Administration.

WHAT IS THE INTERNATIONAL INSTITUTE OF UNIVERSAL RESEARCH AND ADMINISTRATION?—WHEN AND WHY WAS IT ORGANIZED?—WHAT IS ITS PURPOSE AND WHAT HAS IT ACCOMPLISHED?

The above questions are now being asked by "thinking people" in all parts of the world, who desire to be correctly informed upon a subject which is rapidly attracting international attention.

Unless those to whom this explanatory bulletin is presented, have spent some millions of dollars in agricultural, industrial, political or general economic research, and some years of time in world travel, many of the discoveries described herein may seem difficult to believe or to accept. However, we ask the men and women who read these pages, to bear in mind that MILLIONS OF DOLLARS AND YEARS OF TIME HAVE BEEN SPENT BY OUR RESEARCH BUREAU FOR THE PURPOSE OF OBTAINING "THE FACTS" UPON WHICH ITS STATEMENTS ARE PREDICATED. These facts are the demonstrable findings of an international staff of economists and research experts, who are fully prepared to prove them to the world in the manner and at the time specified herein. Their warnings, recommendations and promises, deserve the careful consideration of the world's most "ENLIGH-TENED THINKERS," and it is primarily for them that this information has been prepared.

Inasmuch as the program of The International Institute of Universal Research and Administration, is one of almost indescribably vast extent, it would be quite impossible to impart a full understanding of its practical operations in this small volume. We therefore ask that you reserve your judgment regarding the practicability of the plans, which are but briefly described, until the conclusion of our Research Department's International

30-day proclamation and program mentioned herein. However, after you have carefully studied the following pages, you should have no difficulty in judging the "IDEALS OF SERVICE" for which we stand. If these ideals are such that you feel warranted in extending us your good will and moral support, then we ask that you most alertly guard against permitting skepticism, doubt or distrust, to enter your thought because of a possible inability to understand how the startling results we promise, can be brought to pass. Moving pictures, lectures, radio-broadcasts and printed reports, will be made available to you—"without cost"—for your examination and consideration during The Institute's worldwide 30-day program. We therefore request that you keep constantly in mind, during your perusal of this bulletin, the oft-repeated fact, that [1]"There is a principle, which is a bar against all information, which is proof against all argument, and which cannot fail to keep man in everlasting ignorance; this principle is—Contempt—Prior to Examination."

While granting us your undivided and unbiased thought during the time you are scanning these pages, it will be well to occasionally recall the present-day widely-accepted fact, that unless the industrious and clear-thinking people of this earth quickly awaken to the seriousness of world conditions, and the necessity of immediately uniting their efforts towards the establishment of an economic system capable of guaranteeing freedom from wars and constant rumors of wars, to the citizens of all nations, and also an assurance of universal financial security, employment and opportunities for self-improvement,—mankind's freedom of thought, speech and action, will soon be relinquished in favor of the autocratic rule of a small handful of dictators with ambition to rule the human race and control its destiny for their own selfish benefit, and with but slight consideration for the welfare of anyone else.

In times of stress and economic confusion, people voluntarily forfeit their rights to freedom of thought, speech and action, into the hands of almost anyone who will promise them food and the temporary provision of their material requirements. The subversive influences which have for generations been secretly in control of world affairs, and which have from well behind the scenes of government and major industries largely controlled human activities and our world's resources, have constantly sought ways and means of placing the world's citizens "under their complete and

---

[1] Herbert Spencer

absolute autocratic control." Wars have been planned and executed by them and numerous depressions have occurred solely as the result of their manipulations, in order that through the effects of fear and despair, mankind might willingly relinquish their birthright of freedom into the hands of those able,—through political avenues,—to temporarily provide the necessities of life.

It is the purpose of this bulletin to partly uncover the causes of the present depression, and the method by which it is being continued in preparation for another world war; a war the principal object of which will not be "profits," but instead, the extermination of some four hundred million (400,000,000) of the world's educated, religious, and intelligently industrious citizens.

The following pages also describe the many discoveries and carefully prepared plans of the Research Department of The International Institute of Universal Research and Administration, and the means by which their acceptance and use, by not less than two hundred million(200,000,000) clear-thinking men and women, will not only prevent the approaching civilization-destroying war, but also, without bloodshed or revolution, disband the world's armies and navies, and literally change their cannon and swords into ploughshares; plans by which wars and rumors of wars will not only cease to be, but will never again come within the power of human beings to plan or cause.

Finally, you will learn of steps now being taken, which will guarantee every man, woman and child on earth,—during this and all future generations,—lifelong financial independence,—the development of individual talents,—leisure,—and literally unlimited opportunities for free world travel and self-improvement.

Lincoln reminded the American people that "A house divided against itself cannot stand," and he preserved the unity of a great nation. The Research Department of The International Institute of Universal Research and Administration, requests the privilege of offering to the people of our age, a 30-day program of its discoveries. Discoveries which will bring about the rebuilding of the nations of the earth, and will force mankind to answer two profoundly important questions; the answers to which will spell either the doom of one more civilization,—lost through human bigotry, selfishness, cruelty and greed,—or will usher in and permanently establish universal peace, security, confidence, and "A United International Brotherhood." Mankind today have the privilege of accepting one of two alternatives: First—to permit the world to continue "arming to the teeth" and preparing day and night for war and the legalized murder of over four hundred million (400,000,000) of its educated citizens, or—Second—to encourage two hundred million (200,000,000) clear-thinking industrious men and women to form into one vast Universal Service Corporation and Protective Association, capable of guaranteeing every man and woman on this earth, a lifetime of financial independence, freedom of thought, speech and constructive action, and powerful enough to put an end to the causes of both war and poverty. It should not be difficult for you to decide upon the second alternative after reading the following pages, inasmuch as we neither ask you to take risks nor to make sacrifices of a dangerous or hazardous nature, yet we offer you an opportunity for which billions upon billions of people have prayed throughout all of the countless centuries of human history.

Again permit us to remind you that the following brief explanation of discoveries, plans and recommendations, will only enable you to pass judgment upon the "Ideals" of the revolutionary world-wide movement which this bulletin describes, and that you must not expect to find sufficient information herein to fully explain the many features relative to the practical operation of the International Business facilities to which we refer,—any more than you would expect a volume of this size to enable you (without previous preparation or experience) to comprehend the numerous factors relative to the construction of a great locomotive or its operation. However, you will gain a glimpse of the magnitude of the program of The International Institute of Universal Research and Administration, and you will be led to form a conclusive judgment, and an acceptance or rejection of the "Ideals" for which it stands. If those ideals are acceptable to you, and if you believe that our world has a sufficient number of efficient executives,—highly-trained and expert workers,— enough inventions, machinery and unused resources—("IF UNSELFISHLY and INTELLIGENTLY CO-ORDINATED")—to uproot poverty and guarantee financial security and abundant leisure, to every man, woman and child on this planet, then we ask that you bring The Institute's 30-day program to the attention of your friends and acquaintances.

In order that you may more readily retain a clear understanding of the subject matter contained herein, we strongly recommend that you arrange to read this bulletin during not to exceed a three-day period. It will require a total of approximately seven hours of your time.

The International Registration Bureau
Pacific Coast Division
Publishers

PLEASE NOTE:

The frequent use herein, of the words "Bulletin" and "Explanatory Bulletin," when referring to this volume, has been adopted because of the fact that the contents hereof constitute the first of a series of official proclamations or "Bulletins" which are to be released to the public by the Research Department of The International Institute of Universal Research and Administration. The remainder of said series will be released during our 30-day program which this book fully describes.

GIVE INSTRUCTION TO A WISE MAN, AND HE
WILL BE YET WISER: TEACH A JUST MAN, AND
HE WILL INCREASE IN LEARNING.

—Proverbs 9:9

OUR EARLY HISTORY AND SIXTY SUCCESSFUL YEARS OF SECRET SERVICE

ON December 25th, in the year 1875, a small group of generous and deeply sincere men and women met for the purpose of dedicating their lives and their fortunes to the establishment of a world-wide commercial organization which would, by its "works" as well as its "words,"—fittingly commemorate the birth of mankind's greatly beloved exemplar and way-shower—Christ Jesus.

He,—in memory of whom the Christian era is dated,—taught men that "The Kingdom of Heaven is at hand,—and not afar off," and that they might enter it at any time they were willing to obey the Golden Rule, and to live in peace and brotherly love, dealing with one another as they would be dealt with. He knew that our world's resources and its glorious attractions existed in limitless inexhaustible abundance and that they had been placed here for the happiness and equal use of all mankind. He knew that there was no need for rivalry or greedy competition.

That mankind might be persuaded to prove Jesus' promises and to practically apply them on a world-wide scale, and in all branches of human relationships, and that there might be erected to His memory a monument capable of exemplifying the "Spirit," as well as the "Letter," of His teachings, this little group of men and women pledged their lives, and their combined fortunes of over sixty millions ($60,000,000.00) of dollars, to the establishment of an organization which would devote its resources and the energies of its members, to a discovery of the basic causes of world-wide poverty,—wars and human suffering.

The program they had determined upon, was quite unlike any ever before attempted. They proposed to deal, not with results or effects called Poverty and War, but with their causes, and if need be to spend their entire fortunes and lives in a world-wide investigation and preparation of plans for the annihilation of what they believed to be humanly directed causes of mankind's endless fears, insecurity and suffering.

They had become convinced that poverty, ignorance, superstition, fear, hate and war were largely, if not entirely, the effects of such humanly directed causes, perpetuated century after century by those individuals who found it financially profitable to do so, and who had reached such—a point of moral idiocy that they no longer considered the sufferings of their victims.

In no way could the men and women who gathered together that Christmas Day, be classified as visionary impractical idealists, although the vision which had gradually dawned in the thoughts of each one of them during a period of many years, could only have been the out-growth of the highest form of unselfed ideals. If we were permitted to mention the names of some of the members of that little group, they would be instantly recognized by the well-informed people of every civilized nation on our earth today.

They each had experienced extreme poverty in earlier years and their attainment to positions of wealth and prominence had not been by visionary dreaming, but by exercising intelligence, industry, and an unyielding determination to break the shackles of such slavery. However, success had not dimmed their memories, or caused them to forget their tortures of hunger and privation, nor the fact that hundreds of millions of men, women and little children were still hungry and poorly clad—and tens of millions of them dying of starvation and exposure each year.

And so, on that Christmas Day, in the year 1875, a world-wide organization was formed and given a name. A name which for over fifty-eight years was to be known only by the members of that group, and their immediate co-workers, but a name which throughout all of future human history will stand as a beacon light of progress, forever reminding the men and women of every age, that the Universe itself is their home, and that there will never come a time when men will be able to say that they know all there is to know, and that there is nothing new to explore or to discover. For never will the Research Department of The International Institute of Universal Research and Administration cease making discoveries of which the human race should be informed, nor cease from striving to be worthy of its name's significance. It will never reach the stage where it has wholly fulfilled its mission to the human race, of serving those whom its founders considered as their brothers and sisters, and desired to benefit. It will never cease growing, nor enlarging its capacity to serve.

The major purpose of The International Institute of Universal Research and Administration was to be the discovery and application of ways and means by which the "Golden Rule" might be "Practically" applied in all human relationships, in order that poverty and wars would no longer occur, and men might learn to live in peace and happiness, in this gloriously beautiful world home of ours. That men might learn to enjoy its abundant resources,—which belong equally to us all, their eyes need only be opened to the inexhaustible nature of the needful or desirable things of life placed here on our earth in such endless variety by our Creator. To open men's eyes to the needlessness of poverty and war, and to prove to them the availability of the earth's limitless resources, this was the task to which The Institute's founders had set their hands.

People who have spent less time, effort or money in economic research, may not yet be willing to heed the warnings which some of The Institute's discoveries necessitate, nor to believe the promises which other discoveries so filled with hope, now justify. Those who are willing, not only to heed our Research Department's warnings and act in accordance with its recommendations, but also to believe and accept its promises, will be able,—(when they are sufficient in number),—to awaken the intelligent right-thinking people of the world in time to prevent another war; a war which is internationally planned by the world's War Lords and actual Rulers for the purpose of exterminating the educated and religious inhabitants of the civilized nations, and of permanently enslaving those who are not slaughtered during this world-wide holocaust of deadly gases, poisons, death rays and searing flames.

The sparks which would release these forces of extermination—would be scattered during the years 1935, 1936 and 1937. By October 1937, enough war equipment would be in use, throughout the nations of the earth, to bring about the complete extermination of over four hundred million (400,000,000) of the world's educated and religious classes.

If the Institute's warnings are heeded and its recommendations accepted quickly enough, there need be no civilization-destroying war, but instead, mankind will experience an era of freedom, security and luxurious abundance of the needful and desirable things of life such as have never before been available to even the world's wealthiest or most fortunate citizens. We are prepared to prove that poverty is perpetuated and wars are fought "solely" for the profit of those who control the world's financial structure.

Men are not inarticulate beasts of the field, incapable of voicing their protests against injustice and needless poverty, nor are they handicapped by the limited intelligence of an ostrich which hides its head in the sand in order that by not seeing approaching danger it may believe itself protected and safe. Intelligent creatures need not hesitate nor be afraid to bring out from under cover the forces of greed, insane ambition and cruelty, which have for so long a time enslaved the human race. The control by these soulless, unfeeling task-masters, expressed as insane dreams of conquest, (by a few individuals whom mankind have unwisely permitted to grow wealthy and influential), can be broken with no more difficulty than that which would be experienced by herds of cattle in overcoming the puny influence of their herders, if they but recognized the strength of their own combined numbers.

On that December Day, long years ago, the founders of The International Institute of Universal Research and Administration (to whom we shall hereafter refer as "Our Sponsors"), were fully aware of the truth of the above statement. It was due to their recognition of the fact that the human race was living in needless bondage to these task-masters of greed and insane ambition, that they pledged their combined wealth of over sixty millions of dollars to the establishment of a great "International Research Bureau," in order that the facts pertaining to the specific nature of this bondage, and the truth regarding the limitless quantity and variety of the world's resources, might be brought—with adequate supporting proofs—to the attention of the intelligent right-thinking people of our world.

Our Sponsors believed, (and their Research Department has since proven), that the principal known resources of the earth had been systematically withheld from mankind's use for many centuries, by a world-wide organization composed of a small group of families in possession of fabulous accumulations of wealth, which they were using to gradually pauperize and enslave the human race. They also believed that these people, through an organization, and an executive board, (to which we shall hereafter refer as "War Lords" or "The World's Hidden Rulers," and its "Money Changers"), possessed complete control through their followers and satellites, of the political parties, governments and major utilities and industries of every civilized nation on earth, and that every revolution or war of any consequence, during the past number of centuries, had been planned and executed under their direction, either for the purpose of financial gain or to safe-guard or strengthen their political strangle-hold upon the world and its citizens. Our Sponsors further believed that revolutions and wars were planned and executed by these subversive influences for the two-fold purpose of perpetuating poverty and of killing off the healthiest males of the human race, each century, in order that the followers and satellites of these Hidden Rulers might more readily exercise their control over the world's resources and its peoples.

They knew that this organization of Hidden World Rulers had at its disposal hundreds of billions of dollars in wealth, consisting of gold, silver and jewelry accumulated during thousands of years, by families, organizations and governments over which it had gradually gained control; and that this incalculably vast accumulation of wealth was under the complete unsupervised jurisdiction of an executive board consisting of men who had dedicated their lives and talents to furthering the plans of its original organizers. Age-old plans to eventually exterminate the world's religious and educated classes, and to destroy its educational, religious and humanitarian institutions, (inasmuch as they constitute the principal forces attempting to overthrow poverty and war), and to place in their stead, an organization composed of these maniacs,—or their descendants or heirs, permanently in control of the human race and the resources of our earth. These insanely ambitious moral idiots, (believing that they or their descendants will some day have principalities of their own, and thousands of personal slaves at their beck and call), willingly lend themselves to the furthering of such a program.

Our Sponsors believed that when a member of the executive board of this organization of Hidden World Rulers passes on, that the remaining members, in order to maintain the necessary quota of executives, select one of their most trusted and ambitious agents to take the place of the deceased, and that for hundreds of years, the subversive plots of this powerful and well hidden group have been successfully approaching the time when the world's educated and religious classes are to be exterminated.

Our Sponsors also believed that there was no possible way of thwarting these plots, other than to replace gold and silver as the world's medium of exchange and basis of currency and money, with some form of money which could never be accumulated in large quantities by any individual or group of people, nor spent by anyone other than the one to whom it was issued. They believed that in no other way could the world-wide stranglehold of the "Hidden Rulers" be broken, since their thousands of years of accumulations of gold, silver, jewels, and other easily stored forms of wealth, had finally reached the point where their complete and absolute control of world governments would soon enable them to bring about the permanent enslavement of the human race through the avenues of war.

As a result of former discoveries, it was believed that two great wars would be fought. Although each of them would be conducted on a world-wide scale, the first one would be planned and executed for the dual purpose of pauperizing the peoples of the earth and of testing out the potential slaughtering capacity of the war machinery which the "War Lords" planned to use in their final war of extermination a few years later. Furthermore, their news-collecting and dispensing agencies would he fully tested and experienced in the promulgation and dissemination of the necessary "Fear and Hate-Generating Propaganda" required for the successful execution of any great war. At the conclusion of the first war, all necessary data would be collected by all nations in reference to any improvements required in the construction of their final war machine, including the publicity facilities as well as the actual munitions, armaments and necessary machinery with which to slaughter vast numbers of human beings. Thereafter, a number of years would be devoted to perfecting their plans and equipment, and further impoverishing the substantial class of the world's citizens and its trained workers in order that the necessary Poverty, Fear, Bitterness and Hate, (which constitute the human fuel upon which the war propaganda machine must feed), would provide an acceptable cause for revolutions and wars in the minds of the citizens of the world's major nations.

Religious, racial, and class antagonisms and hatreds, would in the meantime—through carefully prepared propaganda—be fully inflamed, and the people of these various groups be crying out to be allowed to tear at each other's throats like so many hate-incensed and ravenous wolves. With such preparations, the world's Hidden Rulers would experience but little difficulty in causing their final war of extermination. With every nation fully armed and equipped, on the pretext and seemingly laudable grounds of self-defense, it would be childishly simple to ignite the fuse which would set off their bombs and cannon, and bring about the slaughter of the hundreds of millions of men, women and children whom they desire to exterminate. [1]

In no other way than by murdering the educated and religious classes of the world's population, could these "Hidden World Rulers" hope to bring about the final destruction of their two greatest enemies to permanent and complete world control; namely, Mankind's Educational Systems and their Enlightened Religious Institutions.

On December 25th, in the year 1875, although each, of the men and women—who had met together for the purposes previously referred to—had conducted extensive individual investigations, they had been able to only partly obtain the necessary substantiating data, but they had, nevertheless, become convinced that the subversive influences we have described not only existed but were rapidly consummating their program to enslave the human race. The World War of 1914-18, and subsequent events, constitute at least partial proof of the accuracy of their early conclusions.

Centuries ago, Columbus believed that there was a land across the sea. He not only did not know whether or not this was so, but in addition to his own uncertainty even the most highly educated people of his day ridiculed and persecuted him for this belief. Nevertheless, he searched for the land which his intelligent convictions persuaded him existed, and finally he found it. He no longer just believed that it was there, but he knew and could prove his claims to even the most skeptical of his former tormentors, if they would but listen to his testimony or gaze upon the evidence which he had gathered.

The founders of The International Institute of Universal Research and Administration had even greater reason for their belief that the world's resources existed in such vast abundance and variety that each member of the human race could have over one hundred times as much as he had formerly enjoyed, without exhausting these resources during a period of millions of years. They were also equally convinced that greed, selfishness and cruelty bred into the hearts of men by the world's false system of private profits, utterly unscrupulous competition, and its civilization-

---

[1] Without widespread public co-operation our organization can—at this time—do no more than to temporarily delay this catastrophe.

destroying theory of the "Survival of the Fittest," had given birth to, and nurtured, cruel and insane ambitions in the minds of men, until at that time there existed a group of fabulously wealthy individuals with neither souls nor scruples, who had become moral idiots dreaming of owning the world and enslaving its peoples.

The Institute's founders did not know, in the year 1875, that their beliefs were provable, but the results of previous years of research had convinced them that they were. By the year 1919,—almost forty-four years later, after spending millions of dollars of the money they had donated to the service of humanity, and years of their lives, they no longer just believed but instead, just as in the experience of Columbus in verifying his convictions, they also had searched and found irrefutable evidence and proof of their convictions. They no longer just believed—they knew!!! Not only had they proven their theories (which we have previously described herein) to be correct, but also much of an indescribably startling nature. Even those to whom the evidences and proofs were presented in the form of pictures, photostatic copies of contracts, agreements, and plots for the enslavement of the human race, found it difficult to believe that human beings could become such swinish monsters. And none but those who had seen our Research Department's pictures and authenticated hope-inspiring reports of the world's vast inexhaustible resources, inventions and facilities for a world-wide system of quantity production and equality of distribution of the necessities and luxuries of life, could believe that such limitless abundance could possibly have been kept hidden from the human race for so many thousands of years.

Without the proofs before them, but few men or women would be willing to believe the statement of The Institute's Research Department, that "Mankind United"—within a period of "months"—could not only forever uproot the causes of war and poverty, but that they could usher in such an era of peace, security and luxurious abundance of the necessary or desirable requirements of mortal life, that no one would be obliged to work over four (4) hours a day, four (4) days a week, eight (8) months each year, to earn a salary of not less than $3,000.00 per year, irrespective of nationality, color, religion, education, training or ability. Pensions of $250.00 per month could be given to all those who had worked a total of 11,000 hours or who were sixty (60) years of age or over, and desired to retire from active routine duties; also similar pensions for those who were incapacitated and unable to work.

Without such proofs it would sound fantastic to claim hat free transportation during vacation periods to any part of the world—free education, and free development of talents—could be made available to every man, woman or child on earth, and many of these benefits enjoyed within less than ninety (90) days after the acceptance of the plans and recommendations of our Research Department by not less than two hundred million (200,000,000) of the intelligently industrious class of the world's population.

Because of mankind's inherent distrust of each new idea presented to them, and their age-old resistance to progress, (and because of the fact that the proofs gathered by our Research Department would require a library of hundreds of books to adequately describe), a plan for imparting these findings to the world's civilized peoples, in a manner which would overcome their distrust and win their support, was finally adopted by the executive board of The International Institute of Universal Research and Administration in the year 1919.

The problems which confronted Our Sponsors, when it became necessary to determine upon ways and means by which to place their astounding discoveries in the hands of the world's intelligent and right-thinking people, seemed almost insurmountable. For it must be borne in mind that the men and women comprising the Research Department of The Institute, had been obliged to surround their activities with the utmost secrecy, to prevent detection by some one of the thousands of spies retained by the world's Hidden Rulers. Our Sponsors had successfully evaded detection during many years by the simple expedient of individually remaining wholly unknown in connection with any research activities of an international nature, and of obtaining any necessary information through carefully selected, highly intelligent and trustworthy individuals, who had been appointed through agents for their respective tasks, and who were never permitted to know the name nor the identity of their actual employer.

Each of the men and women who had gathered together on that Christmas Day, in the year 1875, and each of those who had later been invited to become members of The Institute's Research Department, had agreed that if any one of them should ever be suspected of being engaged in activities adverse to the plans and interests of the world's War Lords and Hidden Rulers, that such a one would immediately sever his or her connection with the Research Department of The Institute. Also that none of them would ever divulge the name or the identity of any other member of the group, nor acknowledge their connection therewith, even to the members of their own families or their most intimate acquaintances or associates. They agreed that they would never grant such information to anyone during their lifetime, and that even though they might be forced to submit to forms of torture which would cause their death, they would still keep these vows. They further agreed to never invite anyone to join the Research or Administrative Staff of The Institute, until all of the members thereof had unanimously voted in favor of extending such an invitation, nor until the one who had thus been elected to membership, fully agreed to abide by the rules of conduct and caution which the nature of The Institute's activities required. Needless to say, the selection of a new member for their group was preceded by extensive investigations into the character, dependability and courage of such a one. Finally they had agreed that should their Research Department develop inventions or make discoveries of commercial value, that such inventions or discoveries would under no consideration be used by The Institute or its organizers for their own financial gain, inasmuch as such activities might thereby lead to The Institute's detection by the world's subversive influences.

Each member of the Research Department of The International Institute of Universal Research and Administration, is pledged to the service of the human race without hope of personal profit or remuneration of any kind, nor in fact, even recognition. These men and women seek no honors or benefits of any nature whatsoever for their services. Only by waiving all possibilities of financial gain or public acclaim, could they have even hoped to succeed in making the discoveries they sought, or to complete the plans for the establishment of an economic system capable of saving the world from the horrors of war and ultimate enslavement by those who plot the destruction of the educational and religious institutions of our civilization.

Our Sponsors have obtained the necessary proofs and they no longer "Just Believe," "They Know" that illiteracy, superstition, ignorance, poverty and war are planned, directed and perpetuated for the purposes of financial profit, personal power, and control over the resources and peoples of our earth.

They have also learned that the earth's resources are so limitless in variety and quantity, and civilization's mechanical developments and inventions more than adequate for the production of such an abundance of the necessities and luxuries of life, that the entire human family could live on a scale of luxury exceeding even that now enjoyed by the world's so-called wealthy families.

Our Research Department gradually learned that many idealistic, "but perfectly practical plans" for the alleviation of human suffering and the establishment of an economic system capable of permanently guaranteeing mankind against both war and poverty—have from time to time been developed and presented to the human race throughout the centuries. But one and all, they have wholly failed to uproot the actual causes of poverty or war, and the numerous other "Humanly-planned Sources" from which mankind's ceaseless woes emanate—for, One and All, they have been built around "Human Personality" and a publicly known founder or leader. Therefore, all that has ever been necessary for those in control of world affairs to do, in order to keep mankind in bondage, has been for them to get rid of the leaders, and they have thereby invariably gotten rid of any movements which might in time have developed the strength to oppose their rule.

The destruction of any movement for the relief of human suffering, or which might ultimately bring an end to war and poverty, has always been accomplished by the world's subversive forces in one of four ways;— namely, either by intimidation, bribery, flattery or assassination.

Our Sponsors had learned of the futility of even attempting to uncover the malignant world-wide causes of human suffering by attempting to openly appear as the leaders of a movement to eradicate these evils. The only possibility of their success rested in the source of the information released to the world, and the names or the identities of those who obtained such information, remaining permanently unknown.

The paramount necessity of "Absolute Secrecy" was quite apparent to each of those who comprised The Institute's sponsors, for they had learned that the secret service departments of the information agencies controlled by the world's "Hidden Rulers" contained considerably over 10,000 highly trained and well-paid spies, devoting their entire time to the task of supplying information concerning the activities of the peoples of all nations, and the relationship of such data to the activities of the departments employing them.

Having learned that the vast wealth of the world's "Money Changers" (its "Hidden Rulers") enabled them to readily destroy any movement adverse to their interests—(if they could discover its sponsors and its headquarters or the sources of information from which its plans had been evolved)—our Research Department, shortly after its formation, undertook to discover the exact reasons for the failure of many thoroughly practical plans which had, from time to time, been presented to the human race for the prevention of wars and the cure of poverty. Any one of a number of these plans, if universally adopted, would immediately have succeeded, but they had never been allowed to get beyond the "Discussion" stage. Our Research Department had to know the reason for these failures, in order that it might thereby guard against their repetition in its own experience.

It soon learned that one of four (4) methods are always used by the world's Hidden Rulers. Since any movement at its inception can be destroyed by destroying its leader or obstructing his activities, the subversive forces always resort to one of the four (4) methods to which we have just referred. First they try Intimidation, either through the avenues of ridicule or direct Threats. Should intimidation fail, then they next attempt to Bribe the originator of any plans adverse to their interests, if they think he can be reached in that way. One of these two methods usually succeeds. However, if both fail, then for a time the plans of the organizer or leader are "Aided" until he has gained a following. After that, the glorification of his personality and a program of "Ceaseless Flattery" is systematically conducted, until he becomes thoroughly convinced that he is indeed a super being and deserves the praise and adulation of everyone with whom he comes in contact. It is not long thereafter until he has quite forgotten his ideals of service, and desires only to add to his own prestige. His appetite for adulation and flattery develops so rapidly that he has but little time left in which to accomplish any "constructive" results. He is quite too busy feeding his ego, and thenceforth the "Money Changers" have nothing to fear from him.

If this third method does not succeed, the fourth and last one they use has never, throughout hundreds of years, failed to accomplish the result they desire. If a movement is gaining too much headway, and a leader's ideals of service and his plans for uprooting the causes of war or poverty seem to be succeeding in spite of interference, then the fourth method is used—

"Assassination." This last method has invariably destroyed any movement which depended upon the motivating influence of a human leader for its success.

Countless practical plans, quite able to end both war and poverty, have been presented to the human race by generous, brilliant and deeply sincere men and women. Yet, not one has ever been allowed to progress beyond the "Conversational or Discussional Stage," for all have had a known originator or human leader, who could be thwarted or put out of the way at will.

The Sponsors of The International Institute of Universal Research and Administration fully realized that the only method by which the plots of the world's "Hidden Rulers" could ever be uncovered and brought to the attention of mankind, and the only way by which a plan capable of ending war and poverty would ever be established, would be for those who originated it to remain beyond detection. They knew that no plan to assure peace and happiness to the human race could ever succeed unless the source which provided information to the public, and those responsible for its continuous and uninterrupted release—"Remained Unknown," and thereby beyond the murderous reach of the agents of such subversive influences.

Those who control the world's governments, and its political and industrial structures, and who plan the early extermination of its most enlightened citizens, do not waste their time fighting the followers of a movement; "they deal not with effects but with causes." "To destroy a movement, they destroy its leader;" but they cannot destroy a program built upon the indestructible foundation and leadership of an "Idea" instead of a person. Therefore, our Sponsors determined upon "a grouping of ideas," which would constitute a form of leadership "without any known headquarters or personal leaders to attack;" yet fully capable of ultimately bringing to pass the establishment of an organization with sufficient world-wide influence to uproot and destroy the age-old power of the satellites of selfishness and greed, and those who are now the world's "Hidden Rulers."

A program capable of accomplishing this result and with its headquarters and leaders permanently beyond the reach of the world's subversive forces, was conceived of and adopted by the Sponsors of The International Institute of Universal Research and Administration in the year 1875. The proof that they have been fully successful in guarding and protecting their activities, is the fact that the headquarters and the identities of The Institute's founders and research experts are—"Sixty years Later"—still unknown. The wisdom of this cautious policy is evidenced by the further fact that those who have been appointed to impart The Institute's discoveries to the world and to carry out their program, are now rapidly reaching the culmination of their plans for the successful establishment of a world-wide Co-operatively-owned Universal Service Corporation. An internationally-owned business corporation, powerful and influential enough to permanently prevent any further wars and, for all time to come, to end the rule of those influences of selfishness and greed, personified by people who keep the human race in endless poverty, and—for purposes of financial gain—subjected to utterly needless bloodshed and ceaseless suffering.

During Our Sponsors' many years of preparation for the fulfillment of their plans, and for the establishment of an organization universally influential enough to carry them forward to ultimate success—the most important requirement was a well-equipped Research Department with a staff of experts comprising the most talented available members of each major branch of human endeavor. Exact information—"Facts," not "Theories"—constitutes the only foundation upon which any "lasting" accomplishment can be erected.

To destroy the influences which keep the human race in constant bondage to age-old humanly perpetuated foes, such as war and poverty, it would be necessary to discover the source or sources from which they emanate. It would also be necessary to know exactly, "How"—"What" and by "Whom" they are fed. In other words, to discover the organization or organizations, the materials or elements, and the method or methods responsible for the perpetuation, century after century, of these monstrosities and destroyers of human security and happiness.

Finally, after completing such discoveries—if they were to be of any value to the human race—it would be necessary to perfect a program capable of destroying these enemies and preventing the appearance at some later date of similar ones.

To establish a world-wide economic system in which there would be no room left for either war, poverty, or those who condone them, there was but one plan which could possibly succeed. The production and distribution of the necessities and luxuries of human life would have to be conducted by a profit-sharing, equally-owned, worldwide corporation, on such a vast and efficient scale that no man, woman or child in any part of the world would be denied anything essential, or constructively desirable, for his or her happiness, security or advancement. To bring such universally needed results to pass, would require the whole-hearted tireless efforts of the world's most out-standing and experienced experts and leaders, selected from every branch of human activity, and from every corner of the globe. In addition, such people would be obliged to remain wholly unknown to the world; not only when conducting their investigations and perfecting the plans for their great "Universal Service Corporation," but also permanently thereafter.

If they were to successfully guard against the dangerous influences of jealousy, envy or pride, which might strike at their achievement through the avenues of religious, racial or class antagonisms, it would be necessary that not even the members of their own immediate families ever be allowed to know the identities of those who would constitute The Institute's Research or Administrative Staffs.

At such a time as their plans were fully consummated, neither their own families, their relatives nor descendants, must ever be given the opportunity to expect or receive special favors, privileges or recognition, inasmuch as an economic system based upon the "Golden Rule" and a "Brotherhood of Economic Equality," must provide no room for the "glorification" of human beings or "hero-worship." Although men may respect and gratefully appreciate a worthy human accomplishment, they should worship and glorify God,—not one another.

In other words it was necessary that the members of the Research and Administrative Department of The International Institute of Universal Research and Administration, be composed of men and women possessing not only exceptional qualities of intelligence, together with outstanding executive experience and ability, but also a deeply sincere willingness to serve the human race without hope of financial gain or public recognition or glory, but to do so in exchange for no other reward than the satisfaction which the successful performance of a worthy accomplishment might bring to them.

Towards the close of the year 1919, after a period of forty-four (44) years of continuous effort and an expenditure of many millions of dollars—the Sponsors of The Institute had—(although but gradually)—finally succeeded in completing the formation of a group of executives and Research Experts capable of carrying their original and unaltered program on to its ultimate fulfillment.

During these years, the little group which had gathered together on that Christmas Day so long ago, had drawn ceaselessly and generously upon their talents and the experiences of their successful careers, as well as upon their personal fortunes, in order that the organization they had founded might become so firmly established and so thoroughly and so correctly informed upon the matters to which they had dedicated their lives, that before the advancing years could too greatly reduce their ranks, they would have fully removed all elements of uncertainty or possibilities of failure.

Not only had they made many startling discoveries of incalculable value to the human race—in behalf of our own as well as future generations—but they had also carefully and wisely replaced those of their number who had passed on.

By the end of the year 1919, the Research and Administrative Departments of the Institute had been gradually increased to a total executive force of two hundred (200) people. Selected exclusively from the ranks of men and women who had experienced extreme poverty in their earlier years, but who had proven their qualifications and practical abilities by their successful careers and individually acquired fortunes, this group of two hundred (200) research experts and executives possessed ample qualifications for the accomplishment of the purpose for which they had voluntarily dedicated their lives when the opportunity to do so had been extended to them. It was agreed that until after the end of the year 1936, (at which time their program would be approaching its culmination), a Research and Administrative group of exactly two hundred (200) members would be maintained. Should one of their number pass on, a selection of a man or a woman of similar qualifications to those of the deceased would be made, subject to the "Unanimous Agreement" of the remaining members. The one thus selected would be subject to the same irrevocable pledges, and would be voted upon in the same manner as had each of the group of two hundred (200) chosen during the previous years.

This Executive Board, (to whom we shall continue to refer as "Our Sponsors"), therefore at this time consists of two hundred (200) practical, successful and widely experienced experts and authorities, selected from the agricultural, mining, manufacturing, merchandising, banking, transportation, educational and religious groups of leaders, of the world's most advanced civilized nations.

During the past sixteen (16) years, while waiting for world events and mankind's qualities of thought to reach the point where the authenticity of The Institute's warnings would be self-evident and its recommendations universally understandable, our Research Department has carefully checked, tested and proven the value of each of its discoveries, revolutionary mechanical inventions, policies and contemplated plans of procedure developed during their many years of preparation.

All is now in readiness for a world-wide "Free" 30-day program, during which time The Institute's well-guarded sixty years of discoveries and carefully prepared recommendations will be freely offered to the human race. In two-hour programs repeated day and night, twelve times each twenty-four hours, five days each week, this ambitious international proclamation of warnings and recommendations will be freely given to the two hundred million (200,000,000) clear-thinking men and women throughout the nations of the earth, to whom we are now extending our invitation.

At the conclusion of said thirty-day program, a worldwide election will be conducted and an international vote obtained upon one hundred (100) separate measures, which The Institute will at that time offer to the intelligent right-thinking members of the human race for their acceptance or rejection.

Although no effort has been made to either embellish, elaborate or treat in full detail The Institute's discoveries, and the various aspects of a subject which will require a thirty-day use of moving pictures, radio broadcasts, and much in the nature of charts and supporting statistical reports to comprehensively impart, nevertheless the following pages of this Bulletin are intended to outline a number of the humanly-planned causes of war and poverty, and the basic principle upon which any program for their correction must be established. It has been rightly stated that a carefully-prepared picture can supply as much information as the use of ten thousand words. It can therefore be readily understood why we request that the public postpone its opinion of our claims and recommendations until the conclusion of our free 30-day program, which will—(with the use of moving pictures and other modern and efficient methods of presentation)—provide information which would otherwise require the publication of many hundreds of volumes of highly technical reports. However, a careful reading of this Bulletin will provide sufficient data for those who are unbiased, to form at least a partial opinion of the character, motives and ideals, of those who constitute The Sponsors of this world-wide movement.

THE WORLD'S HIDDEN RULERS

INASMUCH as the power of the world's subversive influences—its "Hidden Rulers"—consists primarily of their vast century-old accumula-tions of gold and silver, and the fact that such metals constitute the basic element supporting the money structures of all civilized nations, no program could possibly succeed which failed to take this major fact into consideration, or which failed to sponsor the universal adoption of a wholly different and unaccumulative form of currency. It has been the boast of the agents of these "Hidden Rulers," that it has seldom been necessary to assassinate any of the world's so-called financial or political leaders, for only infrequently do they find one they cannot either intimidate, flatter or "Buy". However, it occasionally takes a little more money to buy some than others. Therefore, since the "Gold and Silver" reserves under the direct control of these "Hidden World Rulers," at this date exceed those of even the combined governments of the earth, it should not be difficult to understand—with the financial structure and money exchanges of every nation completely under their influence—why every government on earth is today directly or indirectly, wholly and entirely controlled by them; nor to understand why this condition exists, irrespective of the name or nature of the political parties which the public naively vote into office.

Believing that by the use of their vote, they are thereby having some voice in the administration of their country's business and consequently in matters which directly affect their own lives, the world's citizens pay very little attention to what actually takes place in the political affairs of their respective nations, until finally, they lose either their lives through war, or their financial security and happiness through a subtly-planned, and expertly-executed depression.

In recognition of the frequently destructive power of misused wealth, all clear-thinking men and women are aware of the fact that the moneys of the world must be established on a basis other than gold or silver, before the human race can even hope to break its present shackles and bondage to war and poverty, or to prevent its ultimate and complete enslavement to those whose vast accumulations of these metals enable them to hold mankind in endless bondage.

Inasmuch as the age-old curses of illiteracy, ignorance, superstition, autocratic domination, war and poverty, constitute the principal sources of profit for those who have for centuries governed the affairs of the human race, mankind can expect neither peace nor security, until the people whom greed and insane ambition have turned into moral idiots, are no longer able to control the governments and resources of the earth, through accumulations—century after century—of its gold and silver.

Those who are familiar with the manipulations of the international stock exchanges and banking systems of the world, can readily understand how the possession of vast accumulations of gold and silver would enable the individuals in whose hands they rested, to completely dominate and control the lives of men.

With the power to increase or decrease the value of stocks, real estate and the prices of food, clothes and other human necessities at will, through the mediums of carefully planned revolutions and wars together with periods of both national and world-wide depressions, a monopoly of the earth's principal resources and a direct but well hidden control of the financial policies, and therefore the governments of the world's major nations, have been maintained century after century. Mankind will have little or no opportunity to resist this domination as long as gold and silver are enthroned as the world's basis of currency, and as the gods which it worships.

The human race, without realizing it, expends literally its entire efforts and the fruitage of its talents, inventions and progressive developments, merely adding to the wealth and strangle-hold over human life already possessed by those who control the moneys and mediums of exchange required by men in their business transactions with one another. For centuries men have worked, not for themselves and their families, but for the world's "Money Changers,"—its "Hidden" though "Actual" Rulers.

When carefully analyzed it is found that for centuries over ninety-seven (97) out of every one hundred (100) families in the world have expended their entire talents and energies without having received even the barest necessities of a well-rounded life, in payment for their efforts. Although men have continuously been made to feel that the "Private Profit System,"—evolved by the "Money Changers,"—provides everyone with an equal opportunity for compensation and advancement in proportion to his or her respective talents, nevertheless, well planned and expertly executed wars and depressions have always stolen these rewards from them.

The cunningly planned plots and slavery of the "Private Profit System" become self-evident, when we realize that the world's "Money Changers"—through the avenues of revolutions, wars and periodical depressions—get back most of the money they pay out in salaries or business profits to others. They readily retrieve such expenditures through the profits of revolutions, wars—carefully planned unemployment, depressions, continuous and ever-increasing taxation—royalties from the control of major patents—the manipulation of industries and stocks—wheat and food exchanges—together with the almost religiously encouraged money savings of the world's thrifty population, deposited for so-called "safe-keeping" in the "Money Changers'" centrally-controlled international system of banks and "so-called" trust companies. Their method is really quite simple, since all they require to assure their success, is an attitude of indifference on the part of the public, and this mankind themselves generously provide.

Revolutions and wars, together with world-wide poverty, and its endless cycles of depressions and unemployment, comprise the broadest channels through which the "Hidden Rulers'" constantly growing accumulations of gold, silver and jewelry, flow into their treasuries.

When people are out of work and hungry, they will sell not only their old gold, silverware and jewelry but also "their services," for little or nothing, in order that they might thereby obtain food. To bring about such conditions of dire need it is only necessary for the "Money Changers" to cause what the world calls "A Depression". Being in complete control of the international money and credit structure, they need only shut off the flow of credit to the business men, farmers and other employers of human labor,—shut down the major industries of the world,—(most of which they either partly, or entirely control), start calling in the thousands of loans made through their banks and other credit avenues,—manipulate the stock and bond exchanges in such a manner that thousands of banks fail and are forced to close their doors, and the "Money Changers,"—with but slight inconvenience thereafter,—quickly "gather up" the previous few years of so-called "prosperity" savings, accumulated by millions of thrifty people all over the world. It is not long, by the application of such methods, before they have retrieved whatever surplus funds the industrious workers, farmers and business men have gradually accumulated from their "seemingly" generous salaries or business profits.

Those whose savings are not taken through bank failures and other occurrences of a similar nature, are forced—(by means of unemployment)—to gradually use up their surplus funds.

When enough people have been thrown out of work and are no longer able to buy the output of those of the world's factories which may still be continuing to operate, nor to purchase the produce of the farms, then these agricultural and industrial institutions are likewise forced to cease hiring men and women. Soon their surplus stocks are disposed of at whatever they can get for them, in (what has become through lack of buyers),—a rapidly declining market, and they also are left entirely at the mercy of the world's "Money Changers". As soon as it is known that practically all surplus funds have been exhausted, then any loans or mortgages against these people or businesses are called in for payment. Knowing that such people have no funds with which to pay off their loans, the farms and businesses belonging to them are then taken over by these "Money Changers," through their satellites and agents, to be disposed of in accordance with their program for retrieving any accumulations of jewelry, gold or silver, gathered by the world's population during the previous generation, and of gaining control of the new inventions, discoveries, patents, resources or properties, which may be of benefit to them in the exercise of their continued domination over the affairs of men.

When the business, professional, industrial, agricultural and employee groups have, through the process of a long drawn-out depression, been forced to use up whatever form of savings they may not have already lost through bank failures, or some other premeditated form of robbery, they are next obliged to draw upon their emergency reserves of stocks and bonds which they have gradually accumulated through their industrious efforts, frugality and self-denial. Since by that time, few but the very rich have any money left with which to buy even the necessities of life, (to say nothing of such "luxuries" as stocks and bonds), there is, consequently, but very little market for these securities, which have been so carefully put away for the "rainy day." Inasmuch as there are only a few buyers, and therefore little demand, it is not long before the holders of these securities offer them at a reduced price to anyone who will buy. The day soon arrives when those who formerly were not wise enough to sell, are obliged to reduce their prices still further, until stocks and bonds which they purchased at a unit price—let us say, of $10.00—from the "Money Changers"—(through their satellites, the international system of stock exchanges, banks and "so-called" trust companies),—they are very happy to sell back to them at a unit price of $5.00. However, waiting their time, it is not long before the "Money Changers" through their world-wide agencies are able to buy back these securities at not only as low as $5.00, $3.00 or $1.00 per unit, but almost in exchange for a loaf of bread,—if people by that time have become hungry enough to make such sacrifices of their resources.

Men who have lost their homes and have no money with which to buy food, will gladly consent to the passing of local, state or national measures, granting their respective governments the right to issue millions or even billions of dollars in bonds, with which to provide food, clothes and homes for those who have been deprived of such necessities;—knowing these facts, the "Money Changers" soon find that they are quite able,—as the result of their carefully planned depression, to further strengthen their hold upon the governments and industries controlling the lives of such people. In fact, since there are by that time none who are able to underwrite such bonds, (and thereby provide the money with which to feed the unemployed),—other than the financial institutions controlled by these subversive influences, they not only succeed in "Stealing" the most desirable homes, businesses, farms, and properties of the people of an entire nation, and are enabled to buy back stocks or bonds for a few pennies,—which they formerly sold for many dollars per unit,—but they also receive as a reward of their careful plans and financial manipulations, a mortgage upon the resources of an entire nation and the labor of its citizens and their descendants, for generations to come.

In case you should be tempted to believe that people should be grateful to them for buying these bonds,—and thereby providing the money with which to feed and clothe those in need during the depression,—let us remind you that such bonds are purchased with the very money which belonged to the people themselves, but which the "Money Changers" had stolen from them through bank failures, property foreclosures, depreciated bonds, stocks and property values, so carefully premeditated and arranged.

Not only have they thereby succeeded in stealing the peoples' money but also through the medium of endless taxes for the repayment of such bonds and interest, they have likewise caused them to mortgage their future earnings and even the earnings of their descendants.

In the meantime, these manipulators of the world's economic structure,—"its Actual, though Hidden Rulers,"—succeed, not only in acquiring the new inventions, discoveries or properties and other resources they may desire to control, but simultaneously,—through the curtailed production of food and other necessities of human life,—the prices of such commodities are gradually increased until those who control the sources of supply, are able not only to hire labor at their own figure, but also to sell the products of such labor at any price they may determine upon for their profit. Considered from all angles, a depression is certainly a most profitable form of manipulation for those in control of the world's major reserves of gold and silver, and the moneys based thereon. The fact that tens of millions of men, women and little children are obliged to suffer pangs of hunger, exposure, and the loss of the homes for which such men and women may have worked the greater part of their lives, does not cause the slightest concern to those whose only thought is the accumulation of more and ever more of that which they worship as their God;—the only "trinity" to which they ever bow down—"Money," "Power" and "Influence."

And so we find that that which the world has glorified as its greatest stimulant to human progress,—"THE COMPETITIVE PRIVATE PROFIT SYSTEM,"—has once more betrayed its followers into the hands of those who many long centuries ago originated it as a means by which to extract the fruitage of mankind's achievements of brilliancy, genius and industry, without compensation; always holding out the "bait" of "personal profit or financial gain,"—yet knowing that they would never have to pay,—it has been childishly simple for the people who control vast sums of the world's present form of money, to get what they want "without ever losing the bait."

Another broad avenue through which the world's "Hidden Rulers" retain their control over human affairs, and at the same time add to their wealth, is that which carefully planned and executed revolutions and wars provide. Although human lives and grief-stricken broken hearts are the materials they use in these manipulations, their financial gains and increased gold and silver reserves are none-the-less gratifying to them. In addition they thereby also reduce the danger of ultimately being overthrown, inasmuch as their slaughter, each century, of the healthiest, strongest and most courageous males throughout the various civilized nations of the earth, effectually removes a source from which a vigorous and fearless opposition might some day be formed.

The method by which revolutions and wars are brought to pass for the profit and continued reign of these subversive influences, will be but briefly touched upon in this Bulletin. However, during the world-wide free, thirty-day program, by the Research Department of The International Institute of Universal Research and Administration, which is more fully described in the last chapter hereof, a complete exposé of the methods used during many centuries by the world's "Hidden Rulers," through which mankind have been kept in ceaseless bondage, will be placed in the hands of the clear-thinking, intelligent men and women of every nation.

Through the avenues of propaganda the "Hidden Rulers" create either hate or fear in the hearts of the people of various groups or nations, and thereafter with but little difficulty, impress such people with the necessity of spending vast sums of money, through bond issues by their governments, for "defensive" (?) armaments and munitions of war, for what they are pleased to call "Preparedness" against the attack of some neighbor nation. At the same time, such neighbor nation is impregnated with similar qualities of either hate or fear and persuaded to spend thousands of millions of dollars, that its people may likewise build up a defense against the attack Iof the nation, which they themselves,—(according to their neighbor's propaganda),—are supposed to be preparing to attack. Through this method, the people of the entire world are persuaded to part with their earnings and business profits, down the avenues of taxation, in order that their respective nations may be well prepared against the attack of other nations, who are likewise preparing—not for wars of aggression—but,—(so they think),—for purposes of defense. Without this ceaseless flow of hate and fear-generating propaganda, there wouldn't be even one man or woman out of each million citizens of any one of the world's civilized nations, who would have the slightest desire to wage a war of aggression against the people of any other country.

Unless they are deliberately influenced otherwise, human beings in all civilized parts of the world are primarily peace-loving creatures, concerned with their own personal advancement and the happiness of their families through normal avenues of industry and the development of individual talents—not through murdering someone against whom, by the wildest stretch of their imagination, they can have no logical reason for any feelings of antagonism.

Inasmuch as the industries controlling the production and sale of armaments and munitions of war are largely, if not entirely, dominated by the "Money-exchange" structure to which we have referred, most of the huge profits from these industries flow directly into the pockets of those who manipulate the thoughts, emotions,—and thereby, the governmental expenditures of mankind.

By causing wars on the pretext of requiring room for expansion,—or possibly for the much more idealistic purpose of "Ending all Wars,"—the armaments and munitions which have thus been sold are thereby destroyed, and must of course be "quickly" replaced because of the imminent danger of another war, "as we are told." We are led to believe that a war of aggression is being planned by a nation which has been preparing for many years to destroy our people and steal our resources, whereas the fact of the matter is, that most of these "demoniacal human beings,"—(as they are pictured to us),—have probably never even "heard" of our country, or if they have, we mean only a name and a few lines on some world map to them. They are quite too busy trying to make a living, and trying to find just a little normal and deserved happiness for themselves and their families, than to be giving any thought to whether they like or dislike us.

With but few exceptions, there has never been a revolution or a war which would ever have been fought, had not some individual or small group of ambitious and usually insanely cruel and morally depraved human beings, devoted their efforts and resources to stirring up either "fear," "bitterness" or "hate" in the hearts of people whom they desired to use as cannon fodder.

It is doubtful if there has ever been a war which has ever benefited anyone other than those who planned and executed it, in order that they might thereby gain wealth, power or glory for themselves. The "only exceptions" to this statement, would be the revolutions or wars fought to gain personal liberty, freedom of speech and religious freedom, or in order that men might be allowed to form governments which would enable them to enjoy privileges withheld from them by their former tyrannical rulers.

However, our Research Department will prove during its international 30-day program that even the worthy institutions of liberty could have been established without having had to, at any time during the past two hundred (200) years, resort to bloodshed or violence, had those who desired the enjoyment of "life, liberty and the pursuit of happiness," been willing to stand together and express as much unity of purpose in the exercise of intelligently industrious efforts in behalf of the production and equal distribution of the necessities and luxuries of life, as they were willing to "emotionally expend" in venting their bitterness and hate on the fields of battle.

Had the mothers, sisters and wives of those who fought for liberty, been willing to make as many sacrifices in the building of an economic system patterned after the "Spirit" as well as the "Letter" of the "Golden Rule," established upon the foundation of "Economic Equality;" and had they been willing to sell their jewels and melt up their silverware to produce the machinery and equipment for the accomplishment of such a result without bloodshed, in the same manner in which they were willing to make such sacrifices that they might buy uniforms, guns, bullets and swords to send their men folk out upon the fields of battle to be slaughtered or maimed, then no wars during the past two hundred (200) years would have been necessary, even for the noble ideal of "liberty." Nor would the world's Napoleons, and others of their ilk, ever have had the opportunity of causing the murder of millions of men, and the broken hearts and lives of countless millions of mothers, sisters, wives and helpless little children, century after century.

With the establishment of a world-wide system of production and distribution, based upon "Economic Equality" and the spirit of the "Golden Rule," there would be no room nor opportunity for private profit in conflict with the welfare of the majority. Personal ambitions would have to take the form of improved individual abilities, and the development of constructive talents, rather than the accumulation of money or the development of one's egotistical conviction of his own superiority to others. Serving one another,—one for all and all for one,—would take the place of self-glorification, and public acclaim would come, not upon the battlefield for having proven one's self a "better killer" than another, but instead, a "better doer" of deeds of service for the happiness of one's fellowmen, as well as one's self. Those with kindly thoughts, generous hearts and noble aspirations in the direction of human welfare and service, would be the ones who would win the respect of their fellowmen. There would be no room for either the qualities of a bully or those of a swine, and it would be the sons of Beelzebub instead of the sons of men who would have no place to lay their heads.

It is such an economic system, built around the ideal of brotherly love and a desire for the development of constructive individual talents, which Our Sponsors seek the privilege of establishing. Wars are fought for the purpose of stealing mankind's wealth, but we ask no sacrifice of jewels or other prized possessions of the men and women to whom this invitation is being extended. We ask only that the world's right-thinking people permit us to form them into an organization two hundred million (200,000,000) strong; that there may be established a Universal Service Corporation, "equally owned," and its production and distribution of the luxuries and the necessities of life, "equally enjoyed," by not only the people who comprise this group, but likewise all others in any nation of the earth, as soon as they are willing to comply with the ideals of service and brotherly love which its charter will embody.

We ask only that these two hundred million (200,000,000) people combine their influence and the vast buying power of over one thousand million ($1000,000,000) dollars per day, which they now possess, and that they use this readily available power in such a manner that a great "Universal Service Corporation,"—equally owned and equally controlled by each of their number,—may be internationally established, and through its influence succeed in bringing to pass the world-wide acceptance of a type of money which can never be accumulated by any one person or group of persons in large enough quantities to cause either wars or poverty.

We ask only that a type of money be thereby established which will,—for all time to come, stand as a monumental symbol of indignation against a system which could unresistingly condone the slaughter of eight million (8,000,000) of its healthiest and finest young men under the sanctions of war; a system which could condone such legalized murder merely in order that a handful of "swinish moral idiots" might thereby derive over one hundred and twenty billions of dollars ($120,000,000,000.) of the world's wealth, to add to their already bulging treasure chests. Over fifteen thousand dollars ($15,000.00) in net profits for each man killed was,—during the last world war,—their reward for possessing large enough accumulations of gold and silver to influence the thoughts of the entire "so-called" civilized world into consenting to war.

We ask only that the right-thinking people of every land consent to the adoption of a form of money based on a different standard of value than either gold or silver, in order that the age-old power and influence possessed by the world's subversive forces, may thereby be forever taken from them; and that no person or group of persons ever again be allowed to gain enough wealth, influence or power to buy, bribe or mesmerically direct the thoughts of others through avenues of propaganda, into agreeing to the legalized slaughter of human life,—to which men have been taught to consent,—under the name of "War."

Is it too much to ask that the Biblical commandment, "Thou Shalt Not Kill," be "Practically," instead of "Theoretically," embedded—not only into the hearts of men, "but also into the very structure of the economic system tinder which they live"???

Is it too much to ask that a "Monetary System" which permits the accumulation of such vast sums of wealth in the hands of a few men that they have the power to change this Biblical commandment into one which is by law engraved into the very statutes of every civilized nation, and reads,—"Thou Shall Not Kill " unless thou first payest a financial profit to thy masters—the "Money Changers,"—be forever destroyed, and in its place, that there be erected a world-wide economic structure which will take into consideration the fact that many men are as yet "but little more than animals," in their character development; a system which will therefore no longer provide a reward for greed and selfishness by supplying the opportunity for such qualities to profit by a monopolistic control of the world's money?

Is it too much to ask that an economic structure be erected which will take into consideration "the fact that human beings are frequently selfish, greedy and cruel"—and which will therefore make it impossible for men, when expressing such qualities,—to harm anyone other than themselves; a system which will enable men to "Reap what they Sow," and "quickly enough" to soon learn the desirability of sowing "Generosity" instead of "Selfishness,"—"Sharing" in place of "Greed," and "Kindness" instead of "Cruelty"?

The "One and only Reward" which the Sponsors of The International Institute of Universal Research and Administration ask in exchange for the voluntary gift of over sixty millions of dollars ($60,000,000.) of their personal resources, and the many years of their lives which they have devoted to this task, is that the "Profits of War" and the "Profits of Planned Depressions," be forever prevented from recurring in any nation on this earth.

Our Research Department is well prepared to provide a proven method by which this result can be immediately accomplished. It has completed the plans for the early establishment of a great world-wide and equally owned "Universal Service Corporation," capable of producing and distributing the necessities and luxuries of life for the entire human race. A world-wide equally owned co-operative commercial organization which will, for all time to come, be powerful enough to stand as a fortress for the human race, successfully preventing either wars, depressions, unemployment or poverty.

No share in the ownership of such a corporation, other than that which each member of the entire human race will receive, is asked or could be accepted under the terms of its charter by any of the Sponsors or Official Associates of The Institute. After many years of ceaseless research and preparation, they ask only the privilege of being permitted to irrefutably prove the wisdom and vital importance of its immediate world-wide formation.

It should not be difficult to understand why a great commercial co-operative equally-owned Universal Service Corporation, capable of producing the requirements of life for the entire human family is needed, nor why the moneys of the world must by such means be established on a basis other than gold or silver, before the human race can even hope to break its present shackles of war and poverty, or to prevent its ultimate complete enslavement.

Inasmuch as world-wide war and poverty constitute the principal sources of profit for those who have for centuries governed human affairs, mankind can expect neither peace nor security, until those whom greed and insane ambition have turned into moral idiots, are no longer able to control the governments and resources of our earth, through their possession of large quantities of "money."

The Research Department of The International Institute of Universal Research and Administration, has developed a type of money which can never be accumulated by any person or group of persons, for it will have value as currency only for a limited period of time after the date it is issued, and will possess such value only when spent by the person for whom it is specifically prepared. No other type of money will ever overcome war or poverty; both of which are perpetuated solely for financial gain, and by those who have enough money to cause depressions and financial panics, by their manipulation of the political, financial and commercial enterprises of the world, and the influence with which to force any or all of the world's various governments into revolutions or wars whenever, they may so desire.

Only a type of "limited use money,"—the accumulation of which would be of no value to anyone,—can ever permanently uproot the impulses of greed and mad ambition; for it has been truly stated that if all of the money in the world could be divided equally among those who comprise the human race, over seventy-five per cent (75%) of it would,—"within less than one (1) year,"—be, either in the pockets or completely under the control of three per cent (3%) of the world's citizens, and the remainder of the human race would again be as poverty-stricken as it had been before.

If the "Golden Rule" is to be used as the measure of men's relationship with one another, then an economic system must be established which will protect those who have not as yet learned how to protect themselves, and a medium of exchange must be adopted which will protect the world's population against "Greed," "Selfishness" and "Dishonesty," until such qualities no longer exist in human nature.

The International Institute of Universal Research and Administration, during a period of over sixty (60) years, has been quietly but ceaselessly engaged in perfecting plans for the accomplishment of this result, believing that its success would at the same time, disclose the means by which to destroy the strangle-hold of those whom greed and mad ambition have turned into mankind's swinish and depraved "Money Changers and Masters."

Intelligent men and women do not place matches, knives or guns in the hands of those who are known to be insane, neither should they permit the continuation of an economic system which breeds greed, selfishness and insane ambitions in the hearts of men; a competitive private profit system which rewards their qualities of selfishness, arrogance and indescribable cruelty, by freely granting them the power of life or death over their fellow beings, through encouraging their control of the world's money and consequently food, clothes, homes, and in fact the very lives of men; nor a system which makes men forget there is a God, and instead, rewards those who dream of becoming gods themselves, and encourages them to seek the power to send millions of men "tearing at each other's throats," incensed with meaningless hate, planted in the hearts of the various combatants through the money-controlled mediums of propaganda scattered throughout the various nations, yet owned and controlled by a single group of men whom mankind have so richly rewarded with their money. Possessing the financial power and influence with which to cause continuous revolutions, wars or depressions for their profit, the greed of these "Money Changers" has become so great, that they no longer feel either pity or compassion towards the millions of human beings whom their war machines slaughter, nor the slightest concern over the tens of millions of grief-stricken, broken hearts and broken lives, which their money-mad ambitions have caused. Insane lust for money soon becomes their god, and constitutes the only feeling they know.

To dethrone "the god of this world" nurtured by a private profit system which has caused literally all of the wars and most of the poverty suffered by the human race, and to place in its stead a world-wide system of production and distribution, with the "Golden Rule" as its cornerstone,—with guaranteed lifelong financial independence for all, and permanent universal security and peace as its structure,—this is the sole purpose, for which our Research Department was formed and the result which it is now endeavoring to accomplish.

THE INTERNATIONAL LEGION OF VIGILANTES AND THE LEADERSHIP OF ETERNAL RIGHT IDEAS

FOR countless centuries men have accepted or have rejected a new idea,—not from the standpoint of whether the "Idea" was good or bad, but from the wholly unintelligent and idiotically illogical basis, of whether they have or have not liked the one who presented it. If such a one is a member of their profession, their lodge, or their church, and if he is as tall or as short, as stout or as slender as they may prefer; and if the sound of his voice is pleasant and the color of his eyes attractive, then of course the idea he is presenting must be all right, and so from this profound basis of judgment, —they accept it. There is but little thought given as to whether the "Idea" itself is "Right" or "Wrong,"—"Good" or "Bad," since human personality has constituted the major factor in its consideration.

However, if the one who seeks to present a plan or an idea to a group of men, does not happen to "Belong," or if such men do not like the way he combs his hair, there is but little chance that they will even take the time to listen to his idea.

After spending over sixty years of time,—more than sixty millions of dollars ($60,000,000.00).—and (in the case of a number of the members) virtually a lifetime in testing and demonstrating irrefutably and conclusively each and every one of their discoveries,—The Sponsors of The International Institute of Universal Research and Administration have had no intention of giving any person or group of persons, the opportunity of judging their program for the establishment of a much needed new worldwide economic system, from the standpoint of the color of its Sponsors' hair.

Three plus three equals six, and is just as true and just as useful in the working out of a mathematical problem when stated by a "tall man," as it is when stated by a "short one."

It is high time those of us who think that we are intelligent creatures, started using the priceless faculties of "Reason and Independence of

Thought " with which we have been divinely endowed. It is high time that we learned to "judge righteously and justly," and when an idea is presented for our consideration, that we judge its value by whether we think it is good or bad, right or wrong, and not by whether we like or dislike the personality of its sponsors, or the method of its presentation. Therefore, due to the previously described necessity of keeping the headquarters of The Institute and the identities of its Sponsors permanently unknown, and of the further desirability and wisdom of having its program and recommendations judged entirely upon their merits, a plan was finally adopted which complies with both of these requirements, and which will be able to win the requisite approval and support of the two hundred million (200,000,000) intelligent, right-thinking men and women, who will comprise our world-wide audience.

By the year 1919, our Research Department had learned that there was but "One Solution" to mankind's age-old problems of war and poverty, and that the concerted action of not less than two hundred million (200,000,000) people would be required for the successful application of this One and Only Solution. They had learned that The Institute's Sponsors and their organization's headquarters must remain permanently unknown or this plan could not possibly succeed. "The only leaders the world could ever be allowed to know, would have to consist of the Institute's ideas and ideals."

Towards the end of the year 1919, the first steps in the accomplishment of these results were taken. It was decided that some hundreds of young men and women would be chosen from all parts of the world, representing each of the major nationalities and racial groups, each of the agricultural, industrial, professional, vocational and cultural groups, and that they would be selected only after they had proven their sincere desire to serve mankind. These young men and women, chosen for their qualities of morality, integrity, courage, industry, perseverance, education and intelligence, would be invited to undergo a fifteen year part-time course of instruction under the supervision of the various members of The Institute's Research Department. Before being accepted they would each be shown a number of the Research Department's discoveries, to assist them in forming what would be the most vital decision of their entire lives. They would then be offered the opportunity of participating,—as a member of The International Legion of Vigilantes,—in the consummation of The Institute's program. Provided however, that in consideration of the privilege of instruction and the opportunity of directly participating in this great world program, that they would sign a contract of which the following is a partial outline:

1st. To the best of their understanding and ability, to obey the Golden Rule in their relationships with their brother man, and to ceaselessly strive to benefit all mankind, irrespective of race, color, religion, education, training or ability;

2nd. To never reveal their association with The International Institute of Universal Research and Administration, nor to ever attempt to discover the identity of any member thereof (nor to ever seek such information) without the personal authorization of the director in charge of their instruction. Should one's affiliation become known, even to the members of that one's own family, without such previous authorization, or under circumstances beyond his control, he would immediately sever any and all direct relationship with the activities of The Institute;

3rd. To obey without question or delay, any and all orders received from one's director, even though one might thereby jeopardize his freedom or life, provided however, that such orders in no way conflict with Christ Jesus' Sermon on The Mount, The Ten Commandments as written in the King James version of the Old Testament, nor the established laws of any nation which grants its citizens the privileges of free speech and the rights of peaceable assembly;

4th. To neither use, nor purchase for the use of others, any intoxicating liquors, opium, or any form of dope, nor to use any food or drug or indulge in any action which might even temporarily deprive one of the full and unimpaired use of his mental faculties;

5th. To serve The Research and Administrative Departments of The International Institute of Universal Research and Administration, to the best of one's talents and abilities, throughout one's lifetime, without either financial remuneration or monetary profit of any kind whatsoever. To freely render such service in behalf of the human race, that peace and joy might some day erase the age-old signs of suffering and privation, from the fear-lined faces of the world's starving and homeless millions;

6th. When the order is publicly released announcing the program of The International Institute of Universal Research and Administration, to thereafter ceaselessly strive to direct the thoughts of those to whom the program is presented,—not to one's official position, importance or personality,—but wholly to the value of The Institute's program, and to the eternal and unchanging dependability of the leadership of "Constructive Ideas," based upon the "Golden Rule" and equality of economic security for all. To ceaselessly strive to prove to mankind the wisdom of selecting such ideas as the only solid or safe foundation upon which to build a new world-wide economic system and to do so in order that the value of useful and constructive ideas may thereby be recognized as a more dependable type of leadership to support and to follow, than the constantly changing, and seldom dependable qualities of human personality, "which are here for a day and have gone on the morrow."

These vows together with a number of similar and irrevocable pledges, constituted the conditions under which some hundreds of deeply sincere young men and women were selected from the world's various civilized nations, and accepted as co-workers by the members of The Institute's Research and Administration Department.

Before the end of the year 1936, the beneficial influence of this International Legion of Vigilantes was recognized and willingly accepted by many of the clear-thinking men and women of every nation. Although but few of its members will ever be known to the public,—due to the hazard of revealing their identities and the obstructions which would thereafter be invariably placed in their way by subversive influences,—nevertheless, their efforts will be increasingly felt through the avenues of world newspapers, magazines, radio broadcasts, moving pictures, pulpits, and lecture platforms. The world will never know the identity of the individuals "primarily responsible" for the dissemination of the many warnings and recommendations publicly promulgated through such avenues, but the effort of preparing the thoughts of mankind for The Institute's thirty (30) day program, will ceaselessly be going forward. Their ideals,—frequently voiced by ministers, lecturers and writers, who are unknowingly repeating ideas originally released to the world by The Institute's Legion of Vigilantes,—are rapidly preparing public thought for The Institute's inspiring, "War and Poverty-destroying,"—revolutionary proclamation and 30-day program.

During the past fifteen years the members of The International Legion of Vigilantes have not only been obliged to remain entirely unknown to one another, but they have likewise never been permitted to know the identity of any member of The Institute's Research Department. Though trained to recognize certain symbols of identification, which would enable them to know that the one from whom they receive their orders and instructions is fully empowered and authorized to act directly for The Institute, nevertheless, neither the voice nor the physical features of such an individual have ever been known to any member of the Vigilantes. The voice and features of each of the Vigilantes are, of course, familiar to the various members of The Institute,—who have given them their instructions and orders during the past fifteen years,—however, these directors will never be privileged to reveal their own identities in connection with the activities of The Institute to any of their Vigilante co-workers. An insistence upon these extreme precautions has been necessary in order that even under the influences of torture, no member could ever be made to reveal the identity of any official or other direct associate of The International Institute of Universal Research and Administration, or of The International Legion of Vigilantes.

The Pacific Coast Division of North America, is the only branch of The Institute's organization which is authorized to publish information of any kind whatsoever, relative to either The Institute or its Vigilantes. This branch is operated under the name of The International Registration Bureau, and any printed or written statements not emanating from such Pacific Coast Division, and duly copyrighted under the Laws of The United States of America, are wholly unauthorized and spurious.

Although many hundreds of The Institute's Vigilantes have been ceaselessly active during the past fifteen years,—and will continue so until the conclusion of the 30-day proclamation and official program,—the majority of them are none-the-less obliged to withhold any acknowledgment of their official association with either The Institute or its program, both before and after its consummation. In no other way can the danger of "personality leadership" be permanently avoided. In no other way will The Institute's "Ideas and Ideals" be accepted by the public as the only lastingly dependable form of leadership, and that which they should support and work for, rather than the human personality of some individual—be he ever so worthy—who may be here today for men to follow, hut gone by tomorrow.

Three plus three equaled six a million years ago, and it will still equal six a million years from now. True ideas never change and never leave us, they are always here for us to act upon, but people whom we are willing to work for and follow frequently annul the effects of our efforts and sacrifices when they pass on, whereas the efforts we expend to promulgate or advance a constructive idea are lasting and do not lose their beneficial effect when some human being passes on. If mankind had worked for the world's acceptance of good and constructive ideas such as the Golden Rule—Unity of Action for the equal benefit of all etc., instead of striving to help some human being to develop power or influence which would largely disappear within a few weeks after he passed on,—this world would by now have almost become the Heaven which Christ Jesus tried to teach mankind is here and at hand, whenever men will learn to live together as brothers instead of like wolves, and will strive for the universal adoption of right ideas of human relationship instead of the glorification of human personalities.

The "Golden Rule" and all for which it stands, will be indestructibly blended into the structure and charter of the great co-operative corporation which will be formed by a world-wide vote of acceptance at the conclusion of. The Institute's 30-day program. The eternally good,—and by agreement—permanently unchangeable nature of a charter and set of by-laws irrevocably wedded to the Golden Rule and the great universal and changeless laws of God,—to which Christ Jesus referred in His teachings which men have named "The Sermon on the Mount,"—constitute the "One and Only Form of Leadership" which will ever bring war and poverty to an end in the lives of men.

This great co-operatively owned Universal Service Corporation will have its officials and executives, and its Board of Directors selected for office on the basis of their talents and unselfish desires to serve mankind, and not because of favoritism or the fact that they may be relatives or friends of some other official or director. Nor will those who become officials through the majority vote of the employees and of their associate workers, ever be granted the power to alter the corporation's charter or policy of relationship with the public and its members or employees. The men and women who will be invited by formal vote to become the members of an executive board, will occupy such positions, not for personal gain, power or self-glorification, but solely for the purpose of officially directing the production and distribution of the necessities and luxuries of human life, together with the numerous educational and benevolent activities of this world-wide Universal Service Corporation, in behalf of the human race. Inasmuch as their share of its products and benefits will be no greater than even the most lowly employee, there will be no jealousy of them, although it will of course be considered an honor to have attained to such a position of service. Through the adoption of an unalterable feature of the proposed corporation charter, no one will be permitted to occupy any official or honorary position longer than three years. This ruling will not only provide all capable workers with an opportunity to occupy the most desirable positions, but through such rotation in office, it will also prevent envy, jealousy, or the feelings of superiority or self-importance, which frequently arise when one is in charge of others who will never be able to advance as far as such a one.

The task of inviting some two hundred million (200,000,000) of the intelligently industrious and clear-thinking men and women of the principal civilized nations, to indicate their interest in the release of The Institute's free 30-day program, and the establishment of its International Corporation, has been,—without hope of financial remuneration or public recognition of any kind whatsoever,—willingly accepted by each unit of the world-wide membership of The International Legion of Vigilantes.

These men and women who have given generously and unstintingly of the past fifteen years of their lives to what has frequently been a most hazardous form of public service, will never receive either the slightest advantage of salary or position, when they later apply,—unknown as Vigilantes,—to the Corporation's publicly elected Boards of Examiners for a position to which they may believe their capabilities or talents qualify them. Each of these men and women, over fifteen years ago, waived any and all advantages which might normally be expected to accrue to them in recognition of such services as they have rendered. It was the desire to serve mankind which constituted the sole motive of their original acceptance of The Institute's offer to instruct them in its program, and they are willing in this most severe manner to remain unknown, and thereby prove the sincerity of their purpose.

That the world may be given at least a slight concept of what these vows of service have cost those who made them, and that a fuller appreciation of the vitally important and "Unselfed Service-inspiring Nature" of The Institute's program may be universally recognized, this little book is published as a living testimony to the fact that each of the hundreds of men and women who made such vows, would willingly do so again, even though they now know and have felt the full weight of the sacrifices which have resulted therefrom.

That they might aid in bringing to fulfillment the vision of a world in which there would be no more wars,—no more poverty,—no more starving and broken-spirited men, women and little children, the members of The International Legion of Vigilantes, (The Institute's co-workers), have willingly and without complaint or regret sacrificed what the world would term the youthful and most highly-prized years of their lives.

That there might be no more fear-filled, tear-stained faces, or broken hearts from the age-old curses of manmade wars and poverty, these young men and women during the past fifteen years have devoted their Saturday afternoons, their Sundays, holidays and vacation periods, as well as all other leisure hours, in ceaseless study and preparation for the various responsibilities they will be expected to assume during The Institute's 30-day program of public proclamations.

During these past fifteen years they have each had but one vacation period of less than ten (10) days' time. They have also been allowed an average of but three Saturday or Sunday afternoons each year, for their own use. The remainder of their time, when not engaged in their respective vocations or professions, has been freely given to assist The Research Department of The Institute, and to receive their necessary instructions and training.

Without compensation,—or any privilege in the future of ever receiving either financial rewards, expressions of public recognition or any personal forms of appreciation, these young people have voluntarily denied themselves not only their leisure hours, but also the joys of either a home or a family. The world has had to be their home, and its millions of starving, fear-filled homeless little children,—their children.

The world's citizens will be asked to make no such sacrifices, nor to subject themselves to either danger or self-denial, "but they 'ARE' asked for their moral support," good will and encouragement, by carefully and understandingly reading this Bulletin and bringing it to the attention of all clear-thinking men and women throughout the world. Only when this has been done, and when The Institute's Sponsors are assured by its Vigilantes, that at least two hundred million (200,000,000) clear-thinking men and women have received its warnings, and an invitation to attend its 30 days of free, simultaneously-released, world-wide proclamations, can the Research Department safely disclose its discoveries to the human race, or present its program for the establishment of a great, equally-owned, profit-sharing Universal Service Corporation, for a world-wide vote of acceptance or rejection.

Any plan of procedure which did not have such an assurance of simultaneous world-wide attention, and an organization consisting of a sufficient number of people to protect and immediately apply its recommendations through the concerted action of not less than two hundred million (200,000,000) individuals,—and "in all parts of the world simultaneously"— would through lack of sufficient strength or influence,—be doomed to certain destruction by those who control the world's financial structure.

We ask, therefore, only the assurance of public attention during a 30-day period,—the dates of which will be internationally announced in the manner described in the concluding chapter of this Bulletin;—and at the end of said 30-day program, that you cast your vote either for or against The Institute's recommendations in accordance with your own individual and unbiased judgment.

In recognition of the adage that "Like attracts like" The Institute's various co-workers have—since the year 1919—been preparing to organize and draw around them, groups of people who would understand and appreciate similar ideals, and be motivated by aspirations similar to their own. Certain aspects of our program have been gradually imparted to these groups in preparation for the time when Our Research Department, during its international 30-day proclamation, would fully warn mankind of the war of extermination which is planned—by the world's War Lords and its Hidden Rulers—to bring about the slaughter of four hundred million (400,000,000) educated and religious people. The consummation of this plot can only be thwarted by the concerted action of not less than two hundred million (200,000,000) unselfish, intelligent, and clear-thinking men and women. However, it is believed that the present influence of the Institute will succeed in temporarily delaying this orgy of wholesale murder.

Although most of The Institute's preliminarily-formed organizations and groups of people, have not been made aware of the fact that the ideals they have had described to them,—or in other instances, the warnings they have received,—emanate from the Research Staff of The International Institute of Universal Research and Administration,—nor have they even been made aware of the fact that there is such a research bureau in existence,—nevertheless, their thoughts are being gradually prepared through many avenues today, such as newspapers, books, magazines, radio broadcasts, moving pictures, pulpits and lecture platforms, in order that they may be unprejudiced and receptive at such a time as The Institute's sixty (60) years of investigations, discoveries and revolutionary mechanical inventions, are offered to the world.

Many of Our Research Department's discoveries are so startling, that human indignation over the atrocities of greed., selfishness and bestiality, in the lives of those whom the human race has looked to for leadership, will cause the world's intelligently industrious and right-thinking men and women to raise their voices in one mighty worldwide demand for a new medium of currency, and the destruction of a monetary system which makes men into swinish monsters. They will demand that those who uphold "Man's inhumanity to man," be no longer allowed to dictate either the world's financial, industrial, political or educational policies, nor allowed to perpetuate poverty in a world of plenty, and the wholesale slaughter, century after century, of millions upon millions of human beings in revolutions and wars, planned and executed solely for the profit of those who barter in human suffering, that they may thereby add to their power or wealth.

UNIVERSAL SECURITY, PEACE AND HAPPINESS VERSUS POVERTY, FEAR AND WAR

WE all desire happiness,—nor do we begrudge the fulfillment of this desire in the life of any other person—therefore, why should we not help each other to find security, peace and happiness? Why should we not stand together,—"One for All and All for One"?

Since none of us would want anyone or anything to stand in our pathway and obstruct or prevent our happiness; nor have any right-thinking men or women the slightest desire to interfere with the happiness or joy of others,—and since these two correlated statements are indisputably true when applied to the lives and thoughts of any group of people in any country on the face of this globe,—Why then is it also true that so few of us have ever felt securely happy? Why is it that envy, jealousy, hate, bloodshed and war, are observed all about us as the indications of experiences in the lives of everyone, and that these conditions exist today, literally as unabated as they have throughout untold centuries of human life? Why is there so much lack and why such ceaseless fear of losing what little we have?

The Research Department of The International Institute of Universal Research and Administration is prepared to prove that the causes which bring about insecurity, and racial, religious, and class antagonisms, are not the inevitable concomitants of evolution, nor an accidental result, but the plans and purposefully directed plots and programs of those motivated by the desire for power and financial gain, "and who are not the slightest bit concerned about how they accomplish their ends."

Were it not for the "Planned Perpetuation of Antagonisms," causing constant division among the people of various groups, we would by now be living in a world populated by men and women doing their fair share of the world's work, and earning the right,—and thereby worthy,—of sharing with fair equality, its inexhaustible and diversified abundance and loveliness. Man would no longer be a creature of lustful enslaving habits and appetites, nor in bondage to superstitions, unprovable beliefs or undemonstrable creeds. Men would be obeying the "Golden Rule"—not from compulsion but from desire—instead of merely theorizing and preaching about it. They would be thinking, speaking and living, in a clean intelligent, unselfish and kindly manner. Man, loving good more than evil, and assured of the right to develop his talents and constructive abilities, would be worthy of trust, and a law unto himself—free—joyous—and forever unconfined and unlimited.

We have no desire to injure or kill you, nor to cross the oceans to some foreign nation and kill people we have never even seen; people who individually could not,—by the wildest stretch of imagination,—have done anything to harm us. Only collectively could they affect us adversely or injure us, and then only after they had been organized and incensed to thoughts of fear, hate or envy, by the lying tongue of propaganda,—stimulated and made to utter its lies by some one person, or some small group of persons filled with the lust for power, glory or wealth. Only then can people be made,—(through the mesmeric and hypnotic influence upon their emotions of subtle propaganda),—to desire or want to kill men whom they have never even seen. Only by being influenced into believing that we might lose the few crumbs of security or happiness,—patronizingly granted to us by the small group of families who unlawfully control the wealth and power of this globe,—could any of us be persuaded into going out and killing another human being—no matter what his nationality or color might be—English, African, Chinese;—white, black or yellow.

It has required centuries of progress for mankind to reach the place where it is now possible to communicate with a large enough number of people, during any one century, to build up a force of sufficient potency to overcome greed and the lust for power, which have, during countless centuries, been the principal causes of poverty, envy, jealousy, hatred, murder and war. These selfishly perpetuated experiences and qualities of thought make security or happiness utterly impossible of attainment in the life of any human being, whether he be rich or poor.

You will readily recognize as your own the ideas we are going to present to your thought, and we therefore suggest that you spend no more time or years in "wishing, only,"—since the world has now reached an age of enlightenment, and has developed facilities for intercommunication, which make it possible to immediately put mankind's universal ideas of freedom into effect. The fulfillment of these desires can be brought to pass with such a small amount of co-operation, that the world's right-thinking men and women need no longer delay, even one day, in taking the necessary steps for their accomplishment.

It is not vast wealth, power, glory, nor the unsubstantial elements of flattery, that mankind seek. All any normal men or women desire, is freedom to do the things which appear to their thought as worthy of effort, and to have the facilities with which to develop natural talents and express "normal" ambitions. No one, until falsely trained to desire such things, asks for great wealth or power, but only for assured security, peace and financial independence. It is not for purposes of luxurious living that the average human being desires financial independence, but primarily, in order that opportunities fo'r constructive self-expression might thereby be made more readily available.

Man is never a glutton or a beast, unless he has become the creature of enslaving appetites and educated desires cunningly encouraged by influences which profit from such weaknesses.

To love Life, and "to Live" and "to let Live," is as natural an impulse of our thought as it is to breathe, unless one's mentality has been warped by an environment, such as need no longer exist on this earth.

Now let us see whether we can, individually as well as collectively, obtain happiness—permanent security—peace—and financial independence, right here in this present world, without any new discoveries,—(other than those which already exist),—being added to our civilization.

Five hundred million (500,000,000) people are always hungry, and thirty million (30,000,000) of them die each year from lack of food, and yet it has been said, and proofs are readily available,—that enough food could be raised within a "ten-year" period, to feed the population of our entire world for over one hundred (100) years, without any further harvesting of crops or other production of food, if mankind desired to use the present machinery, inventions, and available executive ability, for the accomplishment of such a result.

Millions of men, women and little children die annually from extreme exposure, due to lack of warm clothes, and yet, enough clothing materials could be produced within a ten (10) year period to clothe the entire human race for the rest of this century.

Over one thousand million (1000,000,000) people on our planet,—(one-half of its total population),—have no habitations of their own which they can call their home, yet we claim that there is a great world depression and not enough work for the trained workers of our civilized nations to perform, and that therefore, hundreds of millions of industrious and intelligent men and women must remain idle.

With hundreds of millions of people starving, freezing to death and homeless, mankind must wait while the world's "Swinish Money Changers,"—motivated solely by greed, and indescribable selfishness, stop to figure out just how they can succeed in making men continue to work for the private profit system which they control; a system of "Greed" and "Selfishness," which has been perpetuated century after century, for the exploitation of human beings, and which should have been completely destroyed long ages ago.

Is it the purpose of life to build machines, cannons and battleships, accumulate money, and construct vast office buildings,—where. the Midases may count their gold,—or should the object of life consist in seeking wisdom and happiness? Where did we come from?—Why are we here?—Where are we going? Are not these questions of more importance to each of us than the creating of piles of gold to pour into the laps of a small handful of people who cannot possibly ever take such wealth with them when they leave us, and yet, which—after they are gone—always starts the endless struggle all over again, to see who shall possess it?

Is it not right that we each should have our lives to use as we may choose, so long as we harm no one? Should we not be seeking wisdom and happiness, instead of lifeless money and unsatisfying self-glorification?

The two hundred million (200,000,000) people whom we herein invite to learn how they may form an equally owned and "Universal" service corporation, are at this time spending an average of over one thousand million ($1000,000,000) dollars per day. If they have the courage, wisdom and vision to combine their buying power, they can readily own the world's principal resources of raw materials, from which are produced food, clothes, homes and other necessities of life (as well as its luxuries) and thereafter they will have the power to permanently prevent such requirements of human life from ever again being exploited for private profit. There is no other way on this earth, to stop wars or to eliminate poverty.

The Private Profit System controlled by those who use the world's resources and its man power for the production of their luxurious pleasures, is wholly dependent upon "the demand always exceeding the supply," for in no other way can a profit be collected.

When supply exceeds demand, those who control its sources are glad to get whatever people will pay, but when demand exceeds supply and, for instance, two people want exactly the same article of which there is only enough for one, they will then bid against each other, and if they want it badly enough, will keep on bidding until they pay a thousand times or ten thousand times what it actually cost to produce; but the reverse is also true: When those in control of a large quantity of some article,—the supply of which exceeds the demand,—desire to sell, they have to go out bidding for buyers. If they can't get people to buy at one price, then they offer their merchandise at a still lower price, and keep on lowering the price until someone agrees to buy. Hence, anyone who desires to make a profit on the sources of supply he may control, is of necessity forced to curtail his production so as to never release enough to satisfy everyone, or in other words, so that there will always be a surplus of buyers unable to get what he is producing;—always someone to bid a higher price and start the others bidding, so that even after they have paid many times the article's value they will feel fortunate in having obtained it at any price,—due to its "supposed (?)" scarcity.

This basic formula upon which the "Private Profit System" is perpetuated century after century, is readily understood, when we consider the prices paid for rare paintings. If a famous artist has passed on, and the number of his paintings can never again be increased, people begin wanting what they can no longer get, and they offer those who own the paintings, more money than they paid for them; and then some one else thinks he wants them and he offers still more. Finally people begin to think that the paintings, "Themselves," must possess some great inherent value of their own, when actually, the demand has been created largely because of the fact that the quantity can never be increased. "It isn't the paintings they pay for but only the privilege of having control of them."

In accordance with the "Money Changers'" formula,—that the supply of any necessary article must never be permitted to equal the demand,—we find that during the past twenty-four (24) months, they have used the influences which their vast accumulations of gold and silver enable them to wield, to bring about the destruction of millions of acres of wheat and cotton crops, tens of millions of cattle, and countless millions of tons of other necessary or desirable requirements of human life, in order that they might thereby force the demand to a point so far beyond the available supplies of necessities or luxuries, that they would have no difficulty in obtaining whatever profits they might desire through their control over the principal commercial avenues of production and distribution.

The fact that five hundred million (500,000,000) other human beings will go hungry each day, and that thirty million (30,000,000) of them will starve to death during the following twelve (12) months, is of no concern to these captains of finance. Theirs is a business of making profits, and as long as they can make more money from human beings who are suffering and in need, than they can from those who are secure, peaceful and happy,—mankind may rest assured that just so long as gold and silver can control the destinies of men, no improvement in our economic or political systems which might provide a guarantee of security and happiness to the inhabitants of our world, will ever be brought to pass.

Only through the universal adoption of a medium of exchange based on "Service" rather than on "Gold or Silver," will mankind ever succeed in destroying the swinishly perpetuated spectacle of the wholesale destruction of food and other necessities of life, which is permitted to take place before the very eyes of tortured starving human beings.

To make our world into a garden spot, ever more beautiful as a home for the human race,—to add to the sum total of human happiness, and not just seek what we would individually like to possess, (without consideration for others), but instead, to apply "the Golden Rule" of "One for All and All for One"—as a real desire within our hearts, and not merely words emanating from our lips, is the only ambition truly worthy of intelligent creatures.

Man cannot point to a time since the beginning of human history when there has not existed, somewhere on the globe, a greater abundance of those things which are necessary or desirable for his use, than he could possibly exhaust. However, it has been less than one hundred (100) years since men have awakened to a sufficient degree of comprehension and discernment, to recognize the "infinite abundance" of good which has always been available for their welfare here on earth.

Only by the intelligent application of new ideas, have men discovered ways and means of using a few of the materials which the earth contains in such limitless abundance and variety. The good ideas; which they have welcomed and acted upon, now enable them to communicate almost instantly with one another in any part of the globe. By the use of "right ideas,"—at the rate men have proven their ability to abridge distances during the past twenty-five (25) years,—it is not improbable, that at a not far distant date, men will be able to travel to any part of the world between sunrise and sunset of a single day.

Mankind should therefore no longer be mesmerized by the belief that they are made up of many disconnected links, nationalities, classes or families, but they should now,. recognize the fact that they are, after all, just one family—"The Human Family." Why then, should they not become "Mankind United"? The result of world-wide co-operation, and of such internationally united efforts, would soon be "Mankind Unlimited."

Considering the inexhaustible abundance of the earth's resources, and mankind's present ability to rapidly transport those things which constitute a surplus in one locality, to points where there may seem to be a lack, it is high time that "Mankind United" in order that they might share each other's surplus products, and thereby each enjoy a wider variety of the good things which our earth so abundantly produces.

There never has been, and there never will be, an actual economic cause or reason for the existence of a world-wide condition of poverty—or reasons for men to wage war among themselves, inasmuch as an abundance of everything essential to man's welfare has always existed upon this globe. The proof of this statement is a fact which no one can deny;—namely, that all of the materials which enter into our telephones, radios, airplanes, automobiles, or any other present-day invention,—have been here on this earth throughout countless millions of years waiting for man to use them. Limitless resources and power are always available whenever men are willing to stop fighting among themselves and devote their thoughts and efforts towards the discovery of the blessings which our Creator has placed here for our use; resources in such vast abundance, that men need never fight over which one should have the most, for there is more than mankind can use during a period of millions of years.

There never has been and never can be any reason, due to a difference in the fundamental needs or desires of human beings, nor to a lack of materials for food, clothes, shelter,—or any other requirement for man's welfare,—which could constitute any legitimate cause for the establishment of antagonistic forms of government, or separately owned sources of supply, or separately owned facilities for manufacturing or producing mankind's necessities or luxuries of life.

There is not now, nor could there ever have been in the history of man, a period when the intelligent application of "The Golden Rule" in all human activities and relationships, could not have solved every spiritual, moral, or physical requirement of man. The natural results and effects of brotherly love, and a consequent unshakable trust and confidence in one another, would have uprooted the causes of poverty and war centuries ago, had men applied "The Golden Rule" in their "economic relationships," as constantly as they have referred to it in their philosophical discussions with one another.

Merely because our ancestors failed to discern the practical and economic, as well as idealistic desirability of universal brotherly love (which would long centuries ago have resulted in the destruction of class distinctions—national boundary lines and racial antagonisms)—and merely because they preferred to go out and commit murder, and then after stealing the possessions of their weaker brothers, to evolve a rule of conduct which they called "The Law of the Survival of the Fittest" does not justify us in perpetuating such a rule.

The world was not formed "solely" for the use of "swine," nor solely for the use of human beings who subscribe to "swinish" humanly promulgated rules of conduct worthy only of hogs.

Our Research Department claims that wars, poverty, and most of the disappointments, broken hearts and broken lives of mankind, can be avoided by co-ordinating the combined "demonstrable" wisdom, ideas and efforts, of each member of the human family with all others, and distributing the total products thereof, "equally" among the members of the entire human race,—granting none the privilege of attaining to a degree of power or influence sufficiently great to injure his fellows,—should greed or selfishness gain control of such a one's thoughts.

We believe that all men, women and children, of every nation, should have the privilege of developing their talents for their own as well as for the world's advancement, and the equal use of whatever they might desire of the earth's resources of a constructive nature, for their own individual happiness.

THE GOLDEN RULE—OR—THE RULE OF GOLD WHICH SHALL IT BE?

JUST as long as a type of money is in use which can be accumulated in such vast quantities that those who control it are able to dictate to the governments and the peoples of the earth, and to make or break them at will; and as long as human nature is such that a taste of great power or great wealth frequently develops a ceaseless craving for more,—until the time comes when such people have grown so insanely ambitious that they have reached the stage which can only be described as "moral idiocy;"—it is wholly illogical, and—were it not such a tragedy—even rather ridiculous, to place beautifully couched petitions in their hands, which plead with these monstrosities of greed for reduced armaments,—round-table discussions, (instead of war),—old-age pensions, social security and other similarly worthy desires in the hearts of sane, right-thinking men and women.

Knowing that the political structures of every nation can always be controlled—either by methods of intimidation, bribery, flattery or assassination—by those with sufficient money to accomplish such results; —knowing that vast quantities of gold and silver now rest in the hands of a small group of men who desire more wars and more poverty, that they may, thereby,—through the manipulations of cheap labor or the sale of armaments or other merchandise for the slaughter of human life—not only add to the contents of their already over-flowing treasure chests, but also bring about mankind's complete enslavement;—knowing that such men have learned more tricks of propaganda, and so-called mass psychology, through which to control the activities of any groups of politicians, which have ever, or will,—(under our present private profit competitive system),—ever be elected to office;—knowing that such men have learned more ways and means of controlling the actions of politicians and those who hold public office, than the combined civilian population of the combined so-called civilized governments of the entire world could ever hope to learn during hundreds of years, (through their wholly inadequate and usually politically, capitalistically or subversively controlled mediums of news or sources of information);—knowing all of these facts, is it likewise not rather ridiculous that men and women who call themselves intelligent creatures, should waste the time to even try to correct conditions through sending long petitions to people who are so easily controlled by the insanely ambitious maniacs who govern them? (One might just as well send a request to a rattlesnake asking it not to bite him).

Those of us who believe ourselves to be intelligent creatures can never expect to permanently improve conditions by merely writing little crosses on long pieces of paper, which we call "Ballots," when—after tossing these bundles of ballots around among themselves for their amusement,—the world's "Money Changers" arrange the actions of the new political administration in any way they may desire, and with the power and influence of their money, completely control the new crop of publicly or politically appointed representatives, with not the slightest bit of difficulty, through the use of one or more of their four methods of control; namely,—intimidation, bribery, flattery or assassination, which their accumulations of money enable them to exercise.

Knowing these things, it is high time that those men and women throughout the world, who desire financial independence and security, bind themselves together into the only type of organization which will ever succeed in directing either the governments or the industries of the world in behalf of the happiness of its citizens; namely, a Co-operative, Equally Owned Universal Service Corporation, capable of producing and distributing the necessities and luxuries of life for its members, and with its combined buying power of more than One Thousand Million ($1000,000,000) Dollars per day,—(and the concerted action of Two Hundred Million (200,000,000) equal owners),—capable of bringing to pass the international adoption, through "Commercial" instead of "Political" methods, of a type of money which neither any one person nor any group of persons will ever be able to accumulate in sufficient quantities to destructively dictate either the thoughts or the actions of their fellow beings.

Without seeking financial remuneration, public recognition or reward of any nature,, the sponsors of The International Institute of Universal Research and Administration, after many years of thorough preparation, now invite the world's right-thinking and intelligent citizens to accept their proofs of the feasibility of such an accomplishment.

It has indeed been rightly stated, that "That which is every one's business" is usually "No one's business." Our Sponsors, many years ago, became aware of the fact that although all "sane people" desire to end both war and poverty,—and it is surely the business of every intelligent person to help do so,—nevertheless, no individual nor group of individuals with sufficient understanding of these problems to bring about their solution, had considered them of sufficient importance to warrant an expenditure of either the necessary time or money which would be required before any successful solution could be reached. Our Sponsors and Executive Board of two hundred men and women have, for many years, made it "their business" to discover a practical plan for ending war and poverty. They not only have been successful, but of equal importance is the fact that the solution they have evolved is one which can be applied with inevitable success,—and, within a period of less than ninety (90) days after its acceptance by at least two hundred million (200,000,000) intelligent men and women;—nor will such acceptance require any supreme sacrifices of either time or money.

Realizing that the power and influence of the world's subversive forces,—those who perpetuate both its wars and poverty,—consist solely of the enormous buying power which their century-old accumulations of gold and silver place in their hands, Our Sponsors soon recognized the fact that it would be necessary to "fight fire with fire;" in other words, to combat the buying power of the world's "Money Changers" "with a buying power of even greater potency."

They knew that one of the principal reasons for the adoption of plans by the Hidden Rulers, to bring about the extermination of the world's educated and religious peoples, was the fact that such classes of human beings,—through the avenues of study and the privileges of firsthand observation which present modes of travel have made available to them,—have begun to realize that the untouched resources of the earth and the unused lands which could be cultivated for the production of food are so vast, in variety and extent, that there is not the slightest reason for anyone being obliged to experience either privation, poverty, or a life of drudgery. Such educated people are fully aware of the fact that the earth's resources are so abundant that all of the world's citizens might readily be enabled to enjoy lives of comparative luxury, and have ample leisure time for recreation or the development of individual talents, if each new marvelous discovery and mechanical invention were used,—not for purposes of wasteful and destructive forms of competition,—but instead, for the purposes of production for all mankind, in accordance with each individual's respective needs.

Recognizing the growing discontent of the masses against needless conditions of poverty and drudgery, and realizing that unless such of the population, whose education had made them discontented, were soon exterminated, they would eventually unite and demand a greater share of the world's resources than they had been receiving, the Hidden Rulers determined to destroy such people, and to do so before a demand could be made for the establishment of an economic system which might alter the world's medium of exchange, from gold and silver to one of a more equitable nature.

If gold or silver could no longer buy human labor or merchandise, such a condition would, for all time to come, destroy the influence which these "Money Changers" and their satellites have for so many centuries enjoyed. To prevent such a result—which would spell their doom—it would be necessary not only to slaughter four hundred million (400,000,000) of the educated and religious classes, who constitute the group most persistent in their demand for social equality and justice, but it would also be necessary to destroy the world's educational and religious institutions, and thereafter prevent their re-establishment except on a basis which would destroy the initiative of individuals, and in its place create a standardized type of "mass-thought," which would force the mentalities of the human race into a mold capable of shaping their thinking in accordance with the plans and desires of those who would then be their rulers.

The slavery which the world's Hidden Rulers plan to bring about will be similar to that now experienced by the hundreds of millions of people in India, such as has existed there continuously throughout many thousands of years. However, there will be even less freedom or opportunity for mental development. The model towards which they strive, is the one adopted by the aristocracy of India some thousands of years ago; a principle of Government which has never failed to enable those who practice it, to not only continuously add to their own personal fortunes, but also to readily retain their control over the millions of human beings who thereby permanently become their slaves.

The enslaving principle of Government to which we refer, may be briefly described as one which keeps the masses of people always poverty-stricken and illiterate, in order that they may thereby be readily influenced through the avenues of superstition, and fear of the unknown. When millions of people are unable to either read or write, and when the nameless fears of superstition are systematically planted in their thoughts century after century, it is not difficult to sway them into action or obedience, through either the avenues of fear or intense hate. Likewise, when tens of millions of people are not only poverty-stricken or on the verge of starvation, but are actually dying by the thousands each day, from the tortures of starvation and exposure, it is not difficult to buy their labor for little or nothing; inasmuch as they will literally sell their souls for a piece of bread if they are constantly kept hungry enough.

The billions upon billions of dollars of wealth in the form of gold, silver and jewels, retained and added to century after century by the Rajahs and the wealthy families of India, have fully proven the security which such forms of Government bring to those who are wealthy enough to adopt and consistently perpetuate them. It is also readily understood why education and the Christian religion, (the teachings of the Golden Rule and brotherly love), constitute the only enemies which such rulers fear.

Because of the disobedience some centuries ago, of the representatives and satellites of those who then ruled the peoples of the earth, both the influences of "education" and "the Christian religion" were allowed to start leavening human thought. Ceaseless efforts have since been made to eradicate these influences, but they have, during the past few centuries, and particularly during the era represented by recent generations,—spread with much rapidity. They have resulted in such an increase in mechanical inventions, and mediums through which to abridge distance and communicate with great numbers of people from one central point,—through the use of radio and other modern means of inter-communication,—that the only method left to the world's Hidden Rulers—if they are to succeed in retaining their control over the world and its people—is to exterminate all people who are either educated or religious, or whose thoughts have been touched and enlightened by either one or both of these broadening influences. They feel that there is no other solution to their problem, inasmuch as the ever-growing insistence of these right-thinking people is rapidly bringing to pass a world-wide demand, by hundreds of millions of such individuals, that the earth's resources be fully released for the equal benefit of all, and that the mechanical inventions of our present civilization be universally used for the production and distribution of a greater abundance of such resources, in order that all—instead of only a few of the citizens of our world—may enjoy beautiful homes and educational advantages, as well as an abundance of all of those things which add to the happiness of men during their sojourn here on our earth.

That the world's Rulers have been at least partly successful in preventing the influences of education, religion and universal financial security, from developing sufficient strength to bring about their overthrow,—or the establishment of an economic system which would no longer enable them to retain their control over our world,—is evidenced by the fact that even today, during our so-called enlightened twentieth-century civilization, an average of one out of every two people who populate our earth,—in other words, a total of one thousand million (1000,000,000) human beings,—are not only still unable to read or write, but in addition to their illiteracy, the majority of them are filled with the usual numerous nameless fears which are so easily planted in the ignorant and superstitious thoughts of such illiterates.

That the world's Rulers have likewise been quite successful in keeping the masses of people who are located in the more densely populated parts of the earth, hungry enough to be willing to work for little or nothing, is evidenced by the fact that right at this time,—and continuously throughout countless centuries,—over five hundred million (500,000,000) human beings are hungry every day of their stunted, starved little lives, and over thirty millions (30,000,000) of such men, women and little children, die each year; or, in other words, over eighty thousand (80,000) every twenty-four (24) hours,—over two and one-half millions dying each month, after experiencing weeks, -months or years of the slow excruciating tortures of hunger.

Inasmuch as ignorance and poverty go hand in hand,—as they are intended to by those who perpetuate them,—we find that the majority of deaths from under-nourishment, starvation and exposure, occur in those nations whose Rulers have been most successful in perpetuating illiteracy, ignorance and false superstitious teachings. However, even in the world's advanced civilized countries, the influence of the subversive forces to which we refer, has been sufficient to constantly obstruct and greatly handicap education, free speech, and the privileges of "uncontrolled" religious worship. In fact, the buying power and influence of their money has been so great, that even in this so-called enlightened age, (although they are obliged to spend hundreds of millions of dollars each year to accomplish their purpose), they succeed through the avenues of the newspapers, magazines, publishing houses, industrial and political mediums,—which they either own or control,—in seriously obstructing most of the educational or religious teachings which help human beings to become independent, clear, unbigoted thinkers. Through the avenues we have just described, they likewise succeed in perpetuating poverty, and preventing mankind's use of the many marvelous inventions which have been perfected in spite of ceaseless obstructions to the progress of education.

By drawing upon their inexhaustible reserves of gold and silver, these subversive forces have no more difficulty in buying the control of new inventions and basic patents, than they experience in maintaining their rule over the political structures, (be they ever so advanced),—of the world's most civilized nations.

We therefore find that through these dual forms of control,—added to the weakening influences of the ceaseless revolutions and wars to which they subject the world's so-called civilized peoples,—that even in our most advanced nations, hundreds of thousands of people die each year from starvation and exposure.

Even though enlightened thinking has produced countless marvelous mechanical inventions,—capable of relieving humanity almost entirely of the need for human labor or drudgery,—yet through the ceaseless undermining monetary power of the subversive forces, the limitless abundance of the necessary or desirable things of life, which could thereby be so readily made available to all mankind, is not only withheld from their use, but food and other necessities of human life are actually destroyed right before men's eyes, in order to assure their continued poverty and privation. We find, in line with this policy of action, that the political, agricultural and industrial leaders of the world, have been readily influenced into destroying millions of acres of wheat and cotton crops, tens of millions of cattle, and an incalculable quantity of miscellaneous types of food and other necessities of life during the last twenty-four months, in order that the effect of the world's recent inventions might be offset and poverty be made to retain its hold upon the human race.

The influence of "the Money Changers'" publicity and propaganda disseminating medium is so great, that not only do we find them able to gain the public's consent to a monopolistic control of the world's most valuable mechanical inventions, and to a wholesale destruction of the products of such inventions, but also able to accomplish these results without even one newspaper headline, or other announcement to the public, ever appearing in any part of the civilized world, which might inform the sane and right-thinking members of the human race that while they are voting their consent to the wholesale destructions of food and other necessities of human life,—eighty thousand (80,000) of the men, women, and children of their own and other countries, are lying in the gutters of the world with their stomachs bursting open from starvation. Eighty thousand (80,000) human beings dying of starvation every twenty-four (24) hours, and our leaders not only succeed in hiding this fact from us, but actually make us believe they are justified in destroying our foodstuffs and the products of our factories because of a supposed surplus.

Mankind's Hidden Rulers are fully aware of the fact that those who have been allowed to "correctly" learn the meaning of Christ Jesus' teachings,— relative to "the Golden Rule" and "brotherly love,"—would never permit such world-wide destruction of food if they knew that an average of one out of every four of the world's entire population, (in other words over five hundred million people), suffered from hunger each day, and that over thirty million of them will die this year,—(as have a like number, year after year for centuries); yet hardly a word is allowed to be spoken from even the church pulpits of the world nor a headline to appear in any paper, for fear that right-thinking and generous men and women might thereby learn of such conditions.

The reason for such enforced silence on the part of the sources of information to which the public looks for enlightenment and guidance, is readily understood when we realize that with tens of millions of highly-skilled workers, unemployed and living on government doles,—(which the employed people of such nations must pay through numerous avenues of taxation every time they spend even five cents for a loaf of bread),—and with millions of unused acres of land and thousands of idle factories, it is quite evident that the educated, religious and sane men and women of the world would make such a clamor, that its echo would be heard to the ends of the earth;—not only would they demand that such idle workers, idle factories and idle lands be made to produce the food, clothes, homes, and normal requirements of human life, for those who are unemployed, but also for the hundreds of millions of starving, homeless, unwanted, unloved and "truly forgotten" men, women and helpless little children of "every land."

Knowing these things, and knowing that through the avenues of such of the world's inventions as they have been unable to control, mankind might in time be informed of the manner in which they have been duped,—through their acceptance of the selfishly perpetuated false law of "the survival of the fittest," and its tireless servant, "the Private-Profit System,"—and might then demand a system of greater equality and justice; the world's "Money Changers" realized that they must quickly destroy the discontented classes, or they themselves might soon be overthrown. They knew that it would be as impossible to remove the effects of Christ Jesus' teachings of brotherly love, and those of the world's various enlightened forms of education, from human thought and from the hearts of men, as it would be to extract yeast from a pan of dough once it had been impregnated with it. The only means by which these "moral idiots" could even hope to continue their control over the world and its citizens, would be to deal with education and religion, (the only two forces they have ever feared), in the same manner in which they would have to deal with the pan of dough if they were going to try and get rid of the yeast. In other words they would have to destroy the dough in order to destroy the yeast.

The influences of education and religion have now become so deeply embedded into the thoughts and hearts of men, that there is no possible means by which they can be destroyed other than to slaughter those who have felt their effect. Such people are growing increasingly desirous of ending the age-old curses of war and poverty, and of bringing to pass the universal establishment of an economic system which will be able to abundantly supply the requirements of human life for the people of every land, and without any more bloodshed or bitter rivalries.

Recognizing that a desire to bring about the brotherhood of man, had become almost universally accepted among the people of the world's most advanced nations, and that a widespread demand, not only for economic security but for protection against the ravages of war, had entered the hearts of men, the world's Hidden Rulers determined, many years ago, upon a plan which would not only bring about the extermination of the classes of would actually they desire to destroy, but would enlist the enthusiasm and unquestioning help and support of millions of the citizens of these various civilized nations; a plan which would draw this support from both the educated and religious, as well as the illiterate classes. They decided to start a number of great world movements which would appear to have as their objectives, "The Establishment of a World Brotherhood."

They would finance a number of revolutions and bring about the overthrow of the world's major governments, but they would do so in the name and under the guise of what would seem to be "A Great World Brotherhood." Depending upon the characteristics of thought of the people of these various nations, they would name their movements either "Communism," "Fascism" or "Socialism,"—or give them some other equally euphonious title. However in each instance they would cause the people,—through well-planned propaganda and carefully selected and trained lieutenants,— to believe that the leaders of these new types of government, (inasmuch as they had been selected from the working classes), were devoting their entire efforts to the establishment of a system of "equality" and "the brotherhood of man." Finally, with the acceptance of such beliefs, the public would willingly consent, not only to a regimentation of men and of the activities of agriculture and industry, but also grant their support and co-operation towards the enforcement of such rulings.

Under the mesmeric influence of thinking that they were finally helping to bring to pass economic equality and a great world brotherhood, they would unresistingly permit any forms of cruelty or brutality which their new Rulers might tell them were necessary for the success of their movement. When such people had either voluntarily or through compulsion, submerged their own thinking and individualities in programs which they would be told were for the good of the "State" and when they had been taught that the "State" must come first no matter how much suffering they were individually forced to experience, then—"but not until then"—the combined labor, talents and abilities of such people would be directed into channels for the production of great armaments and munitions of war, and for the development of huge standing armies, which the masses would be made to believe were for the protection and advancement of the "long prayed for brotherhood of man."

At the same time, as quickly as it could be safely brought to pass, the religious institutions of the land would be discredited and prohibited from further activities, excepting those which might be under the special authorization and direction of the State. When this was accomplished, people would be gradually taught to worship the "State" instead of God, and to scorn not only the ideals of the various religions but even the purifying impulses of decency and morality. While these effects were brought to pass, the women and little children, as well as the men, (through the mediums of intensive physical training, outdoor sports and athletics), would be hardened for military service.

Soon thereafter, the sanctity of marriage and the concepts of morality, for which the human race has struggled throughout so many long centuries, would have thereby been largely uprooted, and men taught even to ridicule the concept of marriage, home or church. Should the people occasionally wonder what had become of the ideals of brotherhood, and from time to time remember that the only sources from which they had ever received the teachings or been impregnated with the desires of brotherhood or brotherly love had invariably been in the protected atmosphere of the home, either at their mothers' knees or in the Sunday Schools or Churches,—(which latter, would by that time have ceased to exist, and even be prevented by law from ever attempting any further influence upon the thoughts of those who were supposedly striving to bring to pass economic equality and brotherly love),—and should they start complaining because of the cruelty or injustice of their dictators and officials, they would then be reminded of the fact that their Rulers had been selected from their own working classes, and they should therefore not complain.

In the meantime, people would no longer suspect "Capitalists" or believe that they were responsible for the loss of their homes and churches, their freedom of speech, freedom of assembly, and most of the other liberties which had been granted to them under their previous forms of government for, (although the Dictators and Communist Rulers would previously have been carefully selected by the world's wealthy Hidden Rulers), the public would be made to think that such Rulers had attained to their position through their great love for their fellowman, and had only the welfare of humanity at heart.

Even though their dictators might, with one breath utter inspiring statements about the brotherhood of man, and in the next breath give an order to slaughter some thousands of their own citizens for an infraction of some minor regulation; even though one minute they might sign an official publicity statement describing the great benefits which the new form of Government had brought into the lives of the "Proletariat," and in the next instant affix their signatures to a ruling which would abolish the churches of the various religions, annul the sanctity of marriage, and prohibit freedom of speech, the rights of assembly, or the privileges of a home; nevertheless, the people would be told that all of these actions were taken because of their dictator's great love for them, and his courageous undying desire to assure their economic security and happiness. Due to the gullibility of human thought, the world's Rulers believed that men and women would not awaken,—until it was too late, to the fact that the only sources from which they had ever gained the desire for brotherhood or the generous impulses of brotherly love, were those which by that time would be prohibited by law from having any further influence upon the lives of men; namely, the church, the sanctity of marriage and the home.

With the abolishment of all laws granting individual human rights, these Dictators,—(under orders, day by day, received through the secret agents of the world's Hidden Rulers),—carry forward their plans for the building of great armies and the manufacturing of vast armaments and munitions, in preparation for their share in the war which will, at its conclusion, have slaughtered those who fought for the overthrow of their previous forms of government, and the establishment of that which they had been told was to end the rule of the world's capitalists, end wars and poverty, and usher in an era of brotherhood and equality.

With the abolishment of the rights of free speech and the protection of just laws, those in control of the nations which exchange their respective forms of government for Communism, Fascism, Naziism or some other type of Dictatorship, have little difficulty in controlling the masses and compelling them to obey any and all orders issued by the "Money Changers."

With the power of "Life or Death" over their subjects, and with thousands of spies scattered throughout every corner of their countries, it is only necessary to order the execution of anyone who questions or complains about their authority. If one of their agents orders a man or a woman to dig a ditch, and such a one objects or refuses to do so, either torture or execution is the price that must be paid. Dictators do not take time to argue the enforcement of their orders,—"One either obeys them or dies." That is the price paid by those who think that through the avenues of a Dictatorship, Communism, Fascism, Naziism or the world's present concept of Socialism, they are ushering in the brotherhood of man. The only equality which will be experienced by those who believe that they can forfeit their homes, their churches, their freedom of speech and privileges of assembly, in exchange for these various "isms" and dictatorships, "will be the equality of worms," crushed under the heels of the few who win the right and who have the brutality of temperament to walk on them.

If gold and silver are still to constitute the basis of currency, or to be used as such by any new form of government or any economic system recommended by any person or group of persons appearing at this time before the public with a panacea for its ills, such recommendations either emanate from those who are "wholly ignorant" of the actual causes of war, poverty and similar types of human suffering, or they emanate "directly" from the world's "Money Changers;" its "Hidden Rulers." Inasmuch as any government which continues to use a type of money capable of being accumulated by any person or group of persons, will always be under complete subjection to these Hidden Rulers,—(since their accumulations of these metals now exceed, and through their ceaseless additions to their treasuries,—will always exceed any amount which will ever be accumulated by any Government "other than their own Hidden one, which includes the control of all others"),—the only difference between the so-called "Capitalistic Government," and the "Communistic One," is that under a "Dictatorship" the people "know" they are working for nothing, and that whatever they earn is going into the hands of their Rulers; whereas, under the "Private-Profit System" or so-called "Capitalistic" form of government, they are made to "think" that at least a part of the fruitage of their labors will be theirs to store away in their own little, individual, diminutive treasure chests. And in fact, under this latter form of system, that is exactly what they are encouraged to do, for the "Money Changers" know that they can empty out these little chests into their own big ones through the process of depressions, panics and unemployment, any time they may so desire.

However, with the vehicle of Communism and other forms of dictatorship at their disposal, the world's Hidden Rulers have been able, during the past few years, to travel much more rapidly than they would have otherwise towards their goal of the great war of extermination, which they plan to have reach the fulfillment of its purpose,—the slaughter of the educated, religious and right-thinking human beings of every major nation,—at an early date. Every effort is therefore being made at this time to stir up bitterness and hate among the people of the advanced nations in order that their governments may be overthrown, either through the processes of revolution by armed force, or by means of drastic constitutional changes in the basic foundation of their governmental structure.

With the destruction of the rights of free speech and privilege of assembly, any possible sources of objection or opposition can quickly be uprooted, and the "Money Changers" are then able to proceed without interference with their production of vast armaments, the formation of huge armies, and the use of a nation's entire resources for the development and manufacture of facilities with which to perform its share of the task of extermination during the next world war. [1]

All men, women and children, who are able to read and write, are scheduled to be murdered, excepting those who are either the relatives, immediate associates, or trusted agents of the Hidden Rulers and who will, at the conclusion of their war, occupy the same position and relationship to the remaining members of the human race, who may survive this war, as the relationship which now exists between the Rajahs of India and their starved illiterate masses. The only difference between the government of the Rajahs and that of the Hidden Rulers, is that the program of the latter,—(this twentieth century autocracy, which is planned for our world of to-morrow),will provide its Rulers with even greater luxuries and even more certain control over their subjects; although it will of course correspond fundamentally with the basic principles of the governments in India which keep the masses ignorant and on the point of starvation, in order that they may thereby be more readily controlled.

* * PLEASE NOTE * *

In view of what many people consider to be an advanced civilization, the revelations contained in the following chapter will seem wholly unbelieva-

---

[1] Unless a widespread acceptance of its program is accomplished, the Institute can succeed in only temporarily delaying the consummation of these insane dreams of conquest.

ble to a great number of our readers. Knowing this, our Sponsors debated, at length, the advisability of publishing the statements—comprising Chapter VI.—at this time.

However, after weighing the matter carefully, it was decided to include it as written; for it was assumed that as soon as the message in "Mankind United" was released to the public, copies of said book would be delivered into the hands of the world's Hidden Rulers by some one of their thousands of secret service operatives. In this way the "Money Changers" would learn not only that their most secret plans had been discovered, but that every move they might henceforth make towards the consummation thereof would likewise be revealed to mankind long before destructive action against the public welfare could be successfully undertaken.

Nothing is more disconcerting to the general staff of an army of destroyers than to learn that what they had thought to be their most secret plots and plans of campaigning are known to their opponents.

40,000 PRINCIPALITIES ONE THOUSAND MILLION SLAVES AND DEATH FOR ALL OF THE WORLD'S EDUCATED AND RELIGIOUS PEOPLES. SUCH ARE THE RESULTS WHICH WILL CONSTITUTE THE SUCCESSFUL CULMINATION OF THE CENTURY-OLD PLANS OF MANKIND'S HIDDEN RULERS.

DURING the 30-day program of The Research Department of The International Institute of Universal Research and Administration, photostatic copies of plans will be presented to the two hundred million (200,000,000) men and women who will constitute our audience, which will prove to even the most skeptical of them the necessity of establishing a world-wide economic system based upon some medium of exchange and currency other than gold and silver. The Institute's program will prove to them, that unless the economic system it recommends is universally established at an early date,—(as it can be at any time within ninety (90) days upon the consent of the people to whom it will be presented),—that within less than six (6) months after the conclusion of the next world war there will be,—(with the exception of the Hidden Rulers and their followers),—no educated people, (and in no part of the world any religious ones); nor will there be any educational or religious institutions nor facilities for the development of independence of thought, in any nation on this earth, except among the people who will then constitute its ruling class. [1]

The Institute will prove that at the conclusion of the coming war, those who have plotted it have planned to evolve an economic system which will consist of four (4) levels of human society. To bring this system to pass, the entire world is being armed to the teeth, and even little ten (10) year old children are being trained for its armies.

---

[1] The Institute, through its constantly growing influence, has succeeded in temporarily delaying the catastrophe herein depicted; but only by the widespread acceptance of its recommendations can permanent peace and economic security be assured.

The lowest of these four (4) levels will be made up of men and women who will be trained to perform only such drudgery tasks as may require but little intelligence. The next group above them will consist of the men and women who have been taught to operate machines. The third class will include, (up to eighty (80%) per cent of its numbers), the police force, which will consist of eunuchs who will have the responsibility of compelling obedience to the edicts of the rulers. This third class will also include, (up to twenty (20%) per cent of its numbers), the so-called intelligentsia, consisting of men who will be educated and trained to conduct laboratories and research bureaus through which to develop the requirements and luxuries for their Ruler and themselves. The fourth class will be those for whom the first two groups exist as slaves, and for whom eighty (80%) per cent of the third group act as body-guards and twenty (20%) per cent as students and companions. Each ruling family comprising this fourth group, (of which there will be but forty thousand (40,000) will be allowed twenty thousand (20,000) slaves and a bodyguard and group of student companions of five thousand (5000) men to enforce their orders and provide both entertainment and companionship, when desired.

In other words, a total of twenty-five thousand (25,000) people will be under the jurisdiction and control of each one of these forty thousand (40,000) families; in all, a total of one thousand million (1000,000,000) people. Each unit of twenty-five thousand (25,000) people will consist of five thousand (5000) men in the third group and ten thousand (10,000) men and women in the second group, which will include mechanics and various types of machinists, each trained to do some specific task but prohibited from learning any subject other than that in which specific training has been ordered. In other words, each of this second group will literally be a "human automaton." With ten thousand (10,000) men and women laborers in the first group who will perform all necessary drudgery tasks not taken care of by the machines, these four groups with a total of twenty-five thousand (25,000) people, and the family which rules them, will,—with whatever section of the globe is allocated to them,—constitute a self-contained principality over which the appointed ruler will have complete and absolute autocratic control, with the power of life or death over his subjects.

No marriages will be allowed among the members of the twenty-five thousand (25,000) men and women of any of these four groups. However, after the respective ruler has made his selection of the most attractive young girls of the first two groups for his own harem, then the one thousand (1000) students of the third group will have the privilege of drawing by lot, (but with no other rights of selection), whatever girls they may desire as their concubines. All male children will be emasculated, with the exception of the healthiest and best specimens. These will be selected and trained to replace the educated members of the third group, as said members are retired from active service, or die.

Nurses will be selected from the first two groups, who will be put in charge of all children who have passed the age of six months. During the first six months, the respective mothers will be held responsible, under the supervision of said trained nurses, for the health and care of their babies. The only education which will be granted to the children who are placed in the first two groups,—(or the police force branch of the third group),—to replace those who die, will be limited to the training required for the respective duties they will be expected to perform, in accordance with the degree of their intelligence and potential capabilities as determined by the sociologists and psychologists in the laboratories directed by such scientists of the third group in charge of these activities.

Neither reading nor writing will be taught to any of the persons comprising the first two groups of twenty thousand (20,000) men and women, nor to any of the men within the third group, other than one fifth (1/5th) of their number; in other words, one thousand (1000) of them will be educated and trained to carry on the work of the laboratories and experimental and testing departments together with the various bureaus established in accordance with the requirements, interests, or hobbies of the ruler.

In order that the twenty-five thousand (25,000) slaves and selected associates of each principality, may be readily kept under the immediate observation and control of the respective ruler, these people will all be housed within one gigantic structure of twenty-five stories in height, and with the palace and gardens of its owner constructed on the top thereof. Directly beneath the ruler's palace, occupying from the twenty-fifth (25th) down to and including the tenth (10th) story of each such structure, there will be constructed the numerous laboratories, testing, experimental and research bureaus; television and radio departments; power-control rooms, and educational center, as well as the amusement auditoriums for those comprising the third group. From the ninth (9th) story down to and including the first floor, will be located the machine shops and work rooms of the twenty thousand (20,000) slaves of the first two groups, who will be supervised by the five thousand (5000) members of the third group, in the preparation and production of food, clothes, machinery, amusement paraphernalia, and the general luxuries ordered by the ruler for his use and that of the various members of the third group whom he may, from time to time, favor with some expression of his appreciation for their loyalty and services.

The living quarters for the twenty thousand (20,000) slaves comprising the first two groups, will be located for a distance the equivalent of ten stories directly beneath this gigantic structure. They will be so placed, in order that the ruler might—by merely pressing a button,—release any one of a number of kinds of poisonous gases, and thereby not only succeed in quelling any general uprising, but also readily eliminate any of the group who might become particularly unruly. Such ones could be readily slaughtered by housing them in any one of a number of different sections of the subterranean area of his palace. In this section there will also be located the power plants, water reservoirs and storage rooms, hermetically sealed off from access by any other than the ruler's most trusted slaves.

The living quarters above referred to will contain only the barest requirements for sustaining human life. With the exception of the most attractive girls who may be chosen by the ruler and the one thousand educated members of the third group for their respective harems, the remainder of the men and women slaves in these first two groups will have their mentalities regularly dulled through the use of drugs and dope placed in their food and drinking water, in order that the quality of their thinking may remain on a similar level with that of the dullest and least intelligent creatures of the animal kingdom, and that they may therefore be readily satisfied with the coarsest kinds of food,—little or no amusement,—and a stall with some straw upon which to lie, as the only home they will ever know, or even have enough imagination to desire.

The twenty-five thousand (25,000) slaves and guards, belonging to each of those who will comprise the world's ruling class of forty thousand (40,000) men, will be constantly under the direct observation of their respective ruler, through the use of remotely-controlled television and radio equipment, microphones, television screens, etc., placed in every room and corner of the great structures which will constitute the palace as well as factories and slave quarters belonging to each ruler. At any time of the day or night, by either pressing a button or turning a dial, the ruler will be able to look at or listen to any one of his entire allotment of twenty-five thousand (25,000) slaves.

With the exception of his most trusted body-guards and himself, none of his slaves will be allowed to understand the use of guns or other armaments or facilities with which he will keep himself protected. In order that not even one of the forty thousand (40,000) rulers or their descendants may ever be tempted to increase the number of his slaves, or to gain control of any other principality or part of the earth or its resources, than that which has—by majority vote—been allotted to him, it has been mutually agreed upon by those who constitute the present "Money Changers" and "Hidden Rulers" of our day, that if any one of their number should ever yield to such a temptation, such a one and his entire unit of slaves will be blasted off the face of the earth by the immediate simultaneous attack of the thirty-nine thousand nine hundred and ninety nine (39,999) other rulers, with a combined armed force consisting of whatever proportion of their one hundred and sixty million (160,000,000) bodyguards they may require for the accomplishment of such a result.

It is therefore reasonable to state, that once the world's "Hidden Rulers" have succeeded in slaughtering the present educated and religious peoples of our earth, and have thereby gained not only indirect but absolute and complete "Direct Control" of the world's resources, machinery and remaining illiterate populations, they will have little difficulty in maintaining their rule over mankind as long as they may wish to do so, inasmuch as there would never thereafter be any opportunity for the human race to combine its forces against the rule of such depraved, insane monsters. Nor would there ever be any likelihood of even the overthrow of such a type of rule through the jealousy, envy or dissatisfaction of any of the various "little" kings, inasmuch as the strength of their respective kingdoms and their individual allotment of slaves, would never be sufficient to tempt them into even contemplating an attack upon the approximately one thousand million other human beings owned body and soul by the remaining rulers, and constantly under their direct orders.

Being aware of the fact that the smug complacency of some of the modern educated intellects of this age will feel constrained to reject the foregoing statements as being utterly fantastic and quite impossible of accomplishment, we beg to be permitted to call attention to the present "caste system" of India. With its numerous principalities, this system has—century after century—functioned quite satisfactorily for the fabulously wealthy Maharajahs of that country. Those who are inclined to doubt, might also bear in mind the fact that the economic and governing system of India is the only one that has produced "Multi-billionaires" and maintained them in power generation after generation; nor have any of the "modern trimmings" of recent scientific discoveries been required to perpetuate or to aid its operation.

YES, INDEED, THE NEW ECONOMIC SYSTEM, NOW ABOUT TO BE ESTABLISHED BY THE WORLD'S MONEY CHANGERS, WILL WORK "VICIOUSLY WELL" FOR ITS FEW MASTERS.

The Research Department of The International Institute of Universal Research and Administration is fully prepared—"with irrefutable evidence"—to prove (during its 30-day program) that the plot—which has been but briefly described in the foregoing chapter—will unquestionably be consummated unless a new monetary and economic system is "universally" established.

(See bottom of page 73)

SHALL JESUS—OR—JUDAS PREVAIL?

FOR the benefit of those who although having eyes with which to see and ears with which to hear yet are unwilling to either read or to try to understand "The Signs of the Times," and for the benefit of "Those who refuse to recognize the true meaning" in back of the mad scramble by even the most advanced of the world's civilized nations to build up armaments of warfare and vast quantities of munitions,—capable of slaughtering the entire human race, if it were so desired,—we beg to be allowed to remind such people that the eight million (8,000,000) healthy, intelligent young men who died on the battlefields during the world war of the years 1914 to 1918, also scoffed at the idea that there could ever again be a war which would involve "even one" of the great civilized nations, to say nothing of "all of the major ones," as was actually the case. Yet, that war "was planned and executed" with the consent of the actual Rulers, (although not those whom mankind "thought" to be their leaders), of each of those warring nations, working together as one harmoniously united executive board, merely completing "One" of the numerous tests, which have been going on throughout a number of generations, in preparation for the time when the mechanical inventions and chemical discoveries of the world would provide sufficient power with which to bring to pass,— through the purchasing power and influence of their centuries of accumulated "Gold and Silver,"—the complete and final destruction of those influences which have for so many centuries interfered with the "Hidden Rulers'" complete enslavement of the human race; namely, our civilizations' educational and religious institutions.

To those who may believe that prayers (without the actions which "Christ Jesus' Sermon on the Mount," and most particularly "His Golden Rule," enjoins upon the human race) can save the world from another war,— which will destroy not only the most enlightened members of our present civilization but also all of the educational and religious institutions which have required so many centuries to develop,—we bring to their attention the fact that the combined prayers of the most spiritual and enlightened thinkers of all of the religious movements in all of the civilized nations, throughout the entire world, did not prevent the last world war, nor did not prevent the past six years of depression, nor can they possibly prevent the war which will complete the "Hidden Rulers'" program of extermination, unless every man, woman and child who claims to even believe in God—not only "gets down on his knees and prays," but "also stands up on his feet and acts" some of the "Golden Rule" talked and preached about for so many of the past centuries.

Those of us who utter words of brotherly love, which our actions have not justified, are like the "whited sepulchers" of which Christ Jesus spoke, and which He described as "being filled with all uncleanliness." There is no man or woman on this earth today but who is still obliged,—(if he has any but the qualities of a hypocrite in his consciousness)—to bow his head as did the "Penitent Publican," and pray that he might some day have the courage and goodness of spirit with which to be worthy to partake, in some small part, of that Cup which Christ Jesus "drained to the bitter dregs " that men might thereby be taught the lesson "of doing unto others as they would have others do unto them."

That men might understand and become worthy to receive the blessings described by Christ Jesus' "Sermon On The Mount," and the prayer to which the world now refers as "The Lord's Prayer," the Sponsors and officially selected co-workers of The International Institute of Universal Research and Administration have dedicated their lives to the uncovering of "Spiritual Wickedness In High Places," and the development of a program which might open the eyes of men to the necessity of establishing an economic system which would never again provide the opportunity for any human being to successfully plot the destruction of his brothers nor to contemplate the slaughtering of other human beings for the purpose of financial gain, or to attempt to become some "Puny Little Swinish god" in order that he might satisfy his ego by having brass bands play when he appears before men, or if his brother man displeases him, that he might have the power of deciding upon the life or death of such an individual.

That intelligent men and women can—after nearly two thousand (2000) years—still fail to recognize the necessity of "Absolute Obedience" to the universal law, which commands that "We do unto others as we would have others do unto us," now—in the light of our discoveries—seems almost incomprehensible. For it should be self-evident, that if even "one person" has more of this world's goods—and broader opportunities or privileges than are available to another—then either "Jealousy," "Envy," or "Seeds of

Hate," are thereby propagated, and as all things have a tendency to multiply,—(but most particularly, qualities of thought),—it is not long before those who believe they have been treated unfairly, attempt to take away the goods of the one who appears to have more than they themselves have received. Consequently, the wealthy man is forced to build up walls of protection around his possessions, and construct armaments and implements of warfare with which to fight off those who have received less than he.

However, the greatest danger that results from mankind's unwillingness to erect an economic system based upon an equal distribution of this world's goods to all (and from their disobedience to "The Golden Rule" and the principles of universal law expounded by Christ Jesus' teachings) does not consist of the destructive qualities of "jealousy," "envy" or "hate," but rather is it made up of those known as "Greed," "Selfishness" and "Self-glorification." When a man has once tasted of the dangerous fruit of "power and dominion over his fellows," or of the feeling of "Superiority," which comes from having more clothes, more food, finer homes or a greater variety and a superior quality of possessions than one's fellow beings, the desire to prove that "He is Superior to Others," takes hold of his thought, and soon becomes such an obsession, that he can neither be satisfied nor happy, unless everything he owns is better than the possessions which belong to anyone else. As one egotist vies with another, soon such people no longer hesitate to lie, steal or even murder, in order that they might surpass the ones whom they feel may possibly be in doubt as to their individual superiority to others, until, (under our so greatly glorified "Competitive Private Profit System"), we have almost become a world of egotists, thieves and murderers.

It is to awaken those "who are still sane" and who are not either too selfish, too greedy, too bigoted or too egotistical to heed our warnings and accept our recommendations, that Our Sponsors have ceaselessly striven to uncover the "actual causes of human suffering," and obtain the proofs which now point to the utter futility and needlessness,—as well as the danger,—of attempting to prove our "superiority" over other human beings through the accumulation of possessions, when instead, we should be endeavoring to improve our God-given talents and "our birth-right of intelligence," through study, travel, observation and an industriously-trained faculty of appreciation and gratitude for the vast illimitable and gloriously beautiful universe, which our Creator has given to the human race as its home; an indescribably beautiful estate which God has given to "All Men" in much the same way,—and under quite the same restrictions as a wealthy parent might give his dearly beloved sons a great estate for their mutual enjoyment, subject only to "their equal sharing" of all of its resources, facilities, pleasures and beauties.

After all, there is not the slightest justification for any of us to ever feel any "very great" sense of superiority over our fellow beings, for when we go back through mankind's records of human history, and trace the lives of "thousands upon thousands of billions of human beings who have trod this globe," it is not possible for us to point to even one who had anything to do with creating the sun, moon, stars, our earth or its mountains, seas, flowers, trees, birds or bees, nor in fact, even a single hair upon his own head. In the face of such over-powering evidence, even the most profound egotist would be unable to convince a sane jury composed of any of the moderately intelligent men or women on our globe, that he "actually deserves" any larger share of the world's goods, or any greater honors than those bestowed upon even the most lowly of God's children.

However, there is "over-powering evidence" in justification of the fact that man should bow in humble reverence and recognition before the all-wise Creator "who did fashion" our indescribably beautiful and illimitable universal home. His "wisdom," "power" and "might" should be self-evident, even to the most self-centered atheist who ever received his unappreciated benefits of life on this globe.

The recognition of the fact that the wisdom and versatility of the infinite Creator of all things is so great that throughout the millions of years since the first snowflake fell upon our earth He has never even had to pattern two of them alike,—(nor to design any two of His ideas from the infinitesimal to the infinite after the same pattern),—should cause us to seek an understanding of "Him," rather than praise for ourselves. No, not even the hairs on our head, nor the finger-print designs on the fingers of any two of the men or women of all the billions upon billions of human beings whom He has created, has He ever been forced through lack of versatility or intelligence to form alike.

Is it not a more worthy form of ambition for those calling themselves "The Sons of God," to study and seek, that they may thereby learn to appreciate, love, and protect God's creatures, and the artistry of His handiwork, rather than to strive to become gods themselves? Especially is it so, because of the fact that the only reason for men desiring to become "little gods," is that they may thereby gain the power to destroy what they can of God's creation and whomever they may choose of God's creatures, whenever the insane desire to do so takes possession of the "swinish qualities" of their puny intellects;—(qualities of greed and selfishness which they have so assiduously cultivated, that they might thereby be made assured of their own "superiority" over any other of God's creatures).

Surely Christ Jesus' life work, and the supreme sacrifice which He made in order that men might learn what brotherly love "and true giving" really mean, and that the human race might thus be saved from its own selfish destruction, is not going to be so demoniacally reversed that only those who have naught but selfishness, cruelty and swinish bestiality in their thoughts, are to be the only ones to learn the importance of equality!! Why!—Even the monstrous "Hidden Rulers," who know no other human feelings than those of greed and an insane craving for power, have learned that they must divide the earth's resources, and those who will then be their slaves, in such "an equally proportioned manner" that there will never be any occasion for one ruler to be jealous of another, nor for the qualities of envy or hate to thereby cause a disruption among them which might cause a division in their ranks, and as a result of envy, jealousy or hate, bring about the self-destruction of their kingdoms. Even "their" depraved mentalities have become so conscious of the cumulative dynamically destructive forces of jealousy, envy and hate, and those of greed, selfishness and self-glorification, that they have found it desirable to unite upon the common ground of self-preservation, and a full recognition of the power and might of unity based upon equality. Even "they" have enough intelligence left to agree to stand as one, and as a solid body against any one of their members who might ever attempt to have even one slave more than the others, or the slightest advantage which might cause either envy, jealousy, hate—"or the more dangerous feeling of superiority"—to develop in the mentalities of any of the men, who will,—upon the successful consummation of their plots a short time hence,—become the full owners and unopposed rulers of our world. Even "they"—(although it surely cannot be the slightest quality of unselfed love which motivates them)—have agreed to come to the aid of any of their member rulers, who might have trouble with his slaves, and every one of their respective slaves will feel the sting of instant death, upon the slightest appearance or evidence of any of those destructive qualities to which we have referred.

Each of those slaves will be taught that if he ever so much as harmed even one hair on his master's head, that the combined forces of the rulers' bodyguards of millions of men would search him out and subject him to the tortures of the damned until he died.

YES, EVEN OUR WORLD'S HIDDEN RULERS, WHOM WE CALL THE "MONEY CHANGERS" OF TODAY, HAVE LEARNED ONE ASPECT OF THE PROFOUND LESSONS OF THE MASTER, "CHRIST JESUS;" HE WHO CAME TO BRING "PEACE" AND NOT A "SWORD," "BROTHERLY LOVE," NOT "HATE," AND "UNITY" INSTEAD OF "DIVISION" TO THE HUMAN RACE. EVEN "THEY" HAVE LEARNED THE VALUE OF "UNITY" BASED UPON "EQUAL RIGHTS"! BUT UNFORTUNATELY—FOR THE REST OF HUMANITY—"EQUAL RIGHTS" TO THEM MEAN EQUAL RIGHTS FOR THEMSELVES ALONE, AND SLAVERY FOR ALL OTHERS.

CHRISTIANS WANTED!

IF those who call themselves "Christians" (no matter what denomination they may belong to) have ever even been momentarily inspired by feelings of "brotherly love" and "kindness " and will, therefore, help by their unprejudiced thought, moral support, and good will, to gather together a great world-wide audience for us, of two hundred million (200,000,000) courageous and sincere men and women,—men and women who desire to some day attain to that mind "which was also in Christ Jesus,"—(and who would be willing to "start doing so" by consenting to "Do unto others as they would have others do unto them," and would obey this injunction at least to the extent of consenting to the establishment of business facilities powerful and influential enough to produce and distribute the entire necessities and luxuries of human life, which could—either now or in the future—ever be required or desired by the human race);—AND IF SUCH PEOPLE WILL CONSENT,—UPON OUR PRESENTATION OF THE PROOFS WHICH WE HAVE AT OUR DISPOSAL THROUGH THE RESEARCH DEPARTMENT OF THE INTERNATIONAL INSTITUTE OF UNIVER-SAL RESEARCH AND ADMINISTRATION,—TO AN ECONOMIC SYSTEM BASED UPON "THE GOLDEN RULE" AND "ABSOLUTE ECONOMIC EQUALITY," OUR RESEARCH DEPARTMENT WILL GIVE EACH AND EVERY ONE OF THEM INDISPUTABLE ASSURANCE OF PERMANENT, FINANCIAL INDEPENDENCE.

We are prepared to provide an organization composed of not less than 200,000,000 men and women—(dedicated to the practical application of "The Golden Rule"),—with fully perfected inventions so marvelously constructed that the production of food, clothes, homes, etc., can be brought to pass on a scale so vast that, within less than ten (10) years, enough food will have been produced and properly preserved to feed the entire human race, if need should arise, for a period of over one hundred (100) years, without any additional production of such necessities. During that same 10-year period, with the inventions and discoveries which we are prepared to provide as a gift to such an organization, enough wool, cotton, silk, etc., can be produced to also clothe mankind for an entire century, and enough homes constructed to provide a new home for each family on our earth.

WITHIN LESS THAN ONE YEAR, THE WORLD CAN SET INTO MOTION THE NECESSARY MACHINERY AND BUSINESS FACILITIES FOR PRODUCING OVER ONE HUNDRED (100) TIMES AS MUCH FOOD AND CLOTHING MATERIALS EACH YEAR AS THE ENTIRE POPULATION OF OUR PLANET COULD EVEN HOPE TO USE. Instead of five hundred million (500,000,000) men, women and little children going hungry, and over eighty thousand (80,000) of them dying every twenty-four hours from utterly needless starvation, we are fully prepared to prove that "Right Now—at This Time," enough machinery, perfected inventions, executives, trained workers, ready-to-use resources and raw materials are available with which to produce a twenty (20) course meal, and a full change of wearing apparel, from shoes to hats, every hour of the twenty-four, for every man, woman and child on this earth, if they were capable of using them; and this quantity of mass production could continue for millions upon millions of years without ever even starting to exhaust the last of our planet's resources.

Less than one one-hundredth (1/100th) part of the soil on our earth, which is capable of producing food, has ever been ploughed, and yet, because of the influence of a small group of men who have accumulated a few tons of the metals we call gold and silver, five hundred million (500,000,000) people, century after century, remain hungry every day of their lives.

Wealth is not "gold or silver," nor do people eat either these metals or the paper currency which represent them. THEY ARE ONLY SYMBOLS OF VALUE! THE ACTUAL WEALTH OF THE WORLD CONSISTS OF THE MATERIALS AND RESOURCES OUT OF WHICH WE PRODUCE FOOD, CLOTHES, HOMES, AND THE NUMEROUS OTHER NECESSARY OR DESIRABLE REQUIREMENTS OF HUMAN LIFE. Such wealth exists in inexhaustible abundance for the equal use of the entire human race, and no person, or group of persons, will ever succeed in accumulating more than their rightful share after mankind adopts as their "symbol of value" a type of money capable of being used only by the one to whom it has been issued, and spent only through the avenues of a great producing and distributing commercial organization, equally owned by every human being on our earth and given the power to produce and distribute whatever mankind may choose to use from their "equally owned" actual wealth—"the earth and its resources."

In other words, mankind could not possibly consume even the very smallest part of either the 'available necessities of life, or the luxuries which are here ready for our unlimited use and enjoyment, whenever we open our fear-blinded eyes, and cast off the "educated bigotry" of our thought long enough to act like intelligent creatures, instead of "murderous wolves;"—and whenever we are willing to combine our efforts and guarantee each other the equal distribution of our united labors.

Two hundred million (200,000,000) men and women, drawn from the "middle classes" of population of the world's civilized nations, possess a combined buying power of over one thousand million dollars ($1000,000,000.00) per day, with which they can, at any time they wish, insist upon a full release of the "Real Wealth of the World," which belongs equally to all. NO POWER ON THIS PLANET COULD RESIST SUCH A UNITED DEMAND!!

If every man and woman on earth were to draw the equivalent of $3,000.00 per year, in food, clothes, homes, travel, education, etc., and were to start doing so within one year from the date of the establishment of The Universal Service Corporation,—(which Our Sponsors will invite their audience of two hundred million (200,000,000) people to form at the conclusion of the 30-day program herein described), they would be consuming less than one tenth (1/10th) of the productive capacity of their factories, farms, and service departments, which will be functioning within a matter of months thereafter.

THIRTY THOUSAND ($30,000.00) DOLLARS PER YEAR OF THE NECESSITIES AND LUXURIES OF HUMAN LIFE, CAN BE PRODUCED FOR EVERY ADULT ON OUR EARTH BY THE UNIVERSAL SERVICE CORPORATION, WITHIN A PERIOD OF LESS THAN TEN (10) YEARS FROM THE DATE OF ITS FORMATION. Our Research Department stands ready to prove these statements at any time that two hundred million (200,000,000) people have agreed to receive them, and to cast their vote, either for or against the plans, recommendations and charter of The Universal Service Corporation, which will at that time be offered as a gift to the human race, subject only to the equal distribution to the men and women of every nation of the necessities and luxuries of life which said corporation will produce through the unrestricted and unhampered use of our planet's entire resources.

The marvelous inventions our Research Department has discovered, and which have been fully tested and perfected, are capable of providing every family on earth, within this same ten (10) year period,—not with just a temporary shelter against the elements but with a home, the value of which, together with its immediate grounds and furnishings, will exceed a present-day cost-price of twenty-five thousand dollars ($25,000.00). Each home will contain, not only the finest radio equipment known to man,—"but fully perfected television equipment,"—which will provide the interesting, constructive, or educational news of the world any time—day or night—and also an almost unlimited variety of moving pictures,—(either the various popular classics and entertainment features, or the actual day-by-day news happenings of interest),—"and they will be brought directly into every home, no matter in what part of the world it may be situated."

Each home will also be supplied with automatic vocal- type correspondence equipment, which will enable its user to merely press a button and talk as he would into a dictaphone, but in addition to a record of the exact intonations and inflections of his voice, he will have an automatically prepared and typewritten letter—with as many duplicate copies as he may desire—silently released into the correspondence basket on his desk, either ready for his signature, or already automatically signed, yet without any human being having operated the typewriter or personally prepared his letter through any mechanical means requiring human labor. Whenever he wishes to write a letter he will only be required to dictate it, in order to have it automatically typewritten for him.

Each of these homes will be equipped with automatic news and telephone-recording equipment, which will print the most important items of news, and also record them by voice on a record right in each home, minute by minute, as they occur, in any part of the world. Similar equipment will also both print on paper and record by voice any information which others may desire to leave for you by telephone when you are not at home. They will only have to voice what they may wist to tell you, and their message will be, awaiting you upon your return.

Each home will also provide automatic air-conditioning and air-heating and cooling equipment, which will supply each room in every home with whatever type of temperature or climate its occupants may desire; hot air or cold air, seashore, mountain, or desert air;—and with the exact elements in the air in one's home, as those which might be obtained at a favorite resort of any of these climatic selections.

If it is desired, a home will not only be supplied with some acres of landscaped gardens, but also fruit trees, vegetable gardens, and hot houses, in which one may grow any personally favored fruits or vegetables produced in any part of the globe. In accordance with each one's selection, athletic courts, swimming pools and children's playgrounds, surrounded by trees, shrubbery and beautiful flowers; fountains, streams and miniature waterfalls,—(artificially created in exact reproduction of some beautiful spot one may have visited in one's travels throughout the world),—will gradually—over a period of not to exceed ten (10) years—be designed and built for each family.

These benefits will first be provided for those who are able to read and write, and who will consent to learn the "International Auxiliary language" which will enable the men and women to whom it is taught, to converse and correspond with the educated people of every land. The citizens of each nation will be encouraged to continue learning and teaching their mother tongue, until such a time as they may feel that the universal auxiliary language, (which will be used by the broadcasting and news dispensing agencies of The Universal Service Corporation), is embracing not only just the advantages of their own mother tongue, but also the added advantage of being "universal" in nature, and therefore capable of melting away the misunderstandings which arise from one's inability to understand another. This universal language will quickly bring to pass a closer feeling of universal brotherhood in the hearts of men, as they grow to understand one another's habits and customs, and to realize that after all the people of every nation have much of constructive value to impart to those of different racial background and ancestry.

We are all the children of "The One Creator," and as each idea throughout the universe is different from any other,—(but are all needed to accentuate and complement each other), so likewise, are each of God's children endowed with priceless individual talents. Suitable environment, adequate facilities, and a universally available opportunity for their full and complete development, will bring down an avalanche of blessings upon the lap of "old mother earth," and into the hands of men, such as they have never before even visioned in their most inspired concepts of the Heaven which they have sought for so long a time in some distant place; THE HEAVEN WHICH CHRIST JESUS TOLD US NEARLY TWO THOUSAND (2000) YEARS AGO, WAS "NOT AFAR OFF," BUT RIGHT HERE AND "AT HAND " WHENEVER MEN WOULD FULLY APPLY HIS "GOLDEN RULE" IN THEIR RELATIONSHIPS

WITH ONE ANOTHER, AND WOULD PROVIDE "EQUAL OPPORTUNITIES," "EQUAL FREEDOM," AND "EQUAL WEALTH" FOR ALL.

MANKIND'S SELF-APPOINTED GODS AND THE MONSTER CALLED "GREED"

IS it not a fact that after we arrive here on earth, we are forced within a few short years to leave without ever having actually seen it, or viewed even a small part of its limitless attractions? It is not because of any lack of desire, or of facilities for travel; nor is it lack of appreciation or ingratitude on our part, which prevents us from growing acquainted with and enjoying all of the gloriously beautiful parts of our world home. NO, IT IS SOLELY THE INFLUENCES OF GREED AND SELFISHNESS WHICH WITHHOLD FROM US THE PRIVILEGE OF ENJOYING THE WORLD AND ITS LOVELINESS, FOR THEY SURELY BELONG AS MUCH TO ONE AS TO ANOTHER.

To illustrate the practical importance of Christ Jesus' "Golden Rule," suppose someone were to give you, in common with a number of others, the free use of a palace surrounded with all manner of beautiful gardens, and possessing ample facilities for supplying you with whatever might add to your happiness; assume for the moment that the condition of your occupancy, and the use of this lovely estate, depended upon each of those to whom it had been offered, abiding in strict obedience by the rules of conduct implied by "Moses' Ten Commandments," and "Christ Jesus' Sermon on the Mount." Knowing that no one would be allowed to enjoy this estate who had not at first agreed to these rules of action—and realizing that the palace with its surrounding attractions belonged to another and was freely offered to you for your use,—subject however, to your acceptance of the rules of conduct governing those who occupied it, you would surely be most anxious to not misuse this gift nor be barred from its benefits by your failure to abide by the established laws of conduct.

However, suppose you happened by chance occurrence, quite beyond your control, to make your first entrance into the palace by way of the kitchen door. You are met by one who has also been given the privilege of occupancy,—subject to the established rules of conduct and with no greater or lesser privileges than you,—and yet he meets you at the kitchen door with a ball and chain in his hands, which he fastens on your ankle.

After fastening the other end of the chain at a point in the room where he knows that it will prevent you from getting out of the kitchen, he hands you a dish rag and tells you that the kitchen is now your home, and that it is the only part of the palace you are supposed to occupy. Knowing that you have been given the "equal use" of everything the estate contains,—and any rooms in the palace you might desire to enjoy,—you rebel at your confinement and gradually grow filled with bitterness, yet no ways of escape or means of breaking your chain present themselves.

Under such circumstances, do you think that you could ever grow to really appreciate or know and truly love this beautiful home? Instead, wouldn't you after a time grow to almost hate your life, and also the one who had offered you the use of his lovely estate, feeling that somehow it got been offered to you in good faith at all? However, if your friend happened to be traveling in a far-off country and you did not know how to communicate with him, wouldn't you finally welcome even death itself as a means of escape?

If, after a time, there were ten people chained up in the kitchen, and only "one" free to come and go throughout the palace, while the rest of you did the work, how long, do you suppose, would the ten of you "smilingly" take "his" statement and assurances that the home was just as much yours as his, and that you should be very grateful for it, and should sing praises all the day long to the owner—your mutual friend—who had so graciously granted you the use of his great estate?

If each day the one who was free would come into the kitchen,—(and after telling you how fortunate you were to have the use of the palace, he would then steal even the few particles of food you had been able to gather—and would torture and beat you for objecting to his cruelty)—aren't you inclined to think that you would spend your every waking hour in an attempt to figure out some way of breaking your chains? Knowing that the one who was free could not possibly bind you all at one time, and that once free you would never again be chained to the drudgery you had experienced, DO YOU THINK THAT YOU WOULD HESITATE TO AGREE WITH EACH OF THE OTHER TEN CHAINED IN THE KITCHEN WITH YOU, THAT WHEN YOU ALL HAD GAINED YOUR FREEDOM, YOU WOULD "EQUALLY" SHARE THE NECESSARY DUTIES OF MAINTAINING THE ESTATE, PROVIDED YOU ALSO WERE ASSURED BY EACH OF THE TEN THAT YOU WOULD BE ALLOWED TO ENJOY ALL OF ITS ATTRACTIONS LIKEWISE EQUALLY?

You surely wouldn't fear the one unchained and free tenant, "once 'you all' had won your freedom and broken your chains,"—but—knowing his selfishness, greed and brutality, "you would wait until you all had broken your chains," before attempting to insist that he either do his share of the work or leave the palace to those who were willing to do so. Once you all were free, he wouldn't be a problem for your entire group, but if you tried to attack him singly he might. Being more familiar with the arrangement of the rooms in the palace, he could easily arrange a surprise attack and tie each of you up again, one by one, if you became separated from your group. Therefore, while you were chained up in the kitchen together, "and with ample day by day proofs of the free tenant's selfishness and cruelty," you would of course agree when free, to stay together in "one group," so that when you finally located him you would have no trouble in forcing him to either abide by the rules of conduct established for those who had been given the equal use of the palace, or insist that he go off to some corner of the grounds and live by himself. HOWEVER, EVEN HIS FORMER CRUELTIES WOULD NOT WARRANT YOU IN MAKING A SLAVE OF HIM, NOR IN DISOBEYING THE ESTATE'S "GOLDEN RULES" OF CONDUCT,—EVEN THOUGH REVENGE MIGHT ALMOST SEEM TO BE JUSTIFIED.

This little illustration describes the experiences of the human race today, and indicates the steps mankind must take, if they are ever to gain their freedom from the bondage and slavery forced upon them by the small handful of the world's citizens who have succeeded in enslaving all of the rest of the earth's inhabitants, and limiting their use of the world and its infinitely varied resources by shackles of poverty and the menial tasks of life. There is no use in our attempting to attack the small group of fabulously wealthy and powerful citizens who have the rest of us in bondage, if we are going to do so singly or without organization. They can never be forced to obey the rules of life established by the wisdom of our Creator, until those of us who are willing to abide by such rules, are sufficiently large in number to insist upon obedience by all, and an equal sharing of the world's resources and benefits as well as its duties. Until such a time, there is little use in our expecting any privileges other than the duties of the kitchen.

SHALL WE CONTINUE, CENTURY AFTER CENTURY, FEEDING THE MONSTER CALLED "GREED;"—A MONSTER WHICH IS FED WITH THE FIRST BORN OF OUR EVERY EFFORT, AND YET WHICH WE ARE NEVER ABLE TO SATISFY?

The lust for power, wealth and flattery can never be satisfied, nor can you chain it up and kill an occasional one of its offspring, hoping thereby to put it under control. The causes of greed and their malignant family,—"Selfishness and Self-glorification,"—must be stricken from off the face of this globe and never be allowed to return. Laws must be passed which will effectually prevent the production of any food upon which such monsters can feed. Constant rotation in office—equal distribution of the products of mankind's labor, and no individual ever again allowed to gain power, wealth, or an insane sense of superiority, constitute the only cure for greed and mad ambition.

RECOGNIZING THAT MEN ARE STILL BUT CHANGEABLE LITTLE CHILDREN IN THEIR CHARACTER DEVELOPMENT, IT IS IMPERATIVE THAT AN ECONOMIC SYSTEM BE ESTABLISHED WHICH WILL FOR ALL TIME TO COME PREVENT THE WEAKNESSES OF HUMAN CHARACTER FROM WARPING AND DISTORTING THE LIVES OF THE BILLIONS UPON BILLIONS OF HUMAN BEINGS, TO WHOM THE USE OF OUR GLORIOUSLY BEAUTIFUL WORLD HOME IS EQUALLY GRANTED.

Our arrow is not aimed at the heart of any individual or any group of individuals upon this globe,—for there is already far too great a variety of "class antagonism" and "hate,"—but it is drawn, and straining to be released, that it may pierce and destroy the vital spot of that worldwide parent of man's age-old woes,—that monster with the many names called "Greed" — "Self-glorification" — "Depraved Appetites" — "Jealousy" — "Envy" — "Hate" — "Murder" — "Power" and "Wasteful Wealth;" — in short, THE WORLD'S "GOLD AND SILVER" — "PRIVATE PROFIT" MONETARY SYSTEM.

We do not live our lives for the purpose of self-glorification, for the Bible has truly stated that—"Ye shall have no other Gods before Me." Naught else should be glorified—for there is nothing worthy of glorification that is less in stature than the Creator of the entire universe, and it is God and His complete Creation which we should glorify,—not ourselves or some group of human beings. Possibly we will have earned a little credit or honor, when,—through united world efforts,—mankind have destroyed the swamps of filthy environment, the bondage and slavery to those indescribably cruel taskmasters—"Poverty and War"—which warp the souls of men and make them abhorrent.

When we have destroyed those forces which make life so needlessly confused and hopeless, and cause men to either fear or hate their lives so greatly that suicide seems the only solution to their problems, and when thousands of suicides no longer occur each day in this country and other so-called civilized nations—and when peace and security—trust—confidence—gratitude and appreciation of each other's efforts have uprooted the causes of mankind's broken dreams and broken hearts—possibly then, there might be some slight justification for a "little" self-glorification.

Millions of tons of food are thrown away daily in order that prices may be held up to a level where manipulators

in the world's food supplies can gain a speculative profit, while not only in the foreign so-called uncivilized nations of the world, but also in our own country, people are going hungry each day.

YES! WE CERTAINLY ARE AN ENLIGHTENED PEOPLE, AND OUR PRECIOUS PRIVATE PROFIT SYSTEM A GREAT BOON TO MAN. THE WORLD HAS HAD THOUSANDS OF YEARS TO BRING ABOUT SECURITY AND PROTECTION OF THE RIGHTS OF MEN, THROUGH THE APPLICATION OF THE SO-CALLED "PROFIT" SYSTEM, UNDER THE "EACH WOLF-FOR-HIMSELF PLAN,"—AND YET IT IS NO CLOSER TO THAT RESULT THAN IT WAS 10,000 YEARS AGO, NOR WILL IT BE 10,000 YEARS FROM NOW, UNLESS MANKIND EVOLVE A SYSTEM CAPABLE OF PREVENTING GREED AND SELFISHNESS FROM LOCKING THE DOORS OF OPPORTUNITY AGAINST THOSE WHO OCCUPY OUR WORLD.

"MANKIND UNITED"—ONE SINGLE BROTHERHOOD OF MAN—"ONE FOR ALL AND ALL FOR ONE," WITH "ACTIONS" AS WELL AS "WORDS," AND THE WORLD NO LONGER A HOUSE DIVIDED AGAINST ITSELF,—AND BUILT UPON THE SHIFTING SANDS OF CHANGEABLE HUMAN CHARACTER,—BUT FINALLY ERECTED UPON A SYSTEM OF "EQUALITY" AND "GUARANTEED SAFE-GUARDS" AGAINST THE FRAILTIES OF FALLIBLE HUMAN BEINGS, COMPRISES THE ONLY PLAN WHICH WILL EVER ENDEITHER WARS OR POVERTY. "SUCH IS THE PROGRAM OF THE INTERNATIONAL INSTITUTE OF UNIVERSAL RESEARCH AND ADMINISTRATION."

What is wrong with our "so-called leaders" throughout the world,—with our executives and powerful men of wealth? Have they become so coarsened through the development of their dissipated and depraved senses, that they can no longer see or hear the suffering going on around about them? Do they no longer either "see" or "hear," or does the maintenance of their luxurious physical ease mean more to them than the pitiable cries of hundreds of millions of helpless hungry human beings? Billions of men, women and little children who inhabit this planet century after century—barely existing—living utterly hopeless lives,—wretchedly oblivious to the gorgeous beauties of this infinitely glorious universe— solely because of their under-nourished souls, and starved little bodies,— and yet we sing the praises of leaders who order us to destroy food right before the eyes of these hunger tortured human beings.

There is not "one" of the thousands of this world's competent executives, but who would be justifiably insulted if his ability to produce food, clothes and homes for the entire human family, and distribute them fairly and justly to mankind, were questioned,—provided he could be given absolute control of the production and distribution of the world's sources of supply, and ample facilities for distributing them,—and was allowed to do so "at actual cost figures" without "profit" or "speculative returns" to any one, but instead, for the "equal benefit" of all. Then if the world admittedly has sufficient executive talent, and recognized inexhaustibly abundant resources, why don't the world's executives use their talents for the accomplishment of such a result, and why have they failed to do so throughout the centuries?

Mankind can only blame their suffering upon the falsities of an economic system which encourages insane human desires for personal glory, power or wealth, in those who would otherwise possess the talents and ability with which to meet the world's problem of production and distribution, and its educational and cultural development. "There is no other reason!"

MORTAL MAN WAS NEVER INTENDED TO BECOME AN INDIVIDUAL PERSONALIZED "GOD OR RULER," WITH THE POWER OF SLAVERY OR FREEDOM, LIFE OR DEATH, OVER HIS FELLOW BEINGS.

We have throughout all of our earthly history made the fatal mistake of permitting a sense of "self-importance" and "superiority" to be developed in men and women, and after cultivating such a sense, we have placed in the hands of such depraved, abnormal types of mentality, almost "unlimited power" and authority. This mistake has cost mankind the loss of countless generations of painful progress out of poverty and filth, and as the result of it, one civilization after another has been destroyed, during a period of thousands of years, by those who become insane with the lust for more, and ever more wealth and power."!

Mankind's division into tribes and nations with their consequent development of armaments, machines and powers of destruction, created under the lying guise of "self-preservation,"—(THOUGH ALWAYS ACTUALLY MACHINES OF CONQUEST, THAT THE WEALTHY MIGHT GAIN MORE WEALTH AND "INSANE MORAL IDIOTS" MORE POWER),—has, throughout the centuries, created mountains of "dynamite," with fuses scattered over the face of our planet. Anyone, (for the moment feeling a bit like a Napoleon),—by igniting these fuses, could succeed in blowing up a civilization. UP TO THIS PRESENT DATE IN HUMAN HISTORY THERE HAS NEVER BEEN A CIVILIZATION CAPABLE OF PREVENTING ITS OWN SELF-DESTRUCTION, AND THERE NEVER WILL BE, UNTIL ARMIES AND MACHINES OF DESTRUCTION ARE NO LONGER PERMITTED TO EXIST,—nor until mankind is finally united into one unselfish brotherhood, willing to live "One for All and All for One"—with each inhabitant of our planet desiring the security, independence and happiness of every other inhabitant—and willing to do his part of the task of bringing about this universal result; no one desiring nor striving for dominion over another, nor any form of self-glorification; each one joyously free, having an abundance of every good thing; and glad to be alive and to live and let live, with no desire for self-aggrandizement; each one striving to exceed his own former accomplishments, and not attempting merely to surpass those round about him;—not seeking to prove his superiority "over others," but only his superiority over his own former attainments.

A mad scramble, like so many "wolves,"—to see who can accumulate the greatest number and variety of possessions, eat the most food, wear the most clothes, have the most money,—does not constitute a type of ambition worthy of "intelligent creatures," nor would man be motivated by such false and unsatisfying goals were it not for the limitations and forms of bondage forced upon him by our existing economic system.

THE ONLY AMBITION WORTHY OF MAN, IS TO CEASELESSLY STRIVE TO UNDERSTAND FROM WHENCE HE CAME, WHY HE IS HERE, AND THE

ULTIMATE DESTINY AND PURPOSE OF LIFE; IN OTHER WORDS, WHERE HE IS GOING. Recognizing that all of human progress has come "first in the form of an idea" appearing to the consciousness of some individual,—either as a mechanical invention, a new design for homes, or the vision of harmony gained by way of a musical composition, a poem, or a beautiful painting,—men should strive to understand more about the source from whence ideas emanate. ALWAYS HAS THE AVENUE,—THROUGH WHICH EVERY DESIRABLE OBJECT OF LIFE HAS REACHED MANKIND,—CONSISTED OF "MEN'S THOUGHT PROCESSES"—THE NATURE OF THEIR THINKING.

THE MOTIVES INSPIRING THOUGHT—THE VISIONS WHICH PROMPT MEN TO STRIVE UNCEASINGLY TOWARDS THE ATTAINMENT OF SOME HIGH AND WORTHY GOAL—HAVE ALL COME BY WAY OF THOUGHT. IS IT NOT TRUE THEN, THAT THE ONLY AMBITION TRULY WORTHY OF MAN, CONSISTS IN LEARNING HOW TO "THINK" MORE CONSTRUCTIVELY, MORE INSPIRINGLY, MORE BEAUTIFULLY? Inasmuch as such a statement is indisputably true, should not "the combined efforts of mankind" be directed towards the establishment of an economic system and the passing of laws, rules and regulations, controlling the conduct of men in their relationships with one another, in such a manner that no slightest hindrance or obstruction would even momentarily delay man's progress towards the goal of intelligent right thinking? NO CONDITION SHOULD BE PERMITTED TO EXIST WHICH WOULD FORCE US TO A LOWER LEVEL IN THE USE OF OUR THOUGHT FACULTIES THAN THAT OF WHICH WE ARE WORTHY.

SURELY MEN ARE WORTHY OF THOUGHTS OTHER THAN JUST THOSE PERTAINING TO THE ACCUMULATION OF FOOD AND THE SATISFACTION OF THEIR ANIMAL DESIRES. We do not spend hours each day pumping air into warehouses, nor keep hundreds of thousands of men and women busy with bookkeeping entries to record the amount of air we have accumulated, and yet it is very apparent that no one on earth today has learned how to get along without air. But the reason we are not ceaselessly contemplating the importance of air, and morbidly concentrating our entire efforts upon its accumulation, is traceable to the fact that it exists in such limitless abundance that it is wholly unnecessary to waste either time or effort thinking about its accumulation,—other than to be sincerely grateful for the fact that it is free for our use, and does not require any struggle for us to each receive our individual share of it.

SURELY NEITHER FOOD NOR CLOTHES ARE OF ANY GREATER IMPORTANCE OR ANY MORE ESSENTIAL TO OUR EXISTENCE THAN AIR! THEN WHY SHOULD IT BE, THAT WE HAVE ADVANCED NO FARTHER THAN THE SAVAGES OF ONE HUNDRED THOUSAND (100,000) YEARS AGO, WHOSE ENTIRE LIVES CONSISTED OF DEVISING WAYS AND MEANS OF GETTING FOOD;—SINCE—WITH OUR PRESENT DAY MACHINERY—THE EARTH COULD READILY BE MADE TO PRODUCE A HUNDRED TIMES MORE FOOD EACH YEAR THAN THE ENTIRE HUMAN RACE COULD POSSIBLY REQUIRE OR USE.

Having been endowed with the priceless gift and faculty—"which enables us to think"—and thereby to exist on a slightly higher mental plane than the animals of the field,—"whose thought processes consist wholly of physical impulses and desires,"—why must we be forced to waste this precious gift in living lives of no greater usefulness than the swine in their pigpens? WHY MUST THE MAJORITY OF THE WORLD'S "THINKING CREATURES" BE FORCED BY A HANDFUL OF UTTERLY SELFISH HUMAN BEINGS, TO LEAVE NO MORE WORTHY RECORD OF THEIR EXISTENCE "THAN THE CAST-OFF PHYSICAL BODY" TO WHICH THEY HAVE BEEN COMPELLED TO DEVOTE THEIR ENTIRE THOUGHTS, EFFORTS AND LIVES— (TO FEED, CLOTHE, AND HOUSE IT)—AND YET, WHICH, WHEN THEY DIE, DOES NOT OF ITSELF LEAVE ANY GREATER OR MORE LASTING PROOF OF ITS VALUE, THAN THE PHYSICAL BODY OF EVEN THE LEAST INTELLIGENT OF GOD'S CREATURES?

Surely there must be some more permanent proof,—"than just their cast-off physical bodies,"—that the people of each generation can leave in evidence of the fact that they possessed "the faculty of thought,"—even if such proof consisted only in larger and more beautiful parks, more inspiring poems, songs and paintings capable of raising the level of thought of our descendants slightly above that which we occupied!

After all of men's thousands of years of endless struggles,—"out of complete and utter mental darkness and animalic desires,"—to a level upon which they have made such marvelous discoveries that,—if they would use them,—they would no longer need to give even "a passing thought" to how they are going to get food or clothes or homes,—surely the people of this enlightened age are worthy of such discoveries! WHY SHOULDN'T WE MEASURE UP TO THE LIMITLESS POTENTIALITIES OF

PROGRESS, STRETCHING ETERNALLY BEFORE OUR GAZE, AND CEASE THINKING ON A LEVEL WITH THE HERDS OF SWINE WHICH OCCUPY OUR PIGPENS?

Surely,—even though we have made an art of such things,—we can occasionally raise our thoughts above food, or clothes,—what we are going to wear or how we are going to dress our hair,—the shape or design of our shoes—or the variety and preparation of our food,—and have time to give some slight thought to the discovery of what talents we may possess, and to their development, that we may leave some worthy evidence of having been thinking creatures,—when we finally pass on beyond the gaze of our associates.

Why must we,—who call ourselves "The Children of God," and "Intelligent Thinking Beings,"—spend our entire lives working to feed and perpetuate an economic system which raises to its positions and offices of leadership, those men and women who have least advanced beyond the level of the lowest forms of animal life, and whose every impulse and ambition consists of the "swinish lusts of the flesh,"—an insane driving force which causes them to use all of their wealth and power and influence, solely for the accumulation of vast quantities of food, clothes and luxuries, which neither they nor their children, nor their "children's children," could possibly consume or use,—even with the most fully developed of depraved appetites,—during a period of thousands of years?

Why do we raise those who are still no more than animals,—in their thinking processes,—to positions of leadership, and give them the power to keep the rest of us on a level of life where we are forced to waste our priceless natural talents and thought faculties upon ways and means of getting even "the barest necessities" of life?

Why, when every boy or girl in every civilized nation on this globe, dreams of great accomplishments and goals worthy of intelligent creatures, must they be forced, even before they have attained to their maturity, to adjust their ambitions to studies and mental development unworthy of any creatures other than wolves or pigs? Why must they be forced to learn only those things which will enable them,—like wolves tearing at each other's throats, or pigs pushing other pigs aside with their snouts,—to express their priceless faculty of thought solely for the accumulation of food, clothes and material possessions, when our present-day machinery could produce a hundred times more of these things than the entire human race could possibly consume?

WITH BUT A SMALL PERCENTAGE OF THE EARTHS INHABITANTS REQUIRED TO DEVOTE THEIR THOUGHTS AND EFFORTS,—(LARGELY IN A SUPERVISORY CAPACITY),—THE WORLD'S MARVELOUS INVENTIONS, "FULLY USED," COULD RESULT IN A PRODUCTION OF SUCH VAST QUANTITIES OF THE SO-CALLED NECESSITIES AND LUXURIES OF LIFE, THAT MEN WOULD NO LONGER BE OBLIGED TO GIVE ANY MORE THOUGHT TO THEIR ACCUMULATION, THAN THEY WOULD TO THE ACCUMULATION OR STORAGE OF THE AIR WE BREATHE.

Is it not "barely possible" that man freed from the endless struggle for food,—(which would eternally keep him on a level with the lowest forms of animal life),—might possibly make discoveries, and produce results in the form of engineering and cultural attainments worthy of the creative quality of mentality with which he is indisputably endowed? With thousands of millions of men and women—all freed and enabled to release the creative qualities of their thoughts in grand and noble attainments- is it not possible,—(compared to the results of the few dozen men and women who now leave a record of outstanding accomplishments each century),—that the sum total attainments of the people,—"not just of each century, but of every generation,"—might be so startlingly grand, and gloriously beautiful, that there would shortly come to pass the fulfillment of Christ Jesus' teachings, and men might learn that "The Kingdom of Heaven is not afar off," neither "up nor down,"—"East nor West"—"North nor South," "but here at hand," and ready at any time to be "fully expressed?"

WHEN THE GREAT MASTER STATED,—"THE KINGDOM OF HEAVEN IS WITHIN YOU,"—SURELY HE DID NOT MEAN THE BONES AND MEMBRANES, NOR THE BLOOD WHICH FLOWS THROUGH OUR BODIES; HE COULD ONLY HAVE MEANT "OUR CREATIVE FACULTY OF THOUGHT," AND THROUGH THE EXPRESSION OF WHICH, ENDLESS DISCOVERIES OF GLORIOUS BEAUTY WOULD BE ALWAYS AT HAND FOR US TO ENJOY. IS IT SACRILEGIOUS THEN TO THINK THAT MEN MIGHT EVEN OVERCOME "DEATH ITSELF," INASMUCH AS CHRIST JESUS RAISED THE DEAD AND REFERRED TO DEATH AS "AN ENEMY" WHICH WE WOULD EVENTUALLY DESTROY? Is it not possible that sickness and all of its causes would shortly be done away with, and that grief and human suffering would no longer be a concomitant of life, if men were no longer filled with the fear of poverty, and could unite their talents for purposes other than the mere accumulation of food?

Men and women who are truly grateful that they possess the faculties of "thought,"—instead of merely an accumulation of the lower forms of animal instincts and desires,—should "combine" their talents, strength, and "entire resources,"—and if necessary, "dedicate their very lives" to the establishment of an economic system which will no longer invite into public office, any man or woman motivated by the slightest particle of selfish personal desire for wealth or power. IS IT NOT TIME THAT SUCH OF THE WORLD'S POPULATION AS ARE DESIROUS OF THE PRIVILEGES OF FREEDOM OF THOUGHT, SPEECH AND ACTION, FINALLY UNITE THEIR STRENGTH IN ONE GREAT BODY, ENCIRCLING THE ENTIRE EARTH, AND NO LONGER REQUEST, "BUT DEMAND," THE RIGHT TO LIVE AS INTELLIGENT CREATURES SHOULD LIVE, AND TO BE GRANTED THE BENEFITS OF THE INVENTIONS AND DEVELOPMENTS OF RECENT YEARS, THAT THEY MIGHT NO LONGER BE FORCED TO WASTE THEIR ENTIRE LIVES IN STRUGGLING FOR THOSE THINGS WHICH CAN,—TO A LARGE EXTENT,—BE PRODUCED BY NON-THINKING MACHINES?

Recognizing the fact that there are hundreds of millions of industrious and intelligent clear-thinking men and women, who are fully aware of the availability of economic freedom and complete financial independence, would we be worthy of receiving such freedom, if we were unwilling to become acquainted with such people, and to associate with them?

Knowing that over two hundred million (200,000,000) intelligent and industrious men and women can receive the message contained in this bulletin within a matter of months,—as each one to whom it is given assumes the responsibility of placing it in the hands of others,—and knowing that when said number of people have received this announcement, that information will then be placed in their hands which will enable them to form into "one vast united working force;"—knowing that when this world-wide organization has been fully formed, the buying power of its members will exceed one thousand million dollars ($1000,000,000.00) per day,—(based upon their actual cash expenditures at this time),—and knowing that with this buying power, such an organization, "equally-owned" and "equally-controlled" by each of its two hundred million (200,000,000) members, could vote into existence a system which would permanently outlaw—"not only war—but also poverty;"—KNOWING

THESE THINGS, ARE WE SO "DULL OF MIND" AND "BROKEN OF SPIRIT," THAT WE HAVE NEITHER THE MENTAL ENERGY NOR PHYSICAL VITALITY LEFT, WITH WHICH TO RAISE OUR VOICES IN BEHALF OF SUCH A RESULT?

The International Institute of Universal Research and Administration believes that the right-thinking, clear-minded men and women of the world, are awake to the potentialities and possibilities of "world-wide unity of action," not as a conglomeration of antagonistic movements, but as "a world-wide association of intelligent men and women" meeting on the common ground of identical aspirations and ideals of true brotherhood and freedom; and irrespective of race, color, class, or religious beliefs, willing to become part owners in a world-wide corporation capable of supplying their individual as well as their collective needs;—two hundred million (200,000,000) men and women willing to occupy positions with said corporation, in accordance with their individual talents and training, and willing, after expending of their respective abilities, to receive an equal share of the sum total products of their united labors. Just as thinking creatures make no complaint over the amount of air breathed by their fellow beings, nor have any desire to receive a greater abundance of air than another, so likewise should we be intelligent enough to realize that when the necessities and luxuries of life are produced in such large quantities that we could not even use "the smallest part" of our own share of them, we need hardly begrudge others the privileges of similar abundance.

THE PRICELESS GIFT OF LIFE AND WHAT WE DO WITH IT

THE human race seems to be so busily engaged in honoring and glorifying "so-called great men," that it has had no time to glorify "the greatness of the creative source" from which "all things," including "our own lives " as well as "our entire universe," have emanated. A source and Creator whose limitless wisdom and glorious creations make the handiwork of even the world's combined great thinkers and great doers of all of the many centuries of human progress, seem but the puny efforts of a colony of ants. Throughout all past centuries, up to and including the present era, the human race has glorified its "great men,"—and while sacrificing "the very souls" of its billions upon billions of men, women and helpless little children upon the altar of its murderous and insane theory of "the survival of the fittest,"—it has wasted its energies glorifying those who, (with but few exceptions),—climb above the masses—not because of their benevolent accomplishments, BUT PRIMARILY BECAUSE OF THEIR DOMINEERING BRUTALITY, GREED AND UTTER SELF-CENTEREDNESS.

We have, throughout countless ages, broken the hearts and spirits of "billions" of men and women, that we might retain the questionable privilege of bowing down in sacrilegious worship to a handful of egotists, insane with an uncontrollable desire for "self-glorification." Instead of evolving an economic system which would enable "all mankind" to fully develop their God-given talents and abilities, we waste our lives and energies glorifying a handful of people whom we raise to "imaginary heights of grandeur," and then stand in awe-inspired contemplation of their "vast" and "limitless" wisdom. Worshiping human leaders who have yet to ever make "even an attempt" to try and evolve an economic system capable of "guaranteeing" food, clothes, homes, and an "equality of opportunity for self-development," to the people of every land, and every class, and every religion. If "even one" of these "World Rulers" or "Industrial Magnates," had really attempted to obey "The Golden Rule," or measure up,—"even ever so slightly,"—to Christ Jesus' Sermon on the Mount, they could,—with their limitless wealth and influence,—have brought to pass an economic system which would long centuries ago have ended both war and poverty. HOWEVER, WE IDOLIZE AND GLORIFY THEM—NOT FOR ENDING WAR AND POVERTY BUT FOR SUCCESSFULLY PERPETUATING THESE EVILS.

Napoleon Bonaparte and countless other men before and since his time, are remembered and glorified—(?)—not for the happiness, peace and security they brought into the lives of mankind, "but for the number of men they killed," and for their success in burdening with debt, for endless generations, the men and women who would have to pay the bills of their extravagant and insane wholesale slaughter of human life.

What has continued the injustices, wars, poverty and uncertainties of our present economic system, if it is not greed, selfishness and the cruel ambitions of a few men or women each century, who find—thereby—that they can rise to power and prominence, or attain a questionable form of recognition and honor, because of their brutality and cruelty?

Is it not a fact that mankind—by now—should have learned that we did not create either ourselves or this infinitely glorious and eternal universe which we call our home, and that if any honor or glory is due for our existence here,—then ordinary, every-day curiosity,—(if we as yet possess no higher instincts),—should most certainly prompt us to make some slight effort to learn who or what our "Creator" is, and to glorify "Him,"—"not man" who is but the child of that source from whence all things within the universe have come?

Is it not time that we ceased magnifying the importance, or wisdom, or power of any mortal man, who today is—yet tomorrow when we look - around,—"like the grass of the fields,"—he is shriveled up, passed away and no longer to be found? There must surely be something more dependable, stable and worthy of glorification than the usually selfish and "always vacillating" embodiment called a mortal man!

BEFORE WE CAN EVEN START BEING WORTHY OF HONOR, WE WOULD FIRST HAVE TO EXPRESS "CHANGELESS WISDOM,"—THE DEPENDABLE GOODNESS OF "DIVINE LOVE,"—THE UNALTERABLE PERFECTION OF "ETERNAL TRUTH,"—AND WE ARE QUITE SURE THAT "NONE OF US HAS, AS YET, REACHED SUCH HEIGHTS OF GRANDEUR."

Do you not believe it is high time that all of us commenced thinking more along the lines of those things which will make us worthy of at least our own "self-respect," before we seek honor and glory from our fellows? Have we the courage or unselfish love for our brother man which enables us to see the suffering of our fellow beings on every side, and prompts us to an "uncontrollable desire," to relieve it and bring them happiness? If we have not, then we do not yet deserve even "self-respect," since the world today possesses such limitless means of ready communication with our fellow beings, that there is no longer any justifiable excuse for our failure to bring any widespread sufferings we might observe, to the attention of mankind, with a constructively worked-out remedy and solution for such problems.

We claim to be intelligent creatures, and to have "eyes with which to see" and "ears with which to hear"—therefore it must surely be most apparent to us all, that the world's present facilities of production and distribution have permanently eliminated whatever excuses may have seemed to exist in the past, for the wholesale slaughter we call "War," or the still greater suffering and loss of life which the word "Poverty" describes.

Instead of blowing trumpets in honor of the world's false leaders who have used their power, wealth, and influence to murder our loved ones, (with carefully planned revolutions, wars and depressions), let us sing our praises in honor of the "Omniscient," "Omnipotent" and "Omnipresent Creator,"— towards whom we have shown so little honest "respect," "gratitude" or "love," throughout the ages of mankind's sojourn upon this planet.

NO ONE WITH EYES TO SEE OR EARS TO HEAR THE AGONIZING CRIES OF HELPLESS LITTLE CHILDREN, AND BROKEN-SPIRITED FEAR-STRICKEN MEN AND WOMEN, THE WORLD OVER, HAS TIME OR THE DESIRE TO BE HONORED OR PRAISED. SUCH A ONE IS QUITE TOO BUSY TRYING TO FIND AND DESTROY THE ROOTS OF THOSE THINGS FROM WHICH SPRING THE CAUSES OF HUMANITY'S STRUGGLES AND WOES; QUITE TOO BUSY TO "EITHER DESIRE" OR "HAVE TIME" FOR SELF-GLORIFICATION.

For a few years at least, we believe that all of us, "including our so-called great men and women," might well profit by the example of those few throughout the centuries, who have,—(being truly worthy of honor),— been "much too busy" helping their less fortunate brothers, to take the time to "even receive" the honors prepared for them by their appreciative followers.

This book has been written for those whom we believe will agree with us, that it is time all right-thinking men and women on this globe formed into one compact group,—(waiving and forfeiting all chances of individual glorification, wealth, power or honor),—and dedicated their lives to the "sole purpose" of uprooting and wiping out for all time to come, the world's accursed "humanly-planned," and "humanly-perpetuated" causes of poverty and war.

ONLY A PROFOUNDLY SINCERE DESIRE ON THE PART OF EVERY ONE OF THE MILLIONS OF INTELLIGENT MEN AND WOMEN THROUGHOUT THE MAJOR NATIONS OF THE EARTH, AND ONLY "WORLD-WIDE UNITY OF ACTION," WILL BE "POWERFUL ENOUGH" TO UPROOT THE CAUSES OF MANKIND'S "HUMANLY PERPETUATED" TRIBULATIONS.

None of us can as yet stop the sun in its course, or cause the tides to recede before their time, and the difference between even the most brilliant man or woman on this globe and a South African savage, is still very slight. No one need feel greatly abused if he is not honored above the rest of his brothers, for after all none of us are worthy of even very much of our own "self-respect," to say nothing of "special recognition" or "public acclaim." Any impulse man might have to sing praises, or to glorify something, had better—for the present—be devoted to "humble prayers" and psalms to "Our Creator," in evidence of our recognition of the indescribably glorious, and priceless gift of "Consciousness"—"Life"—the capacity to "See"—and to some slight extent, "Understand"—God's limitless creations and gifts of love prepared for our happiness, and so abundantly surrounding our lives.

All of this brings us to just one point: Wouldn't it truly be a relief to become more "childlike"—to give up the age-old struggle for "Superiority" and to live for the clean, wholesome joy of just "Living," and really "Strive" to become worthy of the "priceless" gift of life;—to have time and unlimited opportunity for travel, and to learn to know and to love this gloriously beautiful world of ours; to work to make it ever cleaner and more beautiful as man's home, and then to strive that we may individually become daily "superior to ourself" of yesterday, instead of merely "superior to others;" seeking not to "surpass one another," but only to overcome the weaknesses of that "most opaque" of all human qualities—"self-love?"

THE TIME AND EFFORT MEN HAVE SPENT THROUGHOUT THE AGES TRYING TO ACCUMULATE POSSESSIONS WHICH THEY KNEW THEY COULD NEVER TAKE WITH THEM WHEN THEY LEFT;—AND STRIVING FOR THOSE THINGS WHICH THEY KNEW THEY COULD NOT POSSIBLY NEED, AND WHICH THEY USUALLY DO NOT EVEN WANT AFTER THEY GET THEM; (OR STRIVING TO GAIN HONOR OR GLORY BELONGING NOT TO THEMSELVES, BUT TO THEIR CREATOR),—WOULD,—IF THEY HAD SPENT THE SAME INTENSITY OF EFFORT TO IMPROVE THE LIVES OF THEIR FELLOWMEN,—HAVE TURNED THIS OLD WORLD OF OURS INTO A VERITABLE "GARDEN OF EDEN," AND MEN INTO BEINGS TRULY WORTHY OF OCCUPYING IT—MANY, MANY CENTURIES AGO.

SHALL WE BE MASTER BUILDERS OR MASTER MURDERERS "EXTERMINATION" OR "ECONOMIC EQUALITY"? MANKIND MUST CHOOSE

WHAT do you think would happen if every one on this earth today would put aside the struggle for individual financial superiority over others for just ten short years? What do you think would happen if all would unite their efforts for the purpose of supplying each family on this earth with a beautiful home, with enough to eat and to wear—with beautiful surroundings and lovely parks in which to spend generous leisure hours, and would build the facilities with which to enable "all people" to travel throughout the world to its many points of interest and beauty; . . . . would establish educational institutions in order that all might be enlightened regarding those things worthy of man's investigation and understanding; and then would strive to live as one great family—"One for All and All for One"—with no "superiority" or "inferiority" complexes ever allowed to develop; . . . . "all people" helping to provide opportunities for the cultivation of strong constructive traits of character which would enable them to look forward with joy,—and "limitless" expectations of happiness,—to their lives, instead of cultivating the weaker qualities of character and the enslaving false appetites which inevitably result in a loathing of one's self, and a final hatred of life—(one's own life and experiences, as well as others)? What do you think would happen if we would develop an educational system which would help to make us ambitious for the future of "mankind" and capable of working for "humanity's benefit" and not just our own; . . . and finally, instead of teaching children that the primal object of life, (and the main purpose for which they live), is to "make more money," or to "gain fame and public acclaim" because of their "superiority" over others—teach them rather that their only ambition should be to each day be a little "kinder," a little "finer" in their thoughts and speech and actions—a little "cleaner"—a little "stronger"—a little "more grateful" to their Creator for their lives and for the universe He has given them as their home;—and each day a little "more worthy" of the countless blessings existing here on our earth in limitless abundance and variety for man's use; . . . AGAIN WE ASK, IF THESE WERE MANKIND'S GOALS, WOULD NOT THE WORLD—SOON THEREAFTER—BE

TRANSFORMED INTO THE GARDEN OF EDEN,—"THE HEAVEN" WE ALL ENJOY THINKING OF AS OUR ETERNAL HOME?

LET US UNITE OUR EFFORTS FOR THE PURPOSE OF PROVIDING "EQUALITY OF OPPORTUNITY FOR ALL," AND THEN WHEN THE TIME COMES TO PASS ALONG TO ANOTHER EXPERIENCE, WE SHALL NOT HAVE TO BE ASHAMED OF THE USE TO WHICH WE HAVE PUT LIFE'S "PRICELESS GIFT" OF INTELLIGENCE,—NOR ASHAMED OF THE WAY WE HAVE LIVED OUR LIVES.

Mankind seem to be laboring under the false impression that there are not enough of the necessary or desirable things of life for everyone on this globe, and that therefore each man must struggle with someone else for what he needs or wants, and that only those who are stronger than their fellows can possibly survive this struggle. Can you not see how either this "conscious" or "subconscious" attitude of mind has, throughout the centuries, caused fear, greed, selfishness, envy, jealousy, resentment, hate, robbery and murder to occur among individuals—resulting in feuds between families and groups, and finally,—(as this attitude expands and takes hold of communities and nations),—the all-consuming flames of jealousy, envy, hate and fear of the people of one nation towards those of another, bring to pass the wars of each generation? And do you not see that these qualities of thought are perpetuated largely by those who acquire "financial gain" from doing so?

Do you not see how the citizens of the various nations are taught to believe that they must go out in armies and kill one another, in order that they may weaken the ones from whom they may desire to steal some possession which they have been "mesmerized" into thinking they can get in no other way,—or that they must "kill" in order to protect their own possessions which they have been taught to think someone might attempt to take from them? It is not difficult to recognize the fact that jealousy, envy, fear, or hate, constitute the "primal causes" of crime, murder and war. NOR IS IT DIFFICULT TO RECOGNIZE THE FACT THAT MANY OF THE WORLD'S MOST WEALTHY AND INFLUENTIAL FAMILIES DERIVE THEIR "ENTIRE PROFITS" FROM STIMULATING AND PERPETUATING THESE QUALITIES OF HUMAN THOUGHT, IN ORDER THAT WARS MAY BE FOUGHT, AND THAT THE ARMAMENTS AND MERCHANDISE OF WAR IN WHICH THEY DEAL, MAY BE BOUGHT FROM THEM.

MENTIONING ONLY ONE OF THE BY-PRODUCTS OF THESE FALSE TEACH-INGS, WE REMIND YOU OF A FACT WHICH IS HARDLY LESS IMPORTANT THAN THE HUMANLY-PLANNED AND DIRECTED CAUSES OF WAR; NAMELY, THAT THE WORLD'S LEADING PSYCHIATRISTS AND PHYSICIANS—AS WELL AS ITS MOST PROMINENT METAPHYSICIANS,—ARE UNANIMOUS IN THEIR AGREEMENT THAT THESE SAME QUALITIES OF FEAR, ENVY, JEALOUSY AND HATE, "CAUSE THE GREATER PART OF MAN'S PHYSICAL AILMENTS," AND "THE DEPLETION OF HIS ENERGIES " AS WELL AS THE DEGENERATION OF HIS CHARACTER.

Looking still further into this struggle to accumulate possessions, we find it causing two distinct qualities of character in men, and both of them abominable and totally unworthy of any intelligent creature; namely, "inferiority" or "superiority" complexes of thought. The one who, through lack of educational or cultural opportunities, has developed a sense of self-depreciation—or who starts losing his individual battle in mankind's needless struggle for existence—is soon forced into a belief of being inferior. With his spirit broken, his confidence in himself completely destroyed, (and without even attempting to estimate his "incalculable" loss of happiness or his loneliness and grief), such a one becomes just so much "dead timber"—a lifeless "dead weight" and burden on the shoulders of mankind;—hopeless and ceasing to try, he soon becomes useless to himself and everyone else.

However, the fact of the matter is, that in nine hundred and ninety-nine instances of ordinarily intelligent men or women out of every one thousand whose spirits have been broken, their failures merely evidence a lack of the necessary talent or ability to keep up their end of the "wolfish struggle" for food. But this does not necessarily mean that they might not have found happiness and become useful to themselves and to the world in some entirely different direction,—for there is ample reason to believe that every individual on this globe possesses some quality of intelligence of value to the human race, and there is not the slightest question but that the world's so-called failures would, in the majority of cases, never have been forced to acknowledge their inferiority had they been helped and educated to find their place in the scheme of things in an activity they could enjoy express-ing.

WHO ARE WE TO JUDGE OTHERS? IS IT NOT POSSIBLE THAT EVERY ONE OF THE COUNTLESS BILLIONS OF MEN AND WOMEN THROUGHOUT THE

CENTURIES—(WHO HAVE MADE A FAILURE OF LIFE)—WOULD HAVE ADDED IMMEASURABLY TO THE SUM TOTAL—NOT ONLY OF THEIR OWN HAPPINESS—BUT TO THAT OF THE ENTIRE HUMAN RACE, HAD THEY BEEN GIVEN THE ADVANTAGES WHICH WOULD HAVE DEVELOPED THEIR PARTICULAR TALENTS OR ABILITIES?

MULTIPLY BY ONE MILLION, THE BEAUTIFUL POEMS, THE GLORIOUS PAINTINGS AND INSPIRING MUSICAL COMPOSITIONS OF THE PAST ONE HUNDRED (100) YEARS; . . . ADD TO THIS TOTAL "A MILLION TIMES" THE NUMBER OF INVENTIONS AND DISCOVERIES IN THE FIELDS OF CHEMISTRY, PHYSICS, AND THE ENGINEERING SCIENCES OF THE DAY,—AND THEN YOU MAY START TO UNDERSTAND WHAT THE "EACH WOLF FOR HIMSELF" PRIVATE PROFIT SYSTEM HAS COST MANKIND. AND YET THIS TOTAL WOULD BE BUT THE SMALLEST FRACTIONAL PART OF THE ACTUAL VOLUME OF BENEFITS WHICH MANKIND MIGHT NOW BE ENJOYING, HAD EVERY MAN AND WOMAN ON OUR GLOBE BEEN ENCOURAGED AND HELPED TO FULLY DEVELOP THEIR LATENT POWERS AND NATURAL TALENTS! THIS BRIEF ILLUSTRATION MAY HELP ONE TO GAIN SOME "SLIGHT" COMPREHENSION OF THE LOSS TO MANKIND, AND THE OPPORTUNITIES FOR HAPPINESS OUT OF WHICH WE HAVE BEEN CHEATED BY THOSE WHO HAVE PERMITTED THE PERPETUATION OF A SYSTEM BUILT UPON THE THEORY OF "THE SURVIVAL OF THE FITTEST;"—A THEORY WORTHY ONLY OF "SWINE" WITH THEIR SNOUTS IN TROUGHS OF SWILL, OR "PACKS OF WOLVES" TEARING AT THE THROATS OF LESS FEROCIOUS ANIMALS.

Is it not possible that "all of us" are created to add something of value—(and that we each really have something to add)—to the happiness and welfare of the entire human race as well as to our own families or ourselves? Is it not possible that nothing more is needed than the removal from around the roots of each one's life, of the weeds of fear, envy, jealousy and hate, in order that there may be revealed the useful natural qualities and talents possessed in abundant measure by even the most lowly of human beings?

A garden is surely lovelier when it is aglow with a variety of shades of color and beauty, than when it is overgrown with weeds, and with but an occasional blossom able to survive. So, also will this world become a place of greater beauty and loveliness, when each one of its occupants receives the advantages which will cultivate latent abilities and truly constructive qualities of character.

When the weeds of fear, envy, jealousy and hate are permanently uprooted and forever destroyed, and one's mental and bodily unfoldment takes place in an atmosphere I of brotherly love and good will, instead of rivalry and distrust, what a vision of joyous beauty our world will soon become.

Why shouldn't mankind build an economic system which would help them to develop into that which they were ordained by their Creator to become? Surely men are not just animals, ceaselessly struggling and fighting to prove their superiority over one another!

SINCE GREED—FEAR—ENVY—JEALOUSY—AND HATE LEAD TO DEPRAVITY, DISEASED MINDS, SICK BODIES—CRIME—MURDER AND WAR, WHY DON'T WE UPROOT THAT WHICH CONSTITUTES THEIR ORIGIN; NAMELY, "POVERTY AND ECONOMIC INEQUALITY?" WHY DON'T WE AT ONCE AND FOR ALL TIME, DESTROY THESE PRIMAL CAUSES OF MAN'S SUFFERING AND WOES? WHAT IS THERE TO HINDER US FROM DOING SO? SURELY THE WORLD HAS ENOUGH MACHINERY, EXECUTIVES, TRAINED WORKERS, AND RESOURCES—AS WELL AS DESIRE—FOR THE ACCOMPLISHMENT OF SUCH A RESULT!

Throughout the centuries there has never been a time when the practical application—on a world-wide scale—of the principle of human relationship to which we refer as "The Golden Rule," would not have amply met the needs of every one on our globe, if coupled with it we had shackled and controlled the insane selfishness and mad ambitions of a small percentage of mankind.

Now let us see what happens to the few who win in the struggle of "the survival of the fittest," or who are born with a thousand times as much money and as many opportunities, or a thousand times more of the abundance of this world's goods than the average man possesses. In most instances, we find that there is planted in their minds an almost unavoidable feeling of their "superiority" over their fellow beings, and soon they develop an "ever-growing" desire to prove this superiority—not over their own "inferior qualities" of character or "animalic natures," but over their brother man. If this feeling of superiority continues for long, there quickly develops an insane desire for personal power,—not that they might thereby glorify their Creator or make the lives of their fellows happier,— but to use for satisfying a ceaseless desire to glorify themselves, or to prove how much more they know or how much more powerful and important they are than others. Gradually such an insistence that mankind recognize their power and superiority takes possession of their mentalities, that even the murder of millions upon millions of their fellow beings seems justified to their depraved intellects. MORAL IDIOCY SOON PLACES "A BLIND OBSESSION" FOR POWER IN FULL CONTROL OF THEIR ACTIONS. They will then unhesitatingly plot and execute a war among the inhabitants of the entire earth, if it becomes necessary to do so, in order to gain more wealth or to further convince themselves of their power and influence. To maintain their prestige, they will even sacrifice their own sons to the "god of War," when the lust for power and public recognition has obsessed and warped their mentalities sufficiently.

THE HUMAN RACE WILL NEVER BE FREED FROM WARS AND WILL NEVER FIND PEACE UNTIL IT RECOGNIZES THE FACT THAT IT IS AS VITAL TO "PREVENT" TOO MUCH POWER FROM REACHING THE HANDS OF THOSE WHO HAVE NOT "FULLY PROVEN THEIR LOVE FOR HUMANITY"—AND THEIR "ABSOLUTE SELFLESSNESS OF CHARACTER"—AS IT IS TO PREVENT THE DANGERS OF POVERTY, JEALOUSY, OR FEAR FROM GENERATING "ENVY" AND "HATE" IN THE HEARTS OF MEN. THE LATTER IS A KILLER IN A SMALL WAY, BUT "INSANE GREED" AND THE CRAVING FOR POWER OR WEALTH CONDUCTS ITS KILLINGS BY THE MILLIONS, AND HAS CONSTI- TUTED THROUGHOUT TENS OF THOUSANDS OF YEARS, A FORCE WHICH HAS INVARIABLY DESTROYED EACH AND EVERY CIVILIZATION THAT THE INDUSTRIOUS AND RIGHT-THINKING MEN AND WOMEN OF THE HUMAN RACE HAVE EVER CONSTRUCTED.

Mortal man is not God, nor should he be glorified or worshiped as such. Let his joy and his reward come from bringing greater happiness and security into the lives of his brothers—not from the accumulation of power, excessive wealth, or flattery. Instead, let him be so filled with the desire to make this world ever more joyous and beautiful, that he has no room left within his mentality for a desire to seek praise or to be thanked. Let him forever be turning the thoughts of mankind to gratitude and thanksgiving to the Creator of this vast limitlessly beautiful universe, and to an acquain- tanceship with the "All-wise" and "All-loving" Father and Mother of us all. Let no man desire to draw the attention of others to himself more than to another, for we all have the same "Divine Parent" and this universe—"Our Home"—belongs as much to one as to another. Is it not time then, that the inhabitants of our world unite into one family, with no favorites?

LET THE STRONG GLADLY SHARE THE FRUITAGE OF THEIR GREATER TALENTS OR ABILITIES WITH THOSE LESS FORTUNATE, AND IT WILL NOT BE LONG BEFORE A CONDITION OF ABUNDANCE, BROTHERLY LOVE, AND AN "EQUALITY OF OPPORTUNITY" FOR SELF-IMPROVEMENT AND MUTUAL RESPECT, APPRECIATION AND CONFIDENCE, WILL UNIVERSALLY EXIST AMONG MEN.

LET NONE BE TOO WEAK NOR NONE TOO STRONG IN HIS OR HER OWN EYES, AND FOR THE PRESENT,—UNTIL WE CAN BE TRULY PROUD OF THE "JUSTICE" AND "EQUALITY" OF THE ECONOMIC SYSTEM UNDER WHICH WE LIVE,—LET ALL HONOR OR PRAISE GO TO THE "ALL-WISE" CREATOR OF THE UNIVERSE FROM WHOM ALL LIFE HAS COME;—HE WHO IS FATHER AND MOTHER OF US ALL,—AND FROM WHENCE COMES ALL OF MAN'S STRENGTH, ALL OF MAN'S CONSTRUCTIVE IDEAS, AND ALL OF HIS WORTHY ACCOMPLISHMENTS.

LIMITLESS FIELDS OF INTEREST A "UNIVERSE" TO EXPLORE

THERE is not the slightest question in the thoughts of any intelligent man or woman, but that "all people" want to see and enjoy as many of the gloriously beautiful and awe-inspiring places of interest on this earth, as their capacity for appreciation can hold. We should start enjoying the world, and its limitless variety of blessings "now," and before our interest in life starts running down, and the world says we have grown old. Old age is more a condition of one's mentality—"a loss of interest in life;"—a condition of boredom resulting from the endlessly monotonous repetition of common-place duties and common-place interests,—much more the outgrowth of such experiences than the direct result of the wearing out of our bodies. Bodily decrepitude and lack of vitality and life would not occur in the experience of the average individual for many years later than they now seem to, were men and women each day making discoveries of new interests, instead of being forced to spend literally "all" of their waking hours in a daily round of monotonous "soul-destroying routine duties." The International Institute of Universal Research and Administration seeks the privilege of "uniting" mankind for the purpose of providing such interests.

AFTER ALL, WHAT A "CRUEL FARCE" IT IS THAT ANY ONE SHOULD EVER GROW BORED WITH LIFE IN A WORLD WHICH CONTAINS SUCH A VARIETY OF INEXHAUSTIBLE INTERESTS AS OUR EARTH. No individual could ever travel to each point of beauty and grandeur which it provides, even if every day of his life were devoted to doing nothing but traveling in search of beauty;—nor could he really learn to know and understand and appreciate all of our earth's varieties of beauty, even if he were able to spend hundreds of years doing nothing else. This same statement might apply to the study of the world's beautiful paintings, its poetry and literature—the study of nature—of animals, and the incalculable variety of expressions of life, from the "infinitesimal" to "The Infinite." Growing acquainted with the habits, actions and interests of the numerous forms of life which occupy this world with us, and with which we can readily become friends, companions and protectors—could never grow monotonous even if we were to spend thousands of years doing that alone.

Those who are inclined towards exploration in the fields of science, are aware of the fact that they have not penetrated even the "outer shell" of Mind's limitless potentialities in that direction. Those who prefer to raise their thoughts above the shaping and forming of objectified expressions, such as machinery and the use of the world's various elements and materials, and seek instead to look out into limitless space, in the study of the and the numerous fascinating discoveries of astronomy, have before them a field of adventure which they could not exhaust during many thousands of years of ceaseless investigation. Those who prefer to take the microscope instead of the telescope in their explorations into the "limitless expressions" of Mind,—(which our Creator has formed in such variety and profusion, beyond the discernment of not only the naked eye, but of even the most highly developed microscopes of today),—have not even started on their journey of discovery in the field of the "infinitesimal expressions" of our Creator's omniscience, and surely they need never fear of wearing out their field of interest.

No, there is not the slightest possibility of a man growing bored with life because of its monotonous sameness, except to the extent that he, himself, closes his eyes and like a little Potato Bug, [1]—becoming satisfied with his own little patch of potatoes,—gradually grows to think that since there is nothing in life but potatoes, and he knows all about them, there is nothing worth living for. Nor should men's mentalities become like another type of Potato Bug which makes no effort towards further exploration of the world and its interests, because of the fact that he quite accidentally crawled out from behind his great big potato one day, and seeing just above his head the bushy leaves of the upper part of his potato plant,—(which no other potato bug had ever before discovered),—grew quite certain—because of the vast area of the potato plant—that there was nothing left to discover, and also quite sure in his own mind that he should be forever honored by all other Potato Bugs for having finally reached the most distant outpost of the universe. Carrying our illustration a bit further, we find that because of the fact that this little Potato Bug's discovery was greater than that of any other Potato Bug before his time, all of the other

---

[1] For purposes of illustration only, we have assumed that "Potatoes" and "Potato Plants" constitute a Potato Bug's sole environment and primary interest in life.

little bugs in the "Potato-bug" world, settled back to live a life of commonplace monotony, because they were quite sure there could be nothing left to discover, and no honors for them; quite sure that there was nothing new under the sun. "Ah yes! Life is just one potato after another;"—and so during that generation of potato bugs, there was no further effort expended in the fields of research or exploration.

However, when the excitement over the "startling" and "colossal" nature of the "vast discovery" represented by the finding of the potato plant had gradually worn away, a little Potato Bug, less satisfied with life than his brothers, decided—after viewing the leaves of the potato plant immediately in front of his gaze—that he would undertake further explorations; so, instead of returning by the pathway leading down among the potatoes, he crawled out three or four inches beyond the shadow of the vast and terrifying potato plant, and looking up, he chanced to see a cornstalk towering into the sky far beyond the limits of his naked eye. So huge and tall was this cornstalk which he gazed upon, that for a minute he actually felt a sense of humility, for he began to realize that only a wisdom "much greater" than his own could possibly have brought to pass such an awe-inspiring spectacle, or any creation of such "colossal dimensions," as that of the cornstalk.

And so we find that these little bugs started to honor and glorify not just the accomplishments of their "Super Potato Bugs," but also the creation of a power and intelligence which,—after much humbling of their egos,—they finally acknowledged to be superior and greater than any Potato Bug could ever hope to become. Thereafter, they no longer wasted all of their lives paying homage to other Potato Bugs, but instead they began an orderly and systematic investigation of the handiwork of a Creator whom they knew must possess power and wisdom far surpassing their own. It was not long before they had traveled beyond the cornstalk and discovered a great big stack of hay. One day while they were contemplating the findings of many generations of their most courageous "Brother Bugs" who had finally completed measuring the length of one side of this vast new spectacle, they looked around its edge and, to and behold, they brought within the range of their highly developed telescopes (?) the full stature of a man. Farmer Jones, himself, had become known to his Potato Bugs!

Beholding something almost as vast as their colossal cornstalk, and yet something able to walk and move around from one place to another, just as they themselves could do, they finally concluded,—after going back to their Potato-Bug Capitol and spending many long Potato-Bug years in discussion and debate,—that they had seen "the Creator of all the world," and that they had beheld the being whom henceforth they would worship as their God. THAT ENDED THE POTATO BUGS' FURTHER EFFORTS AT DISCOVERY, FOR THEY FELT QUITE CERTAIN THAT THERE WAS NOTHING LEFT FOR THEM TO FIND. THEY HAD NEVER DEVELOPED TELESCOPES CAPABLE OF SEEING EVEN TO THE TOP OF A TREE, NOR TO THE LITTLE HOUSE IN WHICH FARMER JONES LIVED. HOWEVER, "THEY WERE SATISFIED," AND THAT IS THE REASON THAT THEIR MENTALITIES ARE STILL JUST THOSE OF "LITTLE POTATO BUGS."

Mankind might well guard against the mental qualities of "smug self-satisfaction;" for unless we are no farther advanced than "Potato Bugs," we must surely realize that we have not yet even started to discover the smallest part of the creations of limitless wisdom, nor to recognize even an infinitesimal part of the power and might of life, nor of that source from which the universe and all that is therein, "truly emanates." Just as the little Potato Bugs had not yet discovered Farmer Jones' home, nor even the boundary or fence line which encircled the field containing their Potato-Bug kingdom,—neither has man, up to this stage in history, explored even his own immediate surroundings, nor the smallest part of the field—(our earth)—in which he lives.

Just as beyond Farmer Jones' field there exists the rest of his farm, and beyond that his neighbor's farm, and then the boundaries of the County and the State, and finally the Nation itself—a part of Farmer Jones' continent in turn bounded by oceans—and beyond them other continents, and so on; . . . likewise there exists beyond the boundaries of our earth, fields of "infinite" exploration, limitless elements, resources and awe-inspiring soul-expanding scenes, which man will never learn to enjoy nor, in fact, even see unless he grows—not just merely "discontented"—but "wholly unsatisfied" with his present attainments, and determines to look far beyond himself and his own handiwork, to those expressions of wisdom and power, might and eternality, which make the works of men seem but foolishness in the sight of God.

Well might men cultivate qualities of humility—cease their futile and puny struggles among and against themselves—and combine what little wisdom they at this time have learned to express, and what few energies and powers they have learned to harness, and in the spirit of brotherly love,—in limitless expectation of incalculable benefits and joys awaiting their efforts,—become "Mankind United."

"One for All and All for One,"—Mankind United could enter upon an adventure truly worthy of intelligent creatures;—the building of a world free from petty and puny human differences;—free from wars, free from racial, class or religious antagonisms, and the wholly needless poverty which forces men into lives of drab, ugly monotony. "Mankind United" will bring immediate rewards of financial independence to all people, and an end to all wars; an end to those experiences which cause men to feel that there is nothing of interest in life. "Mankind United"—can put an end to that attitude of life which suggests that, after all, life is just "one potato after another," with nothing to look forward to and no hope of change.

LET THE POTATO BUG STAY IN HIS PATCH OF POTATOES IF HE SO DESIRES, BUT LET MEN TRAVEL AT LEAST TO THE BOUNDARY LINE AROUND THE FIELD WHICH THEY CALL THEIR EARTH, AND LEARN JUST A LITTLE BIT ABOUT ITS RICH FURNISHINGS AND PRICELESS TREASURES.

How can men and women of wealth, or even those in very moderate circumstances,—but with enough to eat and to wear and a home in which to live, shut their eyes to mankind's suffering, and yet obtain any sense of joy or happiness? How can we even "hope" to find contentment and peace within our thoughts, when in the very midst of God's indescribably glorious universe—all around us here on this earth which we call our home—we find the ugliness of greed and the selfishly-cruel handiwork of men expressed as oppression, and an endless personification of "Man's Inhumanity to Man," with its dirt and filth, its poverty, jealousy, envy, hate, murder and war? The evidences of cruelty—instead of brotherly love—ceaselessly force themselves upon our thoughts whenever love, awakening in our hearts, opens the blindness of our eyes and the deafness of our ears, so that we may see and hear the soul-searing struggles and agonizing cries of men and women beseeching us to help them untangle the hopeless poverty-stricken uselessness of their lives. Multitudes of our fellow beings beseeching some one to show them,—(mind you, right here in the very midst of God's inexhaustible provision of mankind's needs), just "one thing" worth living for.

THE REMAINDER OF THE EARTH'S INHABITANTS ARE IN A CONDITION ALMOST AS PITIABLE,—"WAITING FOR SHIPS TO COME IN" WHICH SELDOM IF EVER ARRIVE. ALWAYS DO MEN THINK THAT THEY WILL START LIVING "TOMORROW" OR THAT SOON—"WHEN CONDITIONS CHANGE FOR THE BETTER"—ALL WILL BE WELL, AND "THEN THEY CAN START LIVING." ALWAYS IT IS TOMORROW, NEXT WEEK, OR NEXT YEAR; "CENTURIES HAVE PASSED AND STILL MANKIND WAIT UNTIL SOME 'FUTURE TIME,' TO START LIVING."

Until we close our eyes and shut our ears to the suffering and cries of anguish on all sides,—and become nothing more than animals selfishly concerned only with our own welfare,—there can never be even any imaginary joy in'ôur hearts. Until we destroy, not merely the "effects" of disappointment, fear or hopelessness in the lives of men, but the age-old antiquated and outgrown "causes" of these conditions;—until every man, woman and child on the face of this earth has enough to eat, enough clothes to wear, a place called home, and the time and opportunity with which to seek and to learn the truths about this glorious adventure called "life;"—until we have the leisure time and the opportunity in which to learn to love this beautiful old world of ours, and to find a variety of interests with which to break the "mesmeric" spell of the monotonous routine of common-place detail duties, there can never be lasting peace, security or joy in the life of any man or woman.

Not even a "brief glimpse" of happiness and real peace—way down deep within our hearts—is ever even momentarily possible, until we first shut our eyes and our ears to the appeals of the hundreds of millions of confused hopeless human beings who are ceaselessly crying out for some one to help them. And yet, such people have just as much right to find peace and happiness here on this earth—and just as much right to draw upon our Creator's limitless resources—as the most "saintly" or the most "successful" man or woman who ever walked upon this or any other planet throughout the universe.

IN THIS WORLD OF YOURS AND OURS, THERE ARE OVER ONE THOUSAND MILLION (1,000,000,000) MEN AND WOMEN UNABLE TO READ OR WRITE AND CONSTANTLY FILLED WITH NAMELESS SUPERSTITIOUS FEARS; AND FIVE HUNDRED MILLION (500,000,000) HUMAN BEINGS ALWAYS HUNGRY, HOMELESS, AND UNWANTED!! ARE SUCH CONDITIONS ACTUALLY NECESSARY? MUST WE GO THROUGH LIFE EITHER AS ONE OF A COUNT-

LESS MULTITUDE OF SUCH HOPELESS CREATURES, OR ONE OF THOSE WHO MUST FOREVER LISTEN TO THEIR CRIES FOR HELP? IS THERE A SOLUTION TO THESE PROBLEMS? IF THERE BE ANY MEANS BY WHICH TO SILENCE THEIR CRIES, IT MUST BE IN A DIRECTION OTHER THAN THE ONES IN WHICH WE HAVE SEARCHED THROUGHOUT THE PAST CENTURIES!! IF AN ECONOMIC SYSTEM CAN BE BUILT WHICH WILL BE CAPABLE OF GUARANTEEING FINANCIAL SECURITY AND OPPORTUNITIES FOR HAPPINESS FOR "ALL" PEOPLE, IT MUST BE ONE "VASTLY DIFFERENT" THAN ANY THE HUMAN RACE HERETOFORE HAS ATTEMPTED TO EVOLVE. THE AUTOCRATIC CAPITALISTIC RULE OF "THE SURVIVAL OF THE FITTEST;" THE COMMUNISTIC SYSTEMS OF "MASS REGIMENTATION;" THE SYSTEM WHICH MAKES MEN TEAR AT EACH OTHER'S THROATS LIKE PACKS OF WOLVES—WHICH WE CALL "OUR PRIVATE PROFIT" OR "COMPETITIVE SYSTEM"—HAVE ALL FAILED.

DOES OUR WORLD BELONG ANY MORE TO ONE THAN TO ANOTHER?

ALL PLANS OF "ECONOMIC SECURITY" WHICH HAVE EVER BEEN ADOPTED BY THE HUMAN RACE—(WHETHER PROPOSED AS A POLICY OF GOVERNMENT OR UNDER THE SPONSORSHIP OF THE VARIOUS RELIGIOUS ORDERS OF THE DAY)—HAVE BEEN TRIED AND TESTED, YET THEY HAVE "ALL" FAILED.

EVERY KNOWN METHOD OF PRODUCING AND DISTRIBUTING THE NECESSITIES AND LUXURIES OF LIFE AND OF PROVIDING PEACE AND SECURITY FOR THE HUMAN RACE HAS BEEN TRIED "EXCEPT ONE;" BUT THIS "ONE" NOT EVEN THE WORLD'S MOST TRUSTED LEADERS HAVE "DARED" TO RECOMMEND,—FOR "SPIRITUAL WICKEDNESS IN HIGH PLACES" HAS PRODUCED A RACE OF "MORAL COWARDS."

Fear of ridicule or criticism occupies such an important place in human thought that no one with influence and power in public life, and to whose voice all the world would listen, has dared to suggest the "One" and "Only" plan of human relationship which—if applied to the production and distribution of the needs of human life—could successfully solve the all-important problem of bringing to pass the "Peace on Earth" and "Good Will Among Men" for which mankind have ceaselessly prayed throughout countless ages.

This "One" solution has never been tried because of the fact that those who know enough to make such a recommendation,—and who have sufficient power and influence to enforce it,—would be obliged to sacrifice their precious egotistical belief in their own "superiority" and the conviction that, because of their exalted positions, they deserve a "greater share" of the world's goods than their fellows. This "One" solution might be described in just "two" words—if men were unselfish enough to recognize and acknowledge their true import and intended meaning. Yes; if the plan for ending poverty and war were founded upon the "Spirit" as well as the "Letter" of Christ Jesus' "Golden Rule," and if men were not too egotistical to accept a system established upon "Absolute Economic Equality,"—the concept of "One for All and All for One,"—then there would be no difficulty in completely describing the solution of these age-old world problems with just two words:—"MANKIND UNITED."

Whether men are black or yellow, white or red, tall or short, stout or thin, they are nevertheless the children of "identically" the same Creator as ourselves and, whether we like it or not, they are still our brothers and sisters, with "identically" the same rights of occupancy of this world home and the use of all it contains as the greatest genius or the most sublime egotist—either man or woman—who has ever trod this globe.

OF THOSE WHO HAVE OCCUPIED EITHER THE "MOST LOWLY" OR THE "MOST SOUGHT AFTER" STATIONS IN HUMAN LIFE, NONE HAVE EVER BROUGHT EVEN ONE LOAF OF BREAD WITH THEM WHEN THEY ARRIVED HERE, NOR HAVE YET SUCCEEDED IN REMOVING OR TAKING EVEN ONE LOAF OF BREAD WITH THEM WHEN THEY LEFT. EACH NORMAL MAN OR WOMAN ARRIVES WITH THE SAME NUMBER OF HANDS AND FEET, BUT THEY COME WITH THEIR HANDS EMPTY AND NO SHOES ON THEIR FEET, AND THEY LEAVE THE SAME WAY. THEY BRING NO PROOFS OF THEIR SUPERIORITY WITH THEM WHEN THEY COME AND THEY TAKE NONE WITH THEM WHEN THEY GO. DURING THEIR LIFETIME HERE, THE SUN GIVES NO EVIDENCE OF DESIRING TO SHINE ON ONE MORE THAN ON ANOTHER, NOR THE EARTH TO FEED OR PROVIDE—OUT OF ITS LIMITLESS TREASURE HOUSE OF GIFTS FOR MANKIND—ANY GREATER GIFTS TO ONE THAN TO ANOTHER.

"Man Only" has assumed the responsibility of classifying one human being as more important than another and has determined what the rewards of such a classification shall be. The only way in which such a system could possess any elements of justice, would be for every man, woman and child on our earth to have an equal voice in determining what the various scales of compensation or reward should be,—both for those who are accepted by their fellows as being superior, and also the rewards of those who arc supposed to have inferior capabilities.

However, the odd part of our economic system,—which permits a greater accumulation of this world's goods for one than for another,—is that the deciding voices in such matters, and the voices which determine just who should be considered as superior, and who shall receive the greatest rewards, have always been the voices, not of those who have rendered the greatest service to the human race;—nor those who have lived the most exemplary lives;—nor composed the world's most beautiful music, poems and literature;—nor painted its grandest pictures;—nor developed its most useful inventions, but instead, those who have "actually" had the deciding voice in the distribution of life's luxuries—and even its barest requirements—have—"WITHOUT EVEN ONE EXCEPTION IN HUMAN HISTORY"—been those who have rendered the "least" service to mankind, and left the "fewest" evidences of having brought happiness into the lives of our earth's inhabitants.

IN FACT, THOSE WHO HAVE USUALLY FORMULATED AND ENFORCED THE HUMANLY DEVISED LAWS UNDER WHICH MEN LIVE,—AND WHICH DETERMINE THE AMOUNT OF THIS WORLD'S GOODS THEY MAY POSSESS,—HAVE ALMOST INVARIABLY BEEN THOSE WHO HAVE BROUGHT ABOUT THE WHOLESALE SLAUGHTER OF THE GREATEST NUMBER OF THEIR FELLOW BEINGS, AND PRODUCED THE GREATEST AMOUNT OF HUMAN SUFFERING IN THE FORM OF BROKEN HEARTS AND STARVED BODIES.

The "Napoleons" throughout human history have been the ones that have decided who shall be called superior, and whether life shall be "A Feast" or "A Famine;"—the rest of the human family occupying this earthly home have stood silently by, either too filled with "awe" and "admiration" over the virile qualities of leadership and personality exemplified by these "Napoleons," or too greatly filled with "fear" and the misery of under-fed emaciated starved aching bodies, to demand justice; IN FACT, THEY HAVE USUALLY NOT HAD ENOUGH MENTAL OR PHYSICAL VITALITY WITH WHICH TO EVEN "RAISE THEIR VOICES" IN PROTEST.

Other than those who have become mankind's "self-appointed" rulers—and the "Money Changers" for the race—there are none who would not willingly consent to a sufficiently abundant production and distribution of the world's goods to insure an ample variety and quantity of the needful or desirable requirements of life for the people of every land. With the exception of mankind's "self-appointed" rulers, there are but few who would not joyously welcome a system of human relationship which would value and estimate qualities of "superiority," solely from the standpoint of the greater service to the human race that one might render over another; or who would not willingly agree that such people should receive as a reward, not a greater amount of the world's goods—(which are, after all, lent to each of us equally by our Creator and belong no more to one than to another, neither are they actually ours to give or to take away from each other)—but instead, that they should be appointed as instructors, guides and directors,—in order that they might thereby help others to learn how to constructively seek individual happiness, and yet—at the same time—succeed in serving their brother man more effectually.

Any other method of appointing leaders or of rewarding exemplary service, brings about one of two results; namely, either through "bribery" or "favoritism" incompetent men or women frequently gain positions of authority over their fellows and—"the blind leading the blind"—chaos results; or if rewards are in the form of a greater amount of this world's goods than others are enabled to possess, then jealousy and envy breed bitterness and hate, and bitterness and hate breed murder and war;—NOR CAN THESE EFFECTS "EVER" BE AVOIDED SO LONG AS AN ECONOMIC SYSTEM WHICH PERMITS SUCH INEQUALITIES TO EXIST CONTINUES TO GOVERN THE LIVES OF MEN.

"MANKIND UNITED"—"ONE FOR ALL AND ALL FOR ONE"—"DOING UNTO OTHERS AS WE WOULD HAVE OTHERS DO UNTO US," CONSTITUTES THE "ONE" AND "ONLY" SOLUTION OF THE DUAL CURSES—"POVERTY AND WAR," FROM WHICH HUMAN BEINGS HAVE ENDLESSLY SUFFERED.

Whether or not we think we are "too good" to soil our hands, or to degrade our precious concept of our own "superiority" through association with others whom we believe to be less capable than ourselves, or of a different color of skin, or members of different fraternal or religious associations—as the case may be,—the fact still remains that this world home of ours was provided "equally" for the people of every nation, and for those of every color, and the sun was meant to shine as much upon one as upon another.

WE ARE INDISPUTABLY "OUR BROTHER'S KEEPER" IN THE SENSE OF GRANTING HIM EQUAL RIGHTS TO "LIFE, LIBERTY AND. THE PURSUIT OF HAPPINESS," AND OF PREVENTING SUCH RIGHTS FROM EVER BEING WITHHELD FROM ANY HUMAN BEING ON THIS EARTH.

We have no more right to shut our eyes to the inexcusable suffering caused by greed, selfishness, egotism, and the insanely depraved scramble of a world-wide "pack of wolves" for power, dominion, flattery and wealth, than we would have to sit down and enjoy a delicious meal knowing that our mother, brother or sister were in the next room slowly wasting away from under-nourishment, and gradually starving to death.

Destroying cattle, wheat and other foodstuffs, in a world with five hundred million (500,000,000) people daily suffering from insufficient food and thirty million (30,000,000) human beings "starving to death" each year, is a far greater form of human selfishness and cruelty than any individual could possibly express through the neglect of his immediate family, relatives or friends, yet that is "exactly" what we are permitting our "so-called" leaders to do year after year,—and during an age which we proudly acclaim to be "civilized."

Men will find but little opportunity to develop feelings of security or happiness—(other than those of dumb brutes or self-centered ferocious beasts)—until they feel "at least secure," and in time grow conscious of a sense of "justifiable" self-respect, through feeling that they are not only living "abundantly,"—but also permitting others to do likewise.

MANKIND WILL NEVER FIND HAPPINESS UNTIL THERE IS AN INTELLIGENTLY EXPRESSED SEMBLANCE OF "EQUALITY OF OPPORTUNITY AND FREEDOM," AND A LIMITLESS WORLDWIDE ABUNDANCE—"FOR EVERYONE"—OF THE NECESSARY OR DESIRABLE REQUIREMENTS OF HUMAN LIFE,—TOGETHER WITH THE LEISURE TIME FOR THEIR ENJOYMENT.

EARNINGS—HOURS—EDUCATION GENEROUS BENEFITS AND AMPLE VACATIONS

A "guarantee" of financial independence and security for all can be assured by The Research Department of The International Institute of Universal Research and Administration within a period of but a few months after the formation of The Universal Service Corporation, and the fulfillment of this guarantee can start taking place within ninety (90) days from the date of its general worldwide acceptance. Thereafter, no man or woman on the face of this earth need suffer from a lack of this world's resources, nor be required to work over four (4) hours per day, four (4) days per week, or eight (8) months each year, in order to earn a living.

Upon the acceptance of our Research Department's program, all adults will be guaranteed not less than three (3) days a week and four (4) entire months each year of vacation time with pay. All men and women will receive a minimum yearly salary of not less than three thousand ($3,000.00) dollars, which will gradually be increased to over ten times this amount as mankind's discoveries and capabilities are fully co-ordinated with efficient methods of production and distribution.

Within a matter of months after the public's acceptance of the Corporation Charter of The Universal Service Corporation—(which will constitute the business vehicle of "Mankind United")—we will live in a world where no one will ever again be hungry, cold or homeless; a world in which one hundred million (100,000,000) men and women will spend their full working time planting and caring for gardens, parks and playgrounds, and preparing features of beauty for the enjoyment and happiness of all; a world where none need work more than twenty (20) years of their lives at the rate of four (4) hours per day, four (4) days per week, eight (8) months a year,—or if they prefer to work longer hours "each day,"—they will be required to work only ten (10) years during their lifetime, at the rate of eight (8) hours per day, four (4) days per week, eight (8) months each year. Thereafter, they will be free to travel in any part of the world they may desire to explore, or to develop their talents or further whatever other constructive ambitions they may possess, during the remainder of their lifetime here on our earth.

WITHIN TEN (10) YEARS MANKIND CAN LIVE IN A WORLD IN WHICH PEOPLE WILL BE EDUCATED AND TRAINED FOR THE PRIMARY OBJECT OF DEVELOPING THEIR LATENT TALENTS AND CAPABILITIES, AND OF OBTAINING THE GREATEST POSSIBLE ENJOYMENT AND HAPPINESS FROM LIFE OF WHICH THEY ARE CAPABLE. "INDIVIDUAL" AS WELL AS "COLLECTIVE" WELL-BEING AND HAPPINESS, AND THE DEVELOPMENT OF NATURAL TALENTS, WILL BE CONSIDERED AS THE PRIMAL OBJECT IN LIFE. "JOY"—NOT "STRIFE"—WILL BE RECOGNIZED AS THE NATURAL EXPRESSION OF MAN. WE WILL LIVE IN A WORLD WHEREIN MAN WILL WORK PRIMARILY FOR THE PURPOSE OF ADDING TO HIS OWN HAPPINESS AND THE HAPPINESS OF HIS FELLOWMEN. HE WILL NO LONGER BE FORCED TO LIVE FOR THE "SOLE PURPOSE OF WORKING FOR BREAD TO GET THE STRENGTH TO WORK FOR MORE BREAD," UNTIL HE FINALLY TIRES OF THE ENDLESS STRUGGLE AND DIES.

"MAN DOES NOT LIVE BY BREAD ALONE," NOR CAN HE EVER FIND HAPPINESS OR SATISFACTION IN A LIFE WHICH FORCES HIM TO CONSIDER ITS PREPARATION AS THE MOST IMPORTANT OBJECTIVE OF HIS EXISTENCE.

Again we remind our readers that "right here on our earth" there is over one hundred (100) times as much land—capable of producing food—as mankind now cultivates. But in spite of this fact, over "five hundred million" (500,000,000) people are permitted to remain constantly hungry and over "thirty million" (30,000,000) of them to die of starvation annually. "Hunger and starvation" result solely from "Man's Inhumanity to Man,"— the general "blindness" of the mass of human beings and the wealthy men's frequently complete ignorance of either the "letter" or the "spirit" implied by The Golden Rule.

It has been complacently stated by economists—(who have learned so much, but whose wealthy clients have learned to do so little)—that enough food and enough material for clothes could be produced, stored and preserved, within a ten (10) year period, to feed and clothe the entire human family for the next "one hundred (100) years."

Within the following ten (10) years, in order that the human race may guard against droughts, floods or other unforeseen calamities this will be done, upon mankind's acceptance of our Research Department's charter. However, except for some wholly "unheard-of" form of calamity, men need not ever be deprived of the seasonally grown and freshly prepared foods each year.

NO FOOD WILL EVER AGAIN BE LEFT TO ROT IN THE FIELDS OR ON THE TREES, NOR BE THROWN INTO THE OCEAN, AFTER "MANKIND UNITED" HAVE FORMED THEIR "UNIVERSAL SERVICE CORPORATION."

THOSE OF US WHO HAVE HAD AN ABUNDANCE OF THE GOOD THINGS OF LIFE AND YET HAVE STOOD BY AND WATCHED VAST QUANTITIES OF FOOD BEING DESTROYED WHILE OUR FELLOW BEINGS—IN A HUNDRED DIFFERENT PARTS OF THE EARTH—WERE STARVING TO DEATH, NEED NEVER AGAIN HIDE OUR HEADS IN SHAME OVER SUCH A TRAVESTY ON BROTHERLY LOVE.

Mankind's most experienced farmers, ranchers and producers will have the satisfaction and worthy task of "directing" the production and preparation of vast quantities of food and clothing materials, and of seeing to it that every man, woman and child on this "bountifully fruitful earth" of ours has enough—and to spare—of varied and delicious foods to eat, and warm—"modern"—attractive clothes to wear.

Over five hundred million (500,000,000) people will be kept busy in these various activities, during their four-hour work periods, producing and distributing the requirements of life for all mankind. There will be no idle architects or builders during the ten (10) year period immediately following the formation of "Mankind United" and "The Universal Service Corporation," nor any idle gardeners, inasmuch as all of the world's architects and over one hundred million (100,000,000) gardeners will be formed into a permanent department of The Service Corporation. Over two hundred million (200,000,000) architects, carpenters, building trade mechanics and furniture makers will be kept busy twenty-four (24) hours per day—in four (4) hour shifts—during the following ten (10) years, in order that, by the end of said period, every family on this earth will be enabled to live in a beautiful home, placed in the midst of a lovely park; a home which—if valued at today's valuation—would cost twenty-five thousand ($25,000.00) dollars or more, in buildings, furnishings and surrounding grounds. [1]

---

[1] Over 800,000,000 expert workers will be continuously employed.

As heretofore mentioned,—in addition to the major languages which the citizens of the various nations may desire to retain,—one universal language will also be taught. Within much less than ten (10) years' time the people of every land will be able to readily converse with one another, and the antagonisms resulting from the inability of people to understand each other's habits and customs will thereby be permanently uprooted.

When this one language has been universally learned, most of the instruction in the various branches of human knowledge will be taught by "radio" and "television," and will emanate from one great central department of education. The brilliant scholars and most highly qualified instructors of every nation will meet together and select those most competent of their group to teach us all,—not only the desirable academic subjects of the day,—but also how to live more "intelligently" and "harmoniously" with one another. Such instruction will be amplified with free yearly travel—("during our entire lifetime")—to any part of the world we may either desire to visit, or be required to investigate as a part of the course of study we may individually be pursuing. "FREE" FACILITIES FOR TRAVEL WILL ADD MUCH TO OUR KNOWLEDGE, UNDERSTANDING AND APPRECIATION OF THE HABITS, CUSTOMS AND LIVES OF THE PEOPLES OF THE VARIOUS NATIONS, AND WILL QUICKLY DISPEL THE JEALOUSIES, ENVIES AND ANTAGONISMS WHICH NOW EXIST.

"FREE TRAVEL," "AMPLE LEISURE" AND "ADEQUATE INCOME" WITH WHICH TO OBTAIN FULL ENJOYMENT FROM LIFE, WILL BE AVAILABLE TO EVERYONE ON THIS GLOBE, LONG BEFORE OUR TEN (10) YEAR PROGRAM HAS BEEN COMPLETED.

Every normal man and woman on earth will be expected to spend an average of not less than one hour each work day studying some subject,—(according to each individual's selection),—either by means of radio broadcast, television, or directly under the personal supervision of qualified instructors. The nature of their instruction will be the best that the world can provide, for all nations will be searched for their most highly talented instructors in order that they may be made available for those who desire self-improvement.

The acid tests of "proof and demonstration" will be applied to whatever we sow in the minds of our children, for only that which is constructive and good or true—and thereby "provable"—is worthy to be planted in the fresh clean young intellects of children. Neither war nor warriors,—nor any other kind of "murder" or type of "murderers"—will be glorified, nor those so engaged set up on pedestals for our children to copy as examples in the formation of their qualities of character. "CHRIST JESUS"—NOT "NAPOLEON"—A CHARACTER BUILDER, NOT A WHOLESALE MURDERER, WILL BE THEIR EXEMPLAR. THEY WILL BE TAUGHT TO "BUILD"—NOT TO "DESTROY."

Only by "truly constructive thinking," will the superstitions and groundless fears of mankind be ultimately destroyed. It matters not how abundantly we supply man with "material possessions;"—such things are as but a frame to a picture. If men are not taught what constitutes true happiness—(and only truly intelligent thinking will reveal "true" joy to them)—all of our love-inspired efforts to bring peace, joy and progress to the human race would—within a generation or two—be swallowed up by "greed," insanely futile "mad ambition," and a renewed struggle for self-glorification, personal power and self-gain. Men would once more be under the hypnotic spell of self-centered ambitions;—once more they would be thinking that vast wealth, or selfish personal power, constituted the highway to happiness, and would again have forgotten that we all come here on an "equal" footing—"with no possessions"—and leave unable to take any of our accumulation of material objects with us., Once more men might forget that the world and those in it are not here for the purpose of providing pleasures and luxuries to some small handful of its population—or for the pleasure of some one man; but instead, are here that they might—through . their concerted efforts—assure joy and happiness to "all mankind," as well as to themselves.

UNLESS SUBJECTS OF "TRUE MERIT" ARE TAUGHT, MEN WOULD SOON FORGET THAT IF THEY WOULD FIND HAPPINESS THEMSELVES, THEY MUST SHARE THIS WORLD'S BEAUTY AND BOUNTY EQUALLY WITH ONE ANOTHER. MAN'S ONLY GUARANTEE OF PERMANENT CONTENTMENT AND JOYOUSNESS, RESTS SOLELY UPON HIS CAPACITY TO LEARN—THROUGH THE HIGHER CONCEPTS OF "BROTHERLY LOVE"—WHAT "TRUE HAPPINESS" REALLY IS; FOR SURELY IT CONSISTS AS MUCH IN "GIVING" AS IT DOES IN "GETTING."

To assure mankind's permanent progress, every man, woman and child on this earth must be helped to recognize the importance of regularly studying and searching for wisdom, and of doing so a little "each day." Once man stops growing mentally, he starts growing sensually, and when he starts becoming a slave to his physical appetites and desires, he has lost all chance of finding either "peace" or "happiness" until he first destroys such taskmasters.

Yes; the educational side of The Universal Service Corporation's program,—in its development and production of those things which will bring stability and happiness to the human race,—is indeed going to be by far the most vital and important of its many activities, and it will be but "barely starting" during the following 10-year period, on its endless journey of service.

The name which the Sponsors of this movement selected in designating their organization as "The International Institute of Universal Research and Administration," is intended to convey the "universal" and "endless" nature of the program upon which you will be invited to vote during the 30 days of its final presentation to the public. During the 10-year period in which we have promised that all of the material needs of man will be met and—through the construction of adequate facilities—permanently assured to coming generations, The Universal Service Corporation's program of education will have only commenced.

Organizing and co-ordinating the efforts of the world's most practical, capable and brilliant research economists, industrialists, agricultural experts, and engineers, is a task which any one of hundreds of outstanding business executives of this age could readily accomplish, once he had received the order and authority to "go ahead" from enough people who had definitely decided that they would give up their "questionable chances" of winning great wealth, power or prestige, in exchange for the assurance of "guaranteed economic security" for all. Once two hundred million (200,000,000) clear-thinking intelligently industrious men and women have decided to make this exchange and accept, instead, an abundance of everything any "sane" person could desire—and the leisure time in which to live and enjoy life—then the task of bringing this result to pass is a comparatively simple one, and one which any number of competent executives of today could readily accomplish.

TEN YEARS IS AMPLE TIME FOR FULFILLING THE INSTITUTE'S PROMISES, AND ELIMINATING POVERTY, WAR, AND EVERY OTHER ACCURSED EFFECT OF "MAD AMBITION" AND "ANIMAL GREED" FROM THE FACE OF THIS GLORIOUSLY BEAUTIFUL PLANET. BUT WHEN THIS TASK HAS BEEN

ACCOMPLISHED, AND THE MATERIAL NEEDS OF MEN ARE PERMANENTLY ASSURED, THEN MANKIND WILL HAVE ONLY BARELY STARTED UPON THE ADVENTURE OF LEARNING WHAT "LIFE" AND WHAT "HAPPINESS" TRULY MEAN.

Those who believe that "Mankind United" can obtain a greater degree of security for the individual members of the human race than they could hope to win by their own unaided efforts, are asked to accept the "free gift" of our Research Department's 30-day World-wide Program; during which time they will learn how the establishment of a great Universal Service Corporation can be quickly brought to pass,—and without "bloodshed," "revolution" or the use of "brute force" of any kind. The people who attend our program, will neither be asked to buy stock nor to make any sacrifices other than to spend a few hours of their time in order that they may thereby obtain sufficient information to vote intelligently upon the Corporation's charter.

The undying gratitude of countless generations of human beings will follow the two hundred million (200,000,000) men and women who consent to become equal owners of "The Universal Service Corporation"—(and who will thereby unite as members and supporters of "A True Universal Brotherhood of Man")—for the movement which it will bring to pass; namely,—"Mankind United"—will be preserved for all time to come, as a monument to the "20th Century Birth of Man" in the image and likeness of the divine qualities of intelligence which are his birthright. The names of these two hundred million (200,000,000) men and women,—and all others who unite with them during this generation,—will be preserved throughout countless thousands of years deeply engraved upon tablets of bronze and placed in a gigantic monument erected on the crest of one of the world's tallest peaks; a monument which will forever point upward to greater and grander monuments to the limitless potentialities of "Unity of Effort," when wedded to "Justice" and "Brotherly Love."

In this eternal monument, there will be deposited and sealed within solid blocks of ageless granite—from century to century—each bit of demonstrable Truth or scientific knowledge discovered, tested, and demonstrated by the men and women of each successive generation, in order that their footsteps of progress,—(dating from mankind's first acceptance and "practical application" of Christ Jesus' "Sermon on the Mount" with its "Golden Rules" of human relationship),—may be traced by those of later generations, and may stand forth as an eternal proof to such future generations of the practical value of "Brotherly Love"—"Unity" and "Unselfed Service"—as compared to the "Each-Wolf-For-Himself" Private Profit System of our present generation.

As an indisputable proof of the advantages gained when the inhabitants of the world unite as one family—"One for All and All for One,"—(and, although they may be living in separate and differently furnished rooms—or portions of the world—each individual receives the benefit of the efforts of all the others, and in turn shares the fruitage of his own talents with those who comprise the human family),—this monument will evidence to all future generations—and stand as a permanent reminder to them—that only when mankind had combined their talents and efforts for their "mutual welfare," had their progress been "uninterrupted and continuous"—unbroken either by wars, or other similarly destructive forces, or by any weakening of their unselfishly united energies.

ALSO WITHIN THIS ETERNAL MONUMENT, WILL BE CONTAINED A HUGE MUSEUM FURNISHED WITH THE PROOFS AND EVIDENCES OF "MAD AMBITION," SELFISHNESS, GREED, JEALOUSY, HATE, REVOLUTIONS, WARS, AND THE COUNTLESS OTHER EXPRESSIONS OF UGLINESS WHICH CONSTITUTE "THE NATURAL FRUITAGE" OF "MAN'S INHUMANITY TO MAN"—(WITH ITS RESULTANT JEALOUSIES, ENVIES AND UNCONTROLLABLE HATREDS)—IN ORDER THAT THE PEOPLE OF ALL FUTURE GENERATIONS MAY THEREBY "TAKE HEED," AND THAT THEY MAY NEVER AGAIN BE TEMPTED BY FEELINGS OF "INDIVIDUAL SUPERIORITY," TO SUBSCRIBE TO THOSE HUMANLY CONCEIVED AND PERPETUATED RULES OF RELATIONSHIP BASED UPON THE "JUNGLE LAW" OF "THE SURVIVAL OF THE FITTEST," WHICH THE WORLD NOW CALLS "RUGGED INDIVIDUALISM" AND ITS "PRIVATE PROFIT SYSTEM."

THE UNIVERSAL SERVICE CORPORATION EQUALLY OWNED—EQUALLY CONTROLLED EQUALLY BENEFICIAL

DURING the 30-day program of revelations and recommendations prepared by The International Institute of Universal Research and Administration, each of the Research Department's discoveries and perfected inventions,—to which we have made reference in this bulletin,—will not only be fully described, but will also be offered without cost to those of the human race who associate with The Universal Service Corporation and who will thereby consent to their "equal use," and to the equal unprejudiced distribution of the products and benefits of these numerous discoveries and inventions. An equality which must be subject only to the length of time it will take to teach backward people how to read and write, and how to appreciate and constructively use the world's modern inventions.

THE INSTITUTE'S DISCOVERIES MUST BE MADE AVAILABLE TO THE PEOPLE OF EVERY LAND, NO MATTER HOW "BACKWARD" CERTAIN OF SUCH PEOPLE MAY SEEM TO BE BEFORE THEY ARE TAUGHT THE TRUE VALUE OF "UNITED EFFORT" AND "BROTHERLY LOVE."

Only upon the unequivocal acceptance of such conditions will the inventions and discoveries through which to provide financial independence to the human race be given to the two hundred million (200,000,000) people who will comprise our international audience. Only upon the signed agreement by each of them, that they will permit the products of their "equally-owned" Universal Service Corporation (which they will at that time be helped to form) to be distributed "equally" to the people of every land, irrespective of race, religion, color, class, education, training or ability—subject only to the consent of each new member owner to the same by-laws of brotherly love which will constitute the eternal and unalterable charter of this great Service Corporation—will our Research Department release its revolutionary discoveries into the hands of the Corporation's internationally elected Board of Directors.

THESE DISCOVERIES WILL NEVER BE ALLOWED TO STAND AS A MONUMENT TO THE ACCOMPLISHMENT OF SOME PERSON, OR GROUP OF PERSONS,—(IN ORDER THAT SAID PERSONS MAY BE GLORIFIED OUT OF ALL PROPORTION TO THEIR REAL IMPORTANCE IN THE UNIVERSAL SCHEME OF THINGS),—NOR AS A MONUMENT TO ANY ONE RELIGION, ANY ONE NATION, ANY ONE CLASS, OR ANY ONE PROFESSION; FOR NEVER WILL THOSE WHO REVEALED THEM—AND WHO CONSTITUTE OUR SPONSORS—BE KNOWN TO THE HUMAN RACE; AND THEREFORE, NEVER WILL RELIGIOUS, RACIAL, CLASS, OR PROFESSIONAL RIVALRY HAVE AN OPPORTUNITY THROUGH THE AVENUES OF "BIGOTRY," "JEALOUSY," "ENVY" OR "PRIDE," TO UNDO AN ACHIEVEMENT WHICH ONLY "UNSELFED LOVE" IN THE HEARTS OF "MANY MILLIONS" OF PEOPLE CAN POSSIBLY BRING TO ULTIMATE FULFILLMENT.

Not only will the immediate abundance of the necessities and luxuries of life, to which we have herein referred, start flowing to the human race within a period of months but, with the aid of the world's numerous mechanical inventions and of our Research Department's revolutionary discoveries, they will be produced without the necessity of any of The Corporation's employees ever being obliged—after the first 12 months of its program—to work more than 4 hours per day, 4 days each week, or over 8 months in any one year. This ruling will apply both to "skilled" and "unskilled" labor, as well as to office workers and officials. All employees of said corporation will also receive three (3) days each week and four (4) entire months each year of vacation periods with pay.

BEFORE THE END OF THE FIRST YEAR OF ITS EXISTENCE, THE UNIVERSAL SERVICE CORPORATION WILL BE ABLE TO PAY EACH AND EVERY ONE OF ITS EMPLOYEES,—FROM THE ONES OCCUPYING THE MOST LOWLY POSITIONS, TO THOSE WHO WILL CONSTITUTE ITS EXECUTIVE BOARD OF DIRECTORS,—A MINIMUM SALARY OF THREE THOUSAND ($3,000.00) DOLLARS PER YEAR. WITHIN LESS THAN TEN YEARS FROM THE DATE OF ITS FORMATION EACH EMPLOYEE, FROM THE LOWEST TO THE HIGHEST, WILL BE RECEIVING NOT LESS THAN THIRTY THOUSAND ($30,000.00) DOLLARS PER YEAR, AND EVERY MAN AND WOMAN ON OUR EARTH—IRRESPECTIVE OF RACE, RELIGION CLASS OR COLOR—WILL BE INVITED TO BECOME AN EMPLOYEE AND EQUAL CO-OWNER THEREOF.

To those who will get out their pencil and paper and, within a few minutes of figuring, calculate that there isn't that much money in the entire world,—(nor in fact enough at thirty thousand ($30,000.00) dollars per year—for each one of the earth's hundreds of millions of adult inhabitants—with which to pay them that salary for even the period of one month),—we beg to remind them that people do not eat either gold or silver. DOLLARS ARE ONLY "SYMBOLS" OF VALUE.

If one had a loaf of bread worth ten cents and, after eating it, was still hungry—and decided he could eat ten more loaves—he wouldn't reach into his pocket and expect to satisfy his hunger by chewing up a dollar's worth of ten-cent pieces. Dollars, when converted into that of which they are only the "symbols of value," represent bread and butter, shoes, dresses, suits, hats, automobiles, airplanes, homes, beautiful parks, education, amusements, and all things desired by man.

IT IS NOT DIFFICULT FOR ANY WELL-INFORMED MAN OR WOMAN TO PROVE THAT THE EARTH'S RESOURCES ARE AMPLY ABUNDANT, AND THAT THE WORLD'S HIGHLY EXPERIENCED EXECUTIVES, EXPERTS,. SPECIALISTS, SKILLED AND UNSKILLED LABOR, FACTORIES, MACHINERY AND MARVELOUS MECHANICAL INVENTIONS, COULD PRODUCE NECESSITIES AND LUXURIES OF LIFE FOR THE MEMBERS OF THE HUMAN RACE TO AN EXTENT EXCEEDING "HUNDREDS OF TIMES" THEIR CAPACITY TO USE OR TO CONSUME.

If the world's present number of factories produce—let us say—an average of three hundred ($300.00) dollars worth of necessities and luxuries of life for each of the worlds inhabitants, and such production having proven to be inadequate, mankind votes a salary check of three thousand ($3,000.00) dollars per year for food, clothes, homes, etc., to each man and woman employee and equal co-owner of The Universal Service Corporation,—all that it will be necessary for them to do then, is not to produce more gold or silver—or to print more money—but merely to build more "factories" and "machinery" and produce more food, clothes, homes, etc. When mankind decide that each man or woman should have thirty thousand ($30,000.00) dollars instead of three thousand ($3,000.00) dollars per year, they will again increase the number of their factories, and continue to do so until the desired quantities of necessities and luxuries which they may choose to use, are finally being produced.

The Research Department of The International Institute of Universal Research and Administration will, during its 30-day program of proclamations, "irrefutably" prove to even the most skeptical of men and women, that the factories and the farms of The Universal Service Corporation will be capable, (within a period of less than 12 months from the date of mankind's acceptance of its program), of producing a minimum of three thousand ($3,000.00) dollars worth of commodities, services, etc., per year for every man and woman on this earth, and an average of one thousand ($1,000.00) dollars worth of desired commodities for every member of the human race under 18 years of age. Our Research Department will at that time also prove that the productive capacity of said corporation will exceed an average of thirty thousand ($30,000.00) dollars per year—of the necessities and luxuries of life—per man or woman, within less than ten (10) years from the date of its formation.

WITHIN ONE MONTH AFTER THE CONCLUSION OF OUR RESEARCH DEPARTMENT'S 30-DAY PROGRAM, WHEN A SUFFICIENT PERCENTAGE OF ITS AUDIENCE OF TWO HUNDRED MILLION (200,000,000) MEN AND WOMEN HAS VOTED IN FAVOR OF THE ESTABLISHMENT OF BUSINESS FACILITIES THROUGH THE FORMATION OF THE UNIVERSAL SERVICE CORPORATION, OUR RESEARCH DEPARTMENT "GUARANTEES" THAT SAID CORPORATION'S NUMEROUS DEPARTMENTS WILL THEN BE CAPABLE OF "IMMEDIATELY" HIRING THE UNEMPLOYED MEN AND WOMEN OF THE WORLD'S CIVILIZED NATIONS, AT THE RATE OF CONSIDERABLY OVER TWO MILLION (2,000,000) PEOPLE PER WEEK.

Tens of millions of unemployed men and women throughout the major nations of the world, have been forced into idleness and hardships by the manipulations of the "Money Changers," not only for reasons which have been described in the previous pages hereof, but most particularly for the purpose of causing resentment, bitterness and hate in their hearts against their present governments, in order that they might thereby more readily be influenced into drastically altering their various governmental structures and accepting dictatorships in their stead or, if sufficiently embittered, be influenced into joining the ranks of the Communists and—(through a carefully staged revolution, planned and financed by the Money Changers)—bring about the complete overthrow of their former governments and appoint Communist dictators as their leaders and governors.

All well-informed people are fully aware of the fact that these plans to cause discontent and bitterness in the hearts of millions of people have already reached the point where there are some millions of Communists and Fascists in France, other millions in England, and over ten million (10,000,000) members of these various radical groups even in the "United States of America," which already provides its people with greater liberty and freedom than have ever before been enjoyed by the citizens of any nation.

ALL WELL-INFORMED INDIVIDUALS A R E ALSO FULLY AWARE OF THE FACT THAT THE UNEMPLOYED OF EVERY MAJOR NATION COULD—DURING THE PAST SIX YEARS—HAVE BEEN PROVIDED WITH PERMANENT POSITIONS "AT ANY TIME" WITHIN A PERIOD OF LESS THAN "NINETY DAYS" BY THE POLITICAL LEADERS OF THE RESPECTIVE ADMINISTRATIONS, IF SUCH LEADERS HAD BEEN WILLING OR COURAGEOUS ENOUGH AT ANY ONE TIME TO OVERCOME THE STRANGLE-HOLD AND POLITICAL INFLUENCE OF THE "MONEY CHANGERS" FOR EVEN A PERIOD OF A FEW WEEKS.

THE FACT THAT AFTER "SIX YEARS," NOT EVEN ONE NATION HAS BEEN ABLE TO SUPPLY "PERMANENT" POSITIONS FOR ITS UNEMPLOYED—(OR TO BREAK THE BACKBONE OF THE HIDDEN RULERS' CAREFULLY PLANNED WORLD-WIDE DEPRESSION)-SHOULD PROVIDE SUFFICIENT EVIDENCE FOR ANY INTELLIGENT HUMAN BEING TO PROVE THAT IT IS HOPELESSLY FUTILE TO EVEN ATTEMPT TO IMPROVE CONDITIONS OF HUMAN LIFE ON OUR EARTH THROUGH THE PROCESS OF "WRITING 'LITTLE CROSSES' ON PIECES OF PAPER WHICH WE CALL BALLOTS," AND EXPECT—IN SOME MIRACULOUS MANNER—TO CAUSE THE "LEOPARD" TO CHANGE ITS SPOTS.

THE POLITICAL MACHINES OF THE WORLD HAVE BEEN FOR CENTURIES—AND ARE TODAY—OWNED "BODY AND SOUL" BY THE WORLD'S HIDDEN RULERS, AND ARE FULLY AND COMPLETELY CONTROLLED AT THEIR WILL THROUGH THE AVENUES OF THEIR VAST CENTURY-OLD ACCUMULATIONS OF THE GOLD AND SILVER RESERVES OF THE WORLD.

IF ANY SUPPORTING EVIDENCE IS NEEDED IN JUSTIFICATION OF THE STATEMENT THAT THE UNEMPLOYED COULD BE PUT INTO POSITIONS AT ANY TIME WITHIN NINETY (90) DAYS, IT IS ONLY NECESSARY TO RECALL THE FACT THAT LESS THAN ONE ONE-HUNDREDTH PART OF THE FERTILE SOIL ON OUR PLANET HAS EVER BEEN PLOWED. WITH MILLIONS OF HUMAN BEINGS DYING OF STARVATION EVERY MONTH, SURELY A FEW OF THE UNEMPLOYED COULD BE PUT TO WORK, WITHIN A MATTER OF WEEKS, AND BE GRADUALLY TAUGHT HOW TO PROVIDE FOOD FOR THEMSELVES AS WELL AS FOR THESE STARVING MILLIONS.

The completion of great flood-control and reforestation projects, harbors, highways and air ports; the development of national parks; draining of swamps; and the building of gigantic irrigation systems to take water into the deserts that they might be converted into useful and beautiful spots for the profit and enjoyment of the human race, Would provide work for "hundreds of millions" of men and women for a period of "generations" yet to come. If you should doubt these statements, all that it is necessary? for you to do is to take the time to investigate the thousands of completed engineering plans of projects which are greatly needed by mankind and which—if undertaken—would provide permanent and constructive activity and employment during the entire lifetime of millions who are now looking forward to hopeless and endless years of idleness and unemployment.

Instead these idle millions are filled—(as it has been planned that they should be)—with such "bitterness and hate" that, with but slight additional provocation, they may soon bring about revolutions which will make the "bloody years" of the French Revolution seem like a "children's fight at a Sunday-school picnic" in comparison. For such are the upheavals which are planned as a prologue to the war which is intended to result in the extermination of the world's educated and religious inhabitants, including also those who have been stirred to revolt, and who are to be merely a part of the "cannon fodder" they will be inflamed into creating out of the educated and religious peoples of our earth.

The oft-repeated excuse that no great numbers of unemployed can ever be quickly placed in positions because of the fact that it would take months or years to plan and prepare the engineering studies, blue prints, and specifications for projects with which to keep them engaged, would be quickly dissipated if one were to take the time to glance over the "dust-covered" files of every city, state, and national government throughout the civilized world. Such files—"at this time"—contain completed engineering studies together with blue prints and fully checked specifications, of thousands of thoroughly practical and desirable projects; and most of which are greatly needed by the residents of the respective communities in which they are located.

These various engineering studies have been completed—year after year—at a cost (calculated on a worldwide basis) of "thousands of millions of dollars" of taxpayers' money,—by the duly elected or politically appointed representatives of the people, during periods of their respective administrations. However, before they could establish the necessary budgets with which to buy materials and hire men for the purposes of actual construction—(as they have invariably told us)—these representatives have been voted out of office and new ones, with an entirely "different" group of constituents to please, have started new engineering studies for "entirely different projects" in accordance with promises made to the voters who placed them in office.

The principal reason that these countless thousands of projects have never gotten past the "blue print and specification stage," is traceable to the fact that the majority of the people's political representatives "never actually intended to complete them at all," but only "promised" to do so in order that they might thereby win the necessary votes to put themselves into office. Nevertheless, these completed engineering studies are "instantly available" at any time the public demands their use.

WHENEVER THE "INTELLIGENT" MEN AND WOMEN WHO CONSTITUTE THE WILLING WORKERS AND CONSTRUCTIVE THINKERS OF THE WORLD, "DEMAND" THAT ALL ABLE-BODIED UNEMPLOYED ADULTS BE IMMEDIATELY PROVIDED WITH PERMANENT POSITIONS, AND WHENEVER THEY ESTABLISH "COMMERCIAL FACILITIES"—INSTEAD OF "POLITICAL ONES"—THROUGH WHICH TO "ENFORCE" THEIR DEMANDS, THEN—AND ONLY THEN—WILL THERE BE NEITHER HUNGRY NOR UNEMPLOYED HUMAN BEINGS ON OUR EARTH.

During one of our Research Department's extensive investigations in China, Japan, and certain countries in Europe, it was discovered that a force of over one hundred million (100,000,000) gardeners,—(whose ancestry comes from those who have for centuries lived close to the soil and know and love plant life),—could—within a period of a matter of weeks—be formed into an organization whose members would consent to live in any part of the world or travel to any point to which they might be sent, and who would gladly spend the remaining years of their lives working as gardeners in exchange for no other salary or remuneration than that consisting of the coarsest kinds of food, and the plainest, roughest kind of clothing. And the only homes they ask for are tents or plain board huts. IF ANYONE WOULD GUARANTEE TO FEED THESE PEOPLE AND CONSEQUENTLY QUIET THEIR FEAR OF "STARVATION," THEY WOULD WILLINGLY WORK 16 TO 18 HOURS PER DAY, AND FOR NO MORE REMUNERATION THAN JUST

BARELY ENOUGH TO EAT. WITH THE WORLD'S CIVILIZED (?) NATIONS DESTROYING ALMOST "UNLIMITED" QUANTITIES OF FOOD EACH YEAR, DOES NOT SUCH A PITIABLE CONDITION SEEM AT LEAST "SLIGHTLY" UNJUSTIFIABLE?

In fact, we could almost wish that each of our readers had experienced just a few days of "hopeless poverty" and "ceaseless hunger," in order that each one who reads this statement might thereby be capable of fully appreciating the tragedy of a condition of thought which would cause human beings to offer to "sell" themselves as slaves—(for the duration of their lifetime here on earth)—to anyone who would guarantee them just enough food to keep from "starving to death."

Can you picture the endless miles of beautiful parks and tree-lined highways; the thousands of little artificial lakes and man-made streams—in otherwise arid sections; the playgrounds, athletic fields and recreation centers, which would provide opportunity for the constructive and happy use of leisure hours, if all of the world's "hungry" people were employed for the purpose of producing such results? These advantages could be made readily available for the people of every land, through the activities of a permanent force of one hundred million (100,000,000) men and women trained to design, develop, and permanently maintain thousands of great parks and recreation centers as a protection against the ugliness and lack of beauty which now exist in so many of the world's great cities. The drab and frequently filthy—as well as colorless—immediate environment and surroundings endured by the majority of the earth's inhabitants, have done much throughout the centuries to warp and distort the minds of men.

INASMUCH A S MANKIND'S EXECUTIVE TALENTS WERE QUITE ABLE TO EFFICIENTLY DIRECT AN ARMY OF OVER SIXTY-FIVE MILLION (65,000,000) MEN—ENGAGED IN THE TASK OF "SLAUGHTERING" ONE ANOTHER DURING THE LAST WORLD WAR—SURELY NO ONE CAN QUESTION THE ABILITY OF THE WORLD'S EXECUTIVES TO EFFICIENTLY DIRECT THE ACTIVITIES OF ONE HUNDRED MILLION (100,000,000) MEN AND WOMEN WHO WILL BE ENGAGED IN THE PEACEFUL TASK OF TURNING OUR WORLD INTO A PARADISE OF BEAUTIFUL PARKS.

Knowing the readiness with which our planet could be made to produce an abundance of food for all mankind, our Sponsors have planned—and will recommend to the Universal Service Corporation—that a standing force of not less than one hundred million (100,000,000) men and women landscape architects and gardeners be maintained as a permanent branch of said corporation's activities. Knowing that such workers will receive the same educational benefits and compensation as any other group of employees, and that they will not be required to work any more than the usual 4 hours per day, 4 days a week or over 8 months each year, is it not indeed an inspiring vision—"and an ambition worthy of intelligent creatures"—to contemplate providing such employment for the tens of millions of broken-spirited, fear-filled human beings who now ask no more from life than merely "enough food" to keep from dying?

IT IS TO THOSE WHO THINK THAT SUCH AN AMBITION IS WORTHY OF FULFILLMENT, AND THAT SUCH PLANS FOR THE HAPPINESS OF THE HUMAN RACE JUSTIFY THEIR COOPERATION, THAT WE EXTEND THIS INVITATION TO LEARN OF THE DISCOVERIES AND RECOMMENDATIONS OF THE INTERNATIONAL INSTITUTE OF UNIVERSAL RESEARCH AND ADMINISTRATION.

Yes; our Research Department is well prepared to prove to the clear-thinking men and women of our generation, that every unemployed human being in every civilized nation on our earth, can be placed in permanent positions "at any time" within a period of but a few months—and at the rate of over two million (2,000,000) people per week—starting one month after The Universal Service Corporation has been voted into existence.

When the members of our audience of two hundred million (200,000,000) people have agreed to unite and direct their buying power through what will then be their own mutually and equally owned business facilities, they will have a combined influence of over "one thousand million ($1000,000,000) dollars" per day with which to back up their united demand that "permanent" positions be "immediately" provided for all unemployed. THERE WILL BE NO OCCASION FOR THEM HESITATING TO TAKE SUCH ACTION, INASMUCH AS THEY WILL ALL RECEIVE "EQUAL" BENEFITS THEREFROM.

EACH OWNER OF SAID CORPORATION WILL HAVE AN "EQUAL" VOTE IN ITS MANAGEMENT, AND WILL BE OBLIGED TO CAST HIS VOTE ON ALL MATTERS REQUIRING SUCH ACTION; NOR WILL HE BE PERMITTED TO RETAIN HIS OWNERSHIP THEREIN UNLESS HE TAKES THE TIME TO ATTEND

ALL REGULAR AND SPECIAL BUSINESS MEETINGS OF HIS LOCAL BRANCH OF THE CORPORATION, IN ORDER THAT HE MAY PERSONALLY UNDERSTAND ITS ACTIVITIES AND INTELLIGENTLY VOTE WHEN CALLED UPON TO DO SO. THERE WILL BE NO VOTES BY "PROXY" AND THEREFORE NO OPPORTUNITY FOR ANY "INDIVIDUAL" OR "MINORITY GROUP" TO USE THE BUSINESS FACILITIES OF THE CORPORATION FOR THEIR OWN SELFISH ENDS.

Although the majority of the citizens of many countries regularly vote on the various political issues presented to them, the fact still remains that they are seldom allowed to "actually understand" the issues upon which they vote; and not "one" out of ten thousand of them—at any time—"really knows" what is "actually taking place" on the inside of the world's constantly changing political administrations. The public is therefore readily "duped" into supporting many projects which have been cunningly conceived for purposes directly the reverse of those for which people thought they were voting.

Compulsory attendance at the respective local branch-business meetings of The Universal Service Corporation will be for the purpose of permanently preventing its owners from "unknowingly" consenting to activities of which they may not approve. In due course of time, through the avenues of radio and television equipment placed in each home throughout the world, such business meetings will be conducted from one central point, and each owner of The Universal Service Corporation will be able to vote his acceptance or rejection of the various measures presented to him, right from his own home . . . Through mechanical facilities—which have already been perfected—he will be able to vote by writing his signature and membership number with the use of an electrical device which will enable such information to be instantly recorded in the statistical department of the Corporation's International Headquarters. In other words, at that time it will no longer be necessary for a member to leave his home in order to attend the Corporation's business meetings, or act upon the various measures requiring his vote. Such measures will be described a number of times during each twenty-four hours, until all of the members have had an opportunity to cast their votes. [1] The "universal language"—which will be internationally understood by the world's intelligent and educated citizens within less than twelve months after the formation of The Universal Service

---

[1] These facilities will also be available for those who are traveling or away from their homes.

Corporation—will greatly simplify such activities. Within less than ten years, said "universal language" will be understood and readily used by every civilized man and woman on our earth, for even at this time its principal features are regularly used by well over three hundred million (300,000,000) educated people.

Through a system of "constant rotation in office," in terms of from one to a maximum of three years, a large percentage of the world-wide membership of the Corporation will be given the opportunity of occupying various official positions at the Corporation's International Headquarters and consequently—from first hand observation—will be well qualified to vote intelligently upon matters requiring an expression of their judgment.

IN ORDER THAT "TRUE EQUALITY" AND "JUSTICE" MAY PREVAIL,— "ROTATION IN OFFICE" WILL CONSTITUTE THE PERMANENT AND UNALTERABLE POLICY OF THIS GREAT CO-OPERATIVELY OWNED SERVICE CORPORATION. Its charter will contain specific provisions prohibiting any one, either now or ever in the future, from owning more than one share of its value—from having more than one vote in its management—or from holding an office or occupying any "one" position for a period of over "one" year without the written consent of 80% of the employees directly under such a one's supervision, and in no event, nor under any circumstances whatsoever, over three years.

An executive who is not capable of training his immediate assistant to assume higher responsibilities within not to exceed a three-year period—in order that he himself may be free to advance into broader fields of activity—will not possess the qualifications which our charter will require of its executives.

No employee will be permitted to occupy a position without first agreeing to strive to advance in accordance with such a one's proven qualifications. When one has proven that he possesses the qualifications and the necessary proficiency to occupy an advanced position over the one he is already filling,—and has assisted his immediate understudy to gain the necessary training for the position he desires to leave,—an opportunity for such advancement will constantly be made available in periods of from one to not over three years' time.

In other words all employees, from those occupying the most lowly positions to those who will constitute The Universal Service Corporation's Executive Board, will each be helped to progress in accordance with such employee's respective abilities, and without having to wait for some one in an advanced position either to die—or voluntarily retire—after possibly having obstructed the progress and deserved advancement of numerous other worthy employees for fifteen or twenty years, as they now do under our present economic ("lack of") system.

Unlimited opportunities for study and self-improvement will be made available to all employees, and there will be no need for anyone being obliged to engage in activities for which one may possess neither the natural aptitude nor the potential qualifications. When it is discovered that an employee seems incapable of advancing in a department, in which said employee may be active, immediate and highly specialized assistance will be provided to enable such a "misfit"—or dissatisfied employee—to find the type of work for which he or she may possess the requisite qualifications.

The "Personnel" department of the Corporation will be so conducted that neither the factors of favoritism nor family relationship will enter into the selection of employees for the most highly-prized or desired positions, nor for those of lesser importance. Civil Service examinations and numerous practical tests—conducted by recognized authorities and qualified experts—will be made available for those desiring positions with The Universal Service Corporation.

A SUITABLE AND DESIRABLE POSITION WILL BE GUARANTEED TO EVERY ABLE-BODIED MAN OR WOMAN IN ANY PART OF THE WORLD, IRRESPECTIVE OF RACE, COLOR, CLASS, RELIGION, EDUCATION, TRAINING OR ABILITY.

Although the standard wage scale for all workers, from the lowest to the highest positions, will be calculated at three thousand ($3,000.00) dollars per year each—during the initial stage of the Corporation's existence—it will—however—be gradually increased until within a period of approximately ten years, the Corporation's productive capacity will enable it to distribute approximately thirty thousand ($30,000.00) dollars per year, of the various necessities and luxuries of human life, to every man or woman throughout the world.

Under the proposed new economic system there will be neither creditors nor debtors to keep human beings in bondage to one another, nor to despoil one's life of the natural heritage of freedom and peace. The temptation to endanger one's future happiness by overdrawing one's credit will be prevented, not only through the adoption of a type of currency which only the individual earning or directly receiving it from the Corporation can spend or use, but also through a provision of the Corporation's charter which will prevent any of its employees and owners from ever exceeding their respective allotments of its products. Inasmuch as The Universal Service Corporation will be the only producing and distributing business establishment with which the public will finally be dealing, the exact amounts of credit due each of the earth's inhabitants will always be readily available. Instead of having to refer to the books of many smaller business establishments, in order to determine the amount of unused credit, there will be but "one" bookkeeping account to be taken into consideration and, therefore, but slight opportunity of anyone ever misusing or overdrawing credit.

WHEN THERE IS NO LONGER ANY "FEAR" OR "WORRY" OVER PROBLEMS OF EMPLOYMENT OR INCOME, AND WHEN—ALTHOUGH PEOPLE MAY PURCHASE WHATEVER THEY MAY INDIVIDUALLY DESIRE TO POSSESS—THERE IS NOT ONLY AN ASSURED, BUT ALSO AN "EQUAL" INCOME FOR ALL,—AND WHEN HUMAN BEINGS CONSEQUENTLY HAVE LESS "JEALOUSY, ENVY OR HATE" IN THEIR HEARTS TOWARDS ONE ANOTHER,—WE WILL FIND THAT MOST OF THE "PHYSICAL" AILMENTS OF THE HUMAN RACE WILL ALSO SUDDENLY DISAPPEAR LIKE BANKS OF FOG BEFORE THE RAYS OF THE SUN. MANY OF THE WORLD'S LEADING DOCTORS AND HEALTH SPECIALISTS HAVE IN RECENT YEARS AGREED WITH THE WORLD'S PROMINENT METAPHYSICIANS, THAT NEARLY "ALL" OF MAN'S PHYSICAL AILMENTS AND DISEASES ARE "DIRECTLY" TRACEABLE,—NOT ALONE TO WHAT MEN CALL UNCLEAN THOUGHTS AND ACTIONS, OR TO UNSANITARY CONDITIONS OF HUMAN LIFE,—BUT EQUALLY—"IF NOT EVEN PRIMARILY"—TO THE QUALITIES OF WORRY, FEAR, JEALOUSY, ENVY, HATE, GREED, SELFISHNESS AND FALSE PRIDE, WHICH HAVE FOR SO MANY CENTURIES CEASELESSLY HARASSED AND TORN DOWN THE HARMONY OF MANKIND'S THOUGHTS, AS WELL AS THE HARMONY OF THEIR ACTIONS.

When one observes how the effect of "fear"—"ENTIRELY A MENTAL QUALITY"—causes the blood to "instantly" drain from one's face and causes it to turn almost white;—and then again—when one's thoughts are suddenly filled with "anger or hate"—to observe the blood surge to one's face until its shade of color turns from deep red to almost a purplish tint— "AND THIS CONDITION ALSO CAUSED ENTIRELY BY THOUGHT"—it is not difficult to visualize the extreme action and strain to which the numerous delicately-balanced organs of the body must be subjected before they can cause such effects to appear.

When one contemplates the ceaseless tension and strain caused by men's endless fears and worries,—and the constant jealousy, envy, bitterness, hate, greed and selfishness to which our present economic system of injustice and inequality constantly subjects the thoughts—and consequently the bodily functionings of men—it is not hard to understand the cause of most of mankind's physical ailments.

It is not difficult to envisage the early appearance of a race of clean-thinking, clean-living, wholesome, happy men and women—and fearlessly joyous little children—soon after a "written guarantee" of economic security and equality is placed in the hands of each of the inhabitants of our world; a "lifelong guarantee" signed by the secretary and treasurer of The Universal Service Corporation which will—(with its initial capital of over twenty billions of dollars ($20,000,000,000.00), and the united backing of approximately two hundred million (200,000,000) of the world's most intelligent and industrious citizens)—be quite capable of fulfilling its promises and guarantees.

THROUGH NO OTHER MEANS THAN THAT OF "GUARANTEED FINANCIAL INDEPENDENCE" AND "ABSOLUTE ECONOMIC EQUALITY" CAN MANKIND HOPE TO FIND EITHER "HEALTH," "PEACE," "SECURITY" OR "HAPPINESS."

In addition to the benefits just described, mankind's acceptance of our Research Department's recommendations will also make possible the priceless assurance of "ample leisure" for all. The only arbitrary work requirement, applying to all employees, will consist of a minimum working schedule of not less than 4 hours a day, 4 days each week, during 8 months of each year. At the conclusion of twenty (20) years an employee will be privileged to permanently retire from routine duties if he so desires and yet will receive his or her share of the Corporation's products, services, and benefits for the duration of his or her lifetime. However, all employees will be privileged to earn retirement within a period of only ten (10) years, provided they are willing to work 8 hours a day, 4 days each week, during 8 months of each of said ten (10) years.

FARMERS AND OTHERS,—WHO ARE OBLIGED—"UNDER OUR PRESENT ECONOMIC SYSTEM"—TO WORK FROM BEFORE DAYLIGHT IN THE MORNINGS UNTIL AFTER DARK EACH NIGHT IN ORDER TO EARN A LIVING,—MAY BE TEMPTED TO BELIEVE THAT A FOUR (4)-HOUR WORK DAY COULD NEVER SUCCESSFULLY BE BROUGHT TO PASS. HOWEVER, IF THEY WILL BEAR IN MIND THE FACT THAT FROM "FOUR TO FIVE" MEN OR WOMEN WILL BE HELPING TO PERFORM THE TASKS NOW EXPECTED OF ONLY "ONE" PERSON, AND IF SUCH OF OUR READERS WILL ALSO BEAR IN MIND THE FACT THAT THE "FINEST MACHINERY" AND "LATEST MECHANICAL INVENTIONS" WILL BE USED TO REPLACE MOST OF THE LABORIOUS DRUDGERY OF PRESENT-DAY METHODS, IT SHOULD NOT BE DIFFICULT TO VISUALIZE THE ACCOMPLISHMENT OF NOT ONLY AS LARGE BUT AN INFINITELY LARGER VOLUME OF PRODUCTION THAN HAS EVER BEFORE BEEN ACHIEVED, "AND WITH NO ONE REQUIRED TO WORK OVER FOUR (4) HOURS PER DAY."

In addition to the previously mentioned pensions, there will also be provided a pension benefit consisting of an equal share of the Corporation's products and services for all men or women who are—or who may become—incapacitated and unable to work. Also similar pension benefits for all men and women over sixty years of age—(or over fifty years of age, after the Corporation has been in existence for ten years)—and for those of fifty years of age, or over, who assist in its formation at this time.

All men and women within these classifications-who may desire to retire from routine duties and devote the remaining years of their lives to study, travel or leisure—will be granted pensions of not less than three thousand ($3,000.00) dollars per year.

WHEN WE THINK OF THE ELDERLY PEOPLE WHO ARE FREQUENTLY UNWANTED—AND BUT SELDOM LOVINGLY CARED FOR—THESE PENSION FEATURES OF OUR CORPORATION'S CHARTER WOULD OF THEMSELVES BE SUFFICIENT TO FULLY JUSTIFY THE UNITED ACTIONS OF THE ENTIRE HUMAN RACE TOWARDS THE IMMEDIATE ESTABLISHMENT OF "THE UNIVERSAL SERVICE CORPORATION."

Each employee of the Corporation will be allowed three (3) days each week, and four (4) entire months each year of vacation time. All workers will have their choice of receiving one month out of each three—two consecutive months out of each six—three consecutive months out of each nine—or a four (4) months' vacation at the conclusion of each eight (8) months of continuous work, in accordance with the daily and weekly schedules previously described.

All employees will be entitled to "free transportation" during vacations—(subject to reasonable rules and regulations)—to any part of the civilized world which is now or may in the future be made accessible by regular rail, steamship or air lines. Such unrestricted and free world-wide travel will quickly remove the "racial antagonisms" which result from mankind's lack of familiarity with—and consequent inability to understand—one another's customs and habits. Such a lack of understanding has cast the human race into endless wars and for countless centuries has prevented the "BROTHERHOOD OF MAN" from becoming an actuality. IN ORDER THAT THESE "ENTIRELY UNWARRANTED ANTAGONISMS" MAY BE QUICKLY HEALED, FREE TRANSPORTATION DURING THE CORPORATION'S GENEROUS VACATION PERIODS WILL BE AVAILABLE TO ALL, AND NO ONE WILL BE CONSIDERED "EVEN PARTLY EDUCATED" UNTIL HE HAS PERSONALLY VISITED THE MAJOR NATIONS AND OUTSTANDINGLY INTERESTING PARTS OF OUR INDESCRIBABLY BEAUTIFUL WORLD HOME.

For fear that men might travel and thereby learn of the world's inexhaustible resources,—and that the people of foreign nations are neither murderers nor enemies against whom we must defend ourselves by building vast armaments,—those in charge of the world's governments and its basic economic structure—("through their control of its resources")—have been able to guard against any great number of men or women ever being allowed the privilege of more than one or two weeks of leisure time—"or vacations with pay"—each year. AND THOSE WHO ARE NOW ALLOWED VACATIONS, HAVE USUALLY HAD THEIR MENTAL AND PHYSICAL ENERGIES SO DEPLETED PRIOR THERETO, THAT THEIR PRINCIPAL DESIRE IS TO REST AND SLEEP DURING MOST OF THEIR LEISURE HOURS, OR TO SEEK SOME LIGHT FORM OF AMUSEMENT.

Inasmuch as one of the major objectives of The Universal Service Corporation will be to "melt away"—(instead of to create)—misunderstandings among the various nationalities and classes of human beings, "free" worldwide travel will not only be granted to the Corporation's employees during their vacation periods, but will also be a "compulsory requirement" of the Corporation's educational system for all young men and women under eighteen years of age.

If there are those who may believe that men and women would either get into "mischief" or become "bored" with life, if they were allowed as much vacation time as Our Sponsors have guaranteed to provide,—we beg to remind them of their own earlier dreams, and the yearnings which once filled their hearts with a desire that they might have both the financial means and leisure time, as well as the educational opportunities, with which to develop the natural talents and special capabilities with which they believed themselves to be endowed.

IF ALL PEOPLE WERE ASSURED OF ADEQUATE FINANCIAL INCOME, FREE EDUCATIONAL AND TRAVEL PRIVILEGES, TOGETHER WITH REGULAR PERIODS OF LEISURE, THERE WOULD ONLY BE A FEW OUT OF EACH THOUSAND OF THE WORLD'S POPULATION WHO WOULD NOT MAKE "CONSTRUCTIVE" AND "WHOLESOME" USE OF SUCH LEISURE HOURS AND GENEROUS VACATIONS.

Through the construction of thousands of beautiful parks, athletic fields, playgrounds and recreation centers, limitless opportunities will be provided by the Corporation for the development of clean, wholesome and—consequently—"healthy" habits of thought and action.

We again repeat that if there were no other justification for the establishment of the Universal Service Corporation—recommended by our research department—than the influence which this feature of its program will have upon the formation of "much needed qualities of character," it would warrant the whole-hearted support and co-operation of every clean-thinking, intelligent man and woman in our world today.

Do you know of any "real" fundamental reason why men and women should not be allowed to use at least "one third" of each year to do with as they might desire? It is now possible for any one, if properly equipped with suitable machinery and mechanical appliances, to produce as much during a four-hour work day as our ancestors did by working sixteen hours or more per day. Then why do most people spend eleven and one-half months out of every twelve—and literally all of their daylight hours—

working just for food, clothes, shelter and a possible two weeks' vacation out of each year, which our present system of greed and selfishness generously (?) permits them to call their own? IS IT NOT BECAUSE THE MECHANICAL IMPROVEMENTS AND MARVELOUS INVENTIONS OF OUR GENERATION—WHICH SHOULD HAVE MEANT SECURITY, FREEDOM, AND LEISURE "TO THE ENTIRE HUMAN FAMILY"—ARE CONTROLLED BY "A FEW" AND USED PRIMARILY FOR ACQUIRING EXCESSIVE LUXURIES AND FABULOUS WEALTH FOR THE FAMILIES AND IMMEDIATE FRIENDS OF "THOSE FEW," INSTEAD OF FOR THE WELFARE AND HAPPINESS OF ALL?

Are we justified, however, in blaming the majority of people who take advantage of the world's competitive private profit system for their own personal gain, (and with but little—if any consideration for others,) when it is more than likely that many of those who read this book would gladly—"and quite naturally"—accept and fully enjoy an opportunity for the accumulation of a large amount of wealth themselves? No, we most certainly are not justified in blaming them unless we are willing to raise our voices in protest against an economic system which makes such injustices possible, and such exercise of greed seemingly necessary and desirable.

The privileges of greed and selfishness can no longer be allowed to exist, since they result in ninety-seven out of every one hundred inhabitants of our earth, being inevitably forced to go through life living solely for the purpose of providing "dissipations" or "excessive luxuries" for the other three inhabitants, who—as a result in the majority of instances—are turned into swinish, self-centered, dissipated, depraved human beings. . . . Poor abnormal—unbalanced mortals, who would be healthier, happier and much more satisfied with life, through much more "constructive self-expression," and much, much less "destructive self-indulgence."

NEVER IN ALL OF HUMAN HISTORY HAS MAN HAD SO MANY MECHANICAL INVENTIONS AND FACILITIES, TOGETHER WITH SUCH LIMITLESS OPPORTUNITIES FOR FINDING HAPPINESS. AUTOMOBILES, AIRPLANES, RADIO AND TELEVISION HAVE NOW MADE IT POSSIBLE FOR EACH MEMBER OF THE HUMAN RACE TO ENJOY THE RESOURCES AND BEAUTIES—NOT OF JUST ONE, BUT OF ALL THE WORLD'S NATIONS—AND TO CONSIDER NOT JUST ONE LOCALITY OR COMMUNITY AS HIS HOME, BUT THE "ENTIRE WORLD" WITH ALL THAT IS THEREIN AS "HIS GREAT ESTATE."

ARE WE GOING TO REMAIN IN BONDAGE TO A HANDFUL OF "DEPRAVED MANIACS," WHO THINK THEY HAVE BEEN "DIVINELY ORDAINED" TO OWN OUR WORLD AND DOMINATE ITS INHABITANTS? ARE WE GOING TO LET THEM STEAL THE FRUITAGE OF THE PAST THOUSANDS OF YEARS OF HUMAN PROGRESS WITH ANOTHER OF THEIR DEMONIACALLY PLANNED DEVASTATING WARS, AND SUBMIT TO AN ERA OF UNCONTROLLABLE SLAUGHTER AND INDESCRIBABLE HORROR, MERELY TO SATISFY THEIR INSANE AMBITION TO "OWN THE EARTH" AND TO ENSLAVE ITS INHABITANTS?

The world's Hidden Rulers have no fear of the actions of many "little groups"—or even a few "very large ones"—(led either by sincere but frequently inadequately informed men or women or by those who seek the glorification of their own personalities.)—The only power of which these subversive forces have even the slightest fear, is the power of "Brotherly Love" and "Unity of Purpose," exemplified by Christ Jesus' "Golden Rule," and acted upon by a great number of people at one time.

No group with a financial force in back of them of less than the buying power of a minimum of "two hundred million (200,000,000) people," (which would aggregate a total of over one thousand million ($1000,000,000.00) dollars per day,) could ever exert sufficient influence to establish their own newspapers, their own food supply centers, their own farms and factories, and thereby make themselves not only financially independent of the "Money Changers," but also independently able to provide positions for the world's unemployed whom these Money Changers have thrown out of work and are now rapidly stirring up to revolution and hatred all over the world.

The secret plans to bring about the overthrow of existing governments, and thereby more readily complete—(through the medium of Communism and Dictatorships)—the manufacture of the armaments and munitions of war which must be produced before the "Money Changers" can accomplish the consummation of their final plot, can only be thwarted by the co-operative and concerted "worldwide action" of not less than two hundred million (200,000,000) intelligent and unselfishly-motivated, courageous men and women. THE PEOPLE OF ANY "ONE" NATION, "IRRESPECTIVE OF ITS SIZE," CANNOT COMPETE WITH THE INFLUENCE OF THESE SUBVERSIVE FORCES.

ONLY BY THE INTERNATIONAL ACCEPTANCE OF A TYPE OF CURRENCY BASED UPON SOME MEDIUM OTHER THAN "GOLD OR SILVER," CAN THE WEALTH AND CONSEQUENT POWER OF THE WORLD'S HIDDEN RULERS BE DESTROYED. AN ATTACK UPON A "WORLDWIDE" FRONT—(AND THROUGH THE AVENUE OF AN "ENTIRELY NEW TYPE OF MONEY" WHICH CAN ONLY BE USED BY THE PERSON TO WHOM IT HAS BEEN ISSUED)—CONSTITUTES "THE ONE AND ONLY METHOD" BY WHICH TO PREVENT A CIVILIZATION-DESTROYING WAR.

With the establishment of a Universal Service Corporation which would have a strong enough membership to issue its own money, not only could all of the world's trained workers—who are now unemployed—be put to work within less than ninety days after the formation of such a corporation, but also the absolute and complete control of the principal food supplies of the earth could likewise be readily obtained by the Corporation through the influence of the vast combined buying power of its world-wide owners. With that accomplished, a new form of money could be immediately adopted which would soon make it impossible for the "Money Changers" or their "satellites" to buy even a loaf of bread with their "combined accumulations of gold and silver," or to provide their soldiers with food of any description.

With complete and absolute control of the world's principal "food supplies," and with the. purchase of their own "broadcasting stations" and "newspapers," the 200,000,000 equal owners of The Universal Service Corporation will have but little trouble in bringing about a world-wide demand that the world's armies and navies be disbanded, and that the battleships and armaments of every nation be simultaneously taken to the deepest parts of the Pacific and Atlantic oceans, and there,—(through radio remotely-controlled explosives),—dynamited and blown to the bottom of the seas, where they will no longer menace our civilization.

Previous to this simultaneous destruction of the world's entire armaments and munitions of warfare, and the disbanding of its armies and navies, the Corporation's owners—together with the citizens of the various nations—will have voted the establishment of a world-wide militia with which to maintain law and order, and with which to permanently prevent either revolutions or wars from ever again occurring on our earth. These military police reserves will supplement the then normal but constantly "diminishing" activities of national and local police forces.

For a few years to come, "gold, silver and jewels" will retain a "vanity" and "artistic" value, also perhaps a "sentimental" and "souvenir" value;—but all of which will constantly diminish:—In fact, much more rapidly than one may imagine, once gold and silver are disassociated from the idea of money and are no longer used as a basis or medium of currency. Police departments will then soon find themselves dealing only with crimes of "sudden temper" or "emotion"—which constitute less than 10% of all present-day crime—and even such causes as these will have by that time largely disappeared. There being no need nor incentive to commit crimes for gain—in fact nothing to steal that one could not much more easily and safely earn—the police will find over 90% of their present activities completely eliminated.

The criminals of the world will no longer be able to derive any profit from stealing either gold, silver or jewels, since all of the gold and silver on this planet won't then be able to buy them even a "loaf of bread," inasmuch as whatever is sold or purchased in any corner of the globe, will by that time be produced and distributed by "Mankind United" through their "World-Wide" Universal Service Corporation, for the "equal" benefit of all. WITH THE "PROFIT MOTIVE" GONE, THERE WILL BE BUT LITTLE CRIME!!!

TO PERSONS READILY BEGUILED, THE COMMUNIST PROPAGANDA SUGGESTS THAT COMMUNISM IF ADOPTED WILL ELIMINATE CRIME. COMMUNISM IN RUSSIA HAS THUS FAR ELIMINATED RELIGION, MORALS AND THE SANCTITY OF MARITAL VOWS, BUT HAS YET TO DEMONSTRATE ANY APPRECIABLE CAPACITY TO ELIMINATE EITHER BRUTALITY, SELFISHNESS OR DISHONESTY.

WITH THE FORMATION OF THE UNIVERSAL SERVICE CORPORATION, THE LIVES OF MEN WILL NO LONGER BE ENDANGERED BY GREAT "COMMUNISTIC POLITICAL MACHINES;" POLITICAL MACHINES WHICH NOW FOSTER THE MOST "BRUTAL" OF INSTINCTS AND "CRIMINAL QUALITIES" OF MORTAL THOUGHT AND,—WITH THEIR PERPETUATION OF THE MONETARY SYSTEM OF "GOLD AND SILVER,"—ENCOURAGE THE DEVELOPMENT OF AN EVEN MORE INSIDIOUS TYPE OF RACKETEER AND CRIMINAL THAN THE MUCH— "BUT JUSTLY"—CONDEMNED PRIVATE PROFIT AND COMPETITIVE CAPITALISTIC SYSTEM, WHICH "THEY CLAIM" TO IMPROVE UPON.

NO, THERE WILL BE NO REWARD FOR CRIME IN ANY DEPARTMENT OF THE ECONOMIC SYSTEM OF WHICH THE WORLD WILL BE INFORMED DURING OUR INSTITUTE'S INTERNATIONAL 30-DAY PROGRAM,—FOR A CRIMINAL WILL NEITHER BE ABLE TO SELL HIS STOLEN GOODS NOR TO BUY EVEN FOOD WITH MONEY STOLEN FROM ANOTHER,—AND WHICH HAS BEEN ISSUED TO—"AND CAN ONLY BE SPENT BY"—SUCH A ONE.

IF THE CONCEPT OF HAVING THE WORLD'S "INTELLIGENTLY INDUSTRIOUS CITIZENS" ACQUIRE AND "COMPLETELY OWN" THE PRINCIPAL FOOD SUPPLIES AND OTHER RESOURCES OF OUR EARTH, SEEMS SOMEWHAT STARTLING TO YOUR THOUGHT, WE SUGGEST THAT YOU BEAR IN MIND THE FACT THAT "SOME GROUPS OF PEOPLE" ON OUR PLANET HAVE ALWAYS OWNED AND CONTROLLED SUCH RESOURCES.

Why shouldn't the class of people who have always done the world's work, those who have made its great discoveries, developed its marvelous inventions, established its educational and religious institutions, and have always been responsible for whatever progress the human race may have enjoyed throughout the centuries,—take full charge of the tools and supplies with which they have produced the countless thousands of useful or desirable products mankind have enjoyed? Since the warehouse from which the human family have drawn their raw materials for the production of these useful requirements of life,—(namely, the earth's raw materials and resources),—has had its doors closed and padlocked against them by the "greedy swinish qualities" of human thought possessed by a small group of people who have appointed themselves as "custodians of the key" to the inexhaustible resources within this warehouse, why shouldn't "those who mold and shape such materials for human use"—and "those for whom such products are prepared"—take charge of the "key" themselves, so that they can enter the warehouse at will and take out what the human family may need for its welfare or happiness?

THE "KEY" TO WHICH WE REFER, IS CALLED THE "OWNERSHIP" OR "CONTROL" OF PROPERTY, RAW MATERIALS, ETC: FOR COUNTLESS THOUSANDS OF YEARS THIS "KEY" HAS ALWAYS BEEN HELD BY EITHER ONE OR THE OTHER OF ONLY "TWO" CLASSES OR GROUPS OF OUR WORLD'S INHABITANTS.

The first group has consisted of those who have had the "gold and silver" with which to buy the ownership or title to such resources, after which they have usually stood guard over them like so many "dogs in a manger." Unable to use or sell even the smallest fractional part of the raw materials and resources which their century-old accumulations of gold and silver could purchase, they nevertheless have felt that since they owned the title,—(and had the money with which to coerce the various governments into creating laws and hiring soldiers to protect their title to such resources),—that there was no reason why they should let anyone else use them, unless the user first paid all of the profit to the title holder that he might desire to exact. These "world rulers" have stood idly by, with no other feelings than those of contemptuous amusement or an inflated concept of their own egotistical superiority, while tens of millions of other human beings die from starvation each year, and a majority of the remainder of the human race eke out an existence of privation and fear-filled years, century after century.

The second group,—which has occasionally throughout the past few thousand years succeeded in getting possession of the key—("Ownership")—to the earth's raw materials and resources,—has been, (not some branch of the "fabulously wealthy class") but instead, those of the world's most downtrodden and poverty-stricken "lower classes," who have become so filled with bitterness and hate over their needless privations, that they have risen up in revolution and destroyed their masters. However, with many instances to draw upon, such as the French Revolution and—of more recent date—"Communistic Russia," we find their control of a country's resources is invariably accompanied with a rule of even "greater brutality," "selfishness and greed," than that expressed by their former wealthy masters.

THROUGHOUT COUNTLESS CENTURIES OF GOVERNMENT,—(BY THOSE OF EITHER THE "VERY POOR" OR THE "VERY RICH" DIVISIONS OF THE HUMAN RACE), THOSE WHOM THE WORLD CALLS ITS "MIDDLE CLASSES" OF INHABITANTS, HAVE CONTINUOUSLY BEEN DOING "LITERALLY ALL" OF THE WORLD'S CONSTRUCTIVE THINKING AND PRACTICALLY ALL OF ITS WORK. They have—century after century—. built up its educational, religious and humanitarian institutions, and brought about its priceless discoveries in the numerous fields of research, together with the discovery and development of literally all of its marvelous mechanical inventions. This "middle class," composed—at this time—of those to whom we have herein referred as the "educated and religious groups," have "invariably" been much too busy performing tasks of constructive productive value, to pay any very great amount of attention either to the world's fundamental economic problems or its political departments. HAVING BEEN "MUCH TOO BUSY" TO TAKE THE TIME TO LEARN "WHAT HAS BEEN ACTUALLY GOING ON" IN THE POLITICAL LIFE OF THEIR RESPECTIVE COUNTRIES, THEY HAVE BEEN CONSTANTLY "USED" BY EACH OF THEIR VARIOUS POLITICAL ADMINISTRATIONS—FIRST BY ONE, THEN BY THE OTHER OF THE "TWO" GROUPS ABOVE DESCRIBED. IF THEY HAVE NOT ALWAYS BEEN "WILLING SLAVES" AT LEAST THEY HAVE ALWAYS BEEN "INDUSTRIOUS" ONES.

ALWAYS HAS THIS "MIDDLE CLASS" BEEN TOO "INDUSTRIOUSLY BUSY" PERFORMING LIFE'S CONSTRUCTIVE TASKS—AND TRYING TO BRING HAPPINESS TO THEIR FAMILIES—TO TAKE PART IN THE WORLD'S GOVERNMENTAL ACTIVITIES.

The Sponsors of The International Institute of Universal Research and Administration believed that the "middle classes" of people (who have always constituted "the backbone of every nation") had been held in bondage throughout the centuries, primarily because of the fact that they had been "penny wise" and "pound foolish" in devoting their full time to performing the world's work, and in taking so little time for ascertaining the reasons for their ceaseless bondage to the endless hard laborious tasks which never seemed to get the majority of them beyond the point in life from whence they had started. Through this neglect—of their own basic best interests—the "middle class" inhabitants of our earth have repeatedly permitted the fruitage of their centuries of tireless efforts to be destroyed through revolutions and wars planned for the profit or advancement of either one or the other of the afore-mentioned "wealthy" or "poverty-stricken" groups.

Our Sponsors believe that the control—("ownership")—of the earth's resources,—in other words "the key" to its well-filled warehouses of raw materials,—should be taken over by the intelligently industrious "middle classes" of the world's present population. As soon as the "wealthy" and also the "poverty-stricken" groups have been taught how to perform their share of the world's work—and are willing to do so—then the finished products of such resources, should be divided "equally" through "mutual" and "equal" ownership of a great Universal Service Corporation—"cooperatively owned and managed"—and with every man and woman on our earth entitled to his or her "equal" share of its products, and proportionate control and direction of its policies and management,—subject only to their acceptance and support of the provisions of its charter.

OUR RESEARCH DEPARTMENT STANDS READY TO PROVE THAT TWO HUNDRED MILLION (200,000,000) PEOPLE,—"ACTING SIMULTANEOUSLY" AS A GREAT WORLD-WIDE ORGANIZATION OF MEN AND WOMEN WILLING TO MEET ON THE COMMON GROUND OF THEIR DESIRE TO ENJOY "LIFE, LIBERTY AND THE PURSUIT OF HAPPINESS," UNHAMPERED BY POVERTY, WAR OR RUMORS OF WAR,—CAN SUPPLY PERMANENT POSITIONS FOR ALL OF THE WORLD'S UNEMPLOYED—AS WELL AS FOR THEMSELVES—AND CAN, "WITHIN LESS THAN ONE YEAR," BRING ABOUT THE ESTABLISHMENT OF A UNIVERSAL ECONOMIC SYSTEM WHICH WILL MAKE THE RECURRENCE ON OUR PLANET OF EITHER "WAR" OR "POVERTY"—AN UTTER IMPOSSIBILITY.

BIGOTED SKEPTICISM AND INEVITABLE EXTERMI-NATION OR INTELLIGENT CO-OPERATION AND "ECONOMIC EQUALITY" WHICH SHALL IT BE?

WE seek only the privilege of presenting, as a gift to the human race, the results of our sixty years of investigations, discoveries, and perfected inventions,—all of which have been carefully tested and their value fully proven during the past sixteen years of our Research Department's preparations for its world-wide 30-day proclamation.

Inasmuch as no group of less than two hundred million (200,000,000) clear-thinking and intelligently industrious men and women would have either the buying power or combined influence with which to act upon our recommendations, no further information than that which this book contains will be released to the public until after our Research Department has been assured by its co-workers in The International Legion of Vigilantes, that their Branch Registration Bureaus and 4-4-8-3-4 Clubs (hereinafter described) can guarantee the availability of such an audience.

WE SHALL GIVE NO DETAILED DESCRIPTION OF THE FACILITIES THROUGH WHICH OUR 30-DAY PROGRAM WILL BE IMPARTED TO OUR AUDIENCE, OTHER THAN TO STATE THAT THEY ARE "THOROUGHLY ADEQUATE" FOR THIS PURPOSE.

A "general" does not send a detailed description of his armaments, the position of his army, nor the place nor the time of his contemplated attack, to his enemies. Neither shall our Research Department at this time describe the nature of the discoveries which will enable it to simultaneously communicate its information—"without cost"—to those who previously agree to take the time to cast their votes for or against the various measures which will be recommended for world-wide action at the conclusion of its 30-day program. The world's "Hidden Rulers" have no means by which to ascertain the nature of such discoveries until we introduce their use to our audience. At that time it will be "much too late" for any subversive forces to prevent the release of our program.

THE ONLY ASSISTANCE WE REQUEST IS YOUR GOOD WILL AND UNPREJUDICED AND OPEN THOUGHT, TOGETHER WITH YOUR COOPERATION IN PLACING A COPY OF THIS BOOK IN THE HANDS OF EACH MAN OR WOMAN WHOM YOU FEEL WOULD BE WILLING TO DO AN "EQUAL SHARE" OF THE WORLD'S WORK, AND RECEIVE AN "EQUAL SHARE" OF THE WORLD'S INDESCRIBABLY ABUNDANT RESOURCES IN PREFERENCE TO THE UNCERTAINTIES OF THE "EACH-WOLF-FOR-HIMSELF" PLAN, WHICH THE WORLD NOW CALLS ITS "PRIVATE-PROFIT SYSTEM."

Only those to whom either a direct invitation to receive our Research Department's 30-day program is—or has already been—extended by The International Registration Bureau, or those whose thoughts are prepared for said program through a thorough study and understanding of the contents of this "Explanatory" bulletin entitled "Mankind United"—(which you are now reading)—and who have been sufficiently interested to acquire one or more copies thereof for circulation,—will be invited to receive or to vote upon our recommendations. In accordance with this ruling, a record of each person who is officially registered as above described, or who purchases copies of said bulletin, will be kept until such a time as 200,000,000 men and women have been so listed in The Institute's files. To facilitate the accomplishment of such a result, those who read "Mankind United" are invited to acquire copies thereof for circulation among their friends and acquaintances.

Although this book is, and will continue to be, published "exclusively" by The International Registration Bureau's Pacific Coast Division of North America, it will nevertheless, be circulated far and wide by numerous other branches of The Institute and their associate workers, throughout the civilized nations of our earth. Some single volumes may be read by as many as from fifty to one hundred people, and it is hoped that no volume will stop at just one reader. HOWEVER, IT IS SUGGESTED THAT NO COPY OF SAID BOOK BE PLACED IN THE HANDS OF ANYONE WHO WILL NOT AGREE TO TAKE THE TIME TO CAREFULLY READ IT WITHIN "THREE (3) DAYS" FROM THE DATE OF ITS RECEIPT AND, IMMEDIATELY AFTER DOING SO, RETURN IT TO ITS OWNER FOR FURTHER CIRCULATION.

A selling price of $2.50 has been placed on this volume in order to assist in defraying part of the total expenses of over five hundred million ($500,000,000) dollars, which will be incurred in forming our world-wide audience and in placing a copy of said publication in the hands of each of the 200,000,000 men and women who will constitute a part of said audience. The selling price of $2.50 is also intended to defray part of the costs of preparing the necessary data for recording and classifying such individuals according to their respective professions and vocations on The Institute's carefully guarded official records, and also as a means of compensating those who are helping to place this book in the hands of the 200,000,000 people with whom we desire to communicate.

During our 30-day program, the members of our audience will be supplied with "officially audited" and "properly authenticated" records to prove that no portion of the $2.50 selling price above mentioned, has been retained either as salaries, or in the form of financial profits, by any official of The International Institute of Universal Research and Administration, or by any member of said institute's Research Department;—in fact not even so small an amount as 1/10th of 1 cent. Their services and their lives have been— are now—and will "continuously" be dedicated and donated to this cause.

Due to the urgency of an early release of our 30-day proclamation, and the vital importance of "immediately" creating permanent positions for the needlessly unemployed and idle inhabitants of our earth—(and thereby preventing the world's further preparations for war)—a condition of the release of our program will be that each of the 200,000,000 people who receive it, will agree to permit The Universal Service Corporation to grant a lifetime pension of three thousand ($3,000.00) dollars per year, to each one of the eight million (8,000,000) men and women who are now being invited to assist us in the formation of this necessary audience.

By communicating with the branch registration bureau noted on the last page hereof, you will obtain information as to how you may qualify for one of these honorary pensions. Your principal responsibility will consist of placing not less than twenty-five (25) copies of "Mankind United" in the hands of a similar number of people—who have not previously received a copy thereof—and obtaining a promise from each one of them, that he will also take the time to introduce our message to his friends and acquaintances, by placing one or more copies of said volume in circulation among them.

In other words, eight million (8,000,000) men and women,—an average of one out of every twenty-five of those who will constitute our world-wide audience,—will be granted, as a reward for their assistance, a lifetime pension of three thousand dollars ($3,000.00) per year, to take effect within six months from the date of the formation of the Universal Service Corporation, and the acceptance of its charter by not less than eighty (80%) per cent of the men and women whom they invite to become our audience. Inasmuch as said charter will be based upon the practical application of "The Golden Rule" to the world's commercial activities, and inasmuch as its ideals of "economic equality" will correspond essentially with the general features described herein, there is but little doubt of its acceptance by the above mentioned majority, after they have spent an average of two hours per day—for thirty (30) days—investigating our many discoveries and irrefutable proofs.

Unless mankind possess sufficient gratitude and appreciation for the efforts which will have thus been made, by at least 8,000,000 alert, clear-thinking people, to bring about the successful formation of the audience we require, and unless the members of said audience are willing to grant their consent to the lifetime pension rewards above described,—they would not deserve even the smallest part of the benefits which the successful establishment of the Universal Service Corporation will make available to them and their families, nor would they be given the privilege of receiving such benefits.

Considering the fact that each one of the men and women who thus assist in the formation of said audience, will be obliged to not only donate the time for keeping not less than twenty-five (25) copies of "Mankind United" in circulation, but will also be expected to spend the necessary time to maintain and register an accurate record of the names, addresses, vocations, or professions of the various people who purchase copies as a result thereof; AND CONSIDERING THE ALL-IMPORTANT FACT, THAT WE COULD NOT POSSIBLY FORM AN AUDIENCE AS GIGANTIC AS THE ONE WE REQUIRE,—UNLESS MANY MILLION "INDEPENDENT"—"UNBIGOTED"—"RIGHT-THINKING"—"INDUSTRIOUS" MEN AND WOMEN OFFER US SUCH ASSISTANCE AS MAY BE NEEDED,—SURELY THOSE WHO ARE EITHER "UNWILLING" OR "UNABLE" TO RENDER SUCH ESSENTIAL HELP AT THIS TIME, WILL NOT HESITATE TO ACKNOWLEDGE THE JUSTICE OF OUR RESEARCH DEPARTMENT'S RULING IN THIS MATTER.

Inasmuch as the allocation of honorary pensions is entirely dependent upon the formation of The Universal Service Corporation, we believe that these 8,000,000 pension awards, herein described, should constitute but a very small part of the expression of gratitude mankind will owe to those who thus make possible the consummation of our program and the establishment of this great Service Corporation; therefore, a method has been adopted which will provide an immediate income—at this time—for the men and women who assist The International Registration Bureau in accomplishing this result.

Only those who place not less than four (4) of these books in circulation, through the Branch Registration Bureau noted on the last page of the copy first loaned to them,—will be eligible to form a branch of our International Registration Bureau, or be allowed to qualify for a position which will enable them to receive compensation for their services while helping us to form our world-wide audience. And only those who place not less than twenty-five (25) of said books in circulation, and supply The International Registration Bureau with an authentic record of the names, addresses, vocations or professions of the people who purchase additional copies as a result thereof, will be eligible for the lifetime pensions to which we have previously made reference.

The Branch Registration Bureau, noted on the last page of this volume, will supply you with further information pertaining to the above matters if you will follow the instructions contained thereon when you have finished reading the following chapters.

Inasmuch as there are no other means of preventing the further overturning of existing democracies, or preventing another great world-wide civilization-destroying war—than by mankind immediately taking steps to end universal unemployment and poverty; and inasmuch as those who control the world's currency—(and thereby its governments, through their vast accumulations of gold and silver)—have only one object in view; namely, "the extermination of literally all educated and religious people,"— and since they have the money, and therefore the influence, with which to force the production of the necessary armaments and munitions of war for the accomplishment of this result,—unless the world's "sane" and "right-thinking" inhabitants simultaneously organize in every major nation, and "immediately" establish their own business facilities and "a new type of money" to free them from their age-old bondage to the "war lords" and "money changers" of the world, and unless they thereby completely destroy the value of the century-old accumulations of gold and silver belonging to these hidden world rulers, "it will soon be too late to even talk about doing so." WITH THE WORLDWIDE LOSS OF FREE SPEECH AND THE PRIVILEGES OF ASSEMBLY RAPIDLY BEING BROUGHT TO PASS BY THESE HIDDEN RULERS, THROUGH THEIR CAREFULLY PLANNED AVENUES OF WIDESPREAD UNEMPLOYMENT, COMMUNISM AND FASCISM,—THE EARTH'S INHABITANTS WILL SOON NO LONGER BE ALLOWED TO "EVEN VOICE" THEIR DESIRE FOR PEACE, FINANCIAL SECURITY OR FREEDOM.

Our Research Department therefore feels justified in having adopted a plan for the promulgation of "Mankind United," which will compensate the men and women who co-operate with its International Registration Bureau in the formation of its requisite world-wide audience: a plan which will not only provide an "immediate income" for such co-workers, but will also supply an opportunity for earning the lifetime pension described herein.

To those who may be inclined to think that we should establish a lower selling price for these books,—(and absorb the difference in a price substantially below $2.50, by paying less compensation to the men and women who help us to circulate them,)—we request the privilege of bringing to their attention the fact that not only must these co-workers give generously of their time in exchange for the income which they will receive, but they must also possess the requisite "moral fibre," "courage," and "perseverance," to withstand the attacks of bigotry and sarcasm, and the malicious criticism of unthinking people.—No amount of money can compensate them for these experiences.

There will be many who will do no more than to glance hurriedly through the pages of "Mankind United," and thereafter feel qualified to pass a "profound judgment" of condemnation, upon the merits of a program which even the world's most "brilliant" economists will be wholly unable to "accurately" judge, until after they have seen the moving pictures and numerous authenticated reports and proofs which will be given to the world during our Research Department's 30-day program.

It will take real moral courage to circulate this book and to ignore the skepticism of the type of people who will first have to "actually hear" the deafening roar of hundreds of bomb-laden planes, and wake up in the dead of night with poisonous gases streaming into their rooms and—(like "white-hot coals")—eating out their lungs and tearing the flesh from their bones,—before they will believe that the world's governmental and financial structures are completely under the control of fabulously wealthy "moral idiots;"—or before they will believe that there are men who every second, of every hour, of every day and of every night, are forcing the production of vast quantities of such gases—and other "death dealing" elements—together with the necessary facilities for releasing them in the populated centers of the world;—men who have such world-wide influence, that they are actually paying for such things with the tax money collected from the very people whom they intend to slaughter!!

It is likewise a fact, that until the War Lords' "radio-controlled equipment", now secretly under construction in many parts of the world—(and which was partly assembled and delivered into the hands of their agents during October and November of 1937)—is installed and actually put into operation in the populated centers of the world and—(throughout an area of some hundreds of square miles surrounding the well hidden location of each one of them)—the eyes of millions of people are electrically vibrated from their sockets—AND UNTIL EVERY DROP OF WATER, AND EVERY POUND OF FOOD, IN EVERY THICKLY POPULATED CENTER OF THE CIVILIZED WORLD HAS BEEN POISONED BY ORDER OF THESE "MONEY CHANGERS" DURING THEIR WAR OF EXTERMINATION, WE ARE FULLY AWARE OF THE FACT THAT THERE WILL CONTINUE TO BE MILLIONS OF "OSTRICH-LIKE" HUMAN BEINGS WHO WILL SCOFF—AS THE BOYS BENEATH THE SOD IN THE FIELDS OF FRANCE ONCE SCOFFED—AT THE IDEA THAT THERE COULD EVER AGAIN BE A GREAT WORLD WAR DURING A CIVILIZATION "AS FAR ADVANCED" AS OURS.

THE NEXT WAR WILL NOT BE FOUGHT ON BATTLEFIELDS IN SOME FOREIGN LAND. IT IS TO BE A WAR OF "EXTERMINATION"—NOT FOUGHT BY COURAGEOUS MEN ALONE BUT INSTEAD CONDUCTED BY COWARDS OF THE LOWEST TYPE—FROM "SAFE CONCEALMENTS"—AGAINST MEN, WOMEN AND CHILDREN OF THE EDUCATED CLASSES IN ALL POPULOUS CENTERS OF ALL CIVILIZED NATIONS.

YES, THERE WILL BE MEN AND WOMEN WHO ARE NOT AWARE "OF THE TRUTH" OF THE STATEMENT—IN THE BOOK OF PROVERBS—WHICH WARNS US THAT "WHERE THERE IS NO VISION, THE PEOPLE PERISH,"— AND BECAUSE OF THE "BLINDNESS" OF SUCH PEOPLE, THEY WILL NOT REALIZE THAT THE FACULTY OF "THOUGHT" HAS BEEN GIVEN TO US NOT MERELY THAT WE MIGHT HAVE ENOUGH INTELLIGENCE WITH WHICH "TO GET THE FOOD—TO GET THE STRENGTH—TO GET MORE FOOD,"—BUT

ALSO THAT WE MIGHT DEVELOP THE WISDOM NEEDED FOR OUR "SELF-PRESERVATION" AND "PROGRESS," THROUGH THE "USE"—AS WELL AS THE "DISCUSSION"—OF MIND'S LIMITLESS IDEAS OF VALUE.

OUR RESEARCH DEPARTMENT THEREFORE FEELS THAT BECAUSE OF SUCH QUALITIES OF APATHY–AND THE NUMEROUS FALSE CONCEPTS OF SECURITY UNDER WHICH MANY OF THE EARTH'S INHABITANTS ARE LABORING–THAT IT IS FULLY JUSTIFIED IN CHARGING A PRICE FOR THIS BOOK WHICH WILL ENABLE IT, THROUGH THE AVENUE OF ITS INTERNATIONAL REGISTRATION BUREAU, TO GENEROUSLY COMPENSATE ALL MEN AND WOMEN WHO HAVE SUFFICIENT "INDEPENDENCE OF THOUGHT"—AND THE CONSEQUENT COURAGE—WITH WHICH TO HELP COMBAT NOT ONLY THESE ENEMIES TO MAN'S WELFARE AND PROGRESS BUT ALSO THE WELL HIDDEN FORCES WHICH HAVE, THROUGH THE AVENUES OF "MASS PSYCHOLOGY" AND CEASELESS "PROPAGANDA," PERPETUATED THEIR HOLD UPON THE HUMAN RACE.

WE INVITE THE MEN AND WOMEN WHO READ "MANKIND UNITED," TO HELP US CIRCULATE IT AMONG THEIR MANY FRIENDS AND ACQUAINTANCES, BY GENEROUSLY COMPLYING WITH THE RECOMMENDATIONS CONTAINED ON THE LAST PAGE HEREOF. WE EXTEND THIS INVITATION TO ALL WHO BELIEVE THAT THE WORLD HAS ENOUGH EXECUTIVES, TRAINED WORKERS, MECHANICAL INVENTIONS, UNDEVELOPED LANDS, AND THE RESOURCES WITH WHICH TO PERMANENTLY OVERCOME BOTH POVERTY AND WAR;—AND ENOUGH EDUCATIONAL FACILITIES TO QUICKLY HEAL MANKIND'S ILLITERACY, TOGETHER WITH THEIR RESULTANT SOUL-DESTROYING SUPERSTITIONS. ALL MEN AND WOMEN WHO POSSESS "INDEPENDENCE OF THOUGHT" AND A CLEAR REALIZATION OF THE LIMITLESS POTENTIALITIES OF "UNSELFISHLY MOTIVATED UNITED WORLD-WIDE ACTION," BY THE EARTH'S INTELLIGENTLY INDUSTRIOUS INHABITANTS, ARE INCLUDED IN THIS INVITATION.

ALTHOUGH—IF YOU SO DESIRE—BY COOPERATING WITH US, YOUR IMMEDIATE AS WELL AS YOUR FUTURE FINANCIAL REWARDS WILL BE GRATIFYINGLY SUBSTANTIAL, NEVERTHELESS, YOUR GREATEST AND MOST SATISFYING BLESSING WILL CONSIST OF THE GRATITUDE OF COUNTLESS GENERATIONS OF HUMAN BEINGS, WHO WILL NEVER CEASE TO BLESS YOUR COURAGEOUS GENEROSITY AND VISION.

Only those who are sufficiently interested in the program of The International Institute of Universal Research and Administration, to purchase at least one copy of this book—either for further study or for purposes of circulation in accordance with the instructions contained on the last page hereof—(or who have otherwise qualified as a member of our world-wide audience of 200,000,000 people)—will be notified of the date of our Research Department's 30-day program, or be permitted to vote upon its recommendations—and the charter of The Universal Service Corporation—at the conclusion of said program. For only those who have not only read—but who have also "carefully studied" the contents of this "Explanatory" bulletin, or our other officially released publications, will have had their thoughts adequately prepared to receive the thirty days of proclamations and recommendations which will at that time be put into the hands of our audience.

Prior to the date that the 30-day program is officially announced, none of our branch Registration Bureaus—or their respective secretaries—will be allowed to give out any additional information relative to the discoveries or the plans of our Research Department, nor are they authorized to make any statements other than those either contained herein, or printed and copyrighted by The International Registration Bureau. However, said Branch Registration Bureaus, and their respective secretaries, are supplied with copies of all such necessary printed data, as well as instructions to be given to those who desire to co-operate with us in the formation of our world-wide audience.

In order to protect the time and efforts of the men and women—(whose names appear on the numerous copies of this book now being placed in circulation)—who have been appointed as the secretaries of our various branch Registration Bureaus, and to guard them against the demands of people who may be motivated primarily by "curiosity," said secretaries are specifically prohibited from giving out any information—other than that which this volume contains—(relative either to our general program or the subject of financial remuneration)—to anyone other than those who have first evidenced the sincerity of their interest in our purposes and plans, by having purchased at least one copy of "Mankind United" as a proof of their desire to help us promulgate our message.

MANKIND UNITED-&-THE INTERNATIONAL 4-4-8-3-4 CLUB

THE name "Mankind United," selected as the title for this "Explanatory" bulletin, is also the name of the worldwide organization whose members will comprise the international audience of 200,000,000 men and women, now being formed for the Research Department of The International Institute of Universal Research and Administration, by The International Registration Bureau.

Each purchaser of a copy of this volume, thereby simultaneously becomes an honorary member of "Mankind United," and as such, will be duly notified of the date of our Research Department's 30-day program. When said program date is officially announced, full instructions relative to the steps which you will be invited to take, in order to receive the proclamations and reports of the discoveries of The Institute's Research Department, and full instructions together with the necessary ballots containing one hundred (100) separate measures upon which you will be invited to vote at the conclusion of said free 30-day program—will be duly sent to you.

YOUR MEMBERSHIP IN "MANKIND UNITED" IS ENTIRELY AN HONORARY ONE, AND THERE ARE NEITHER INITIATION FEES, DUES, NOR OBLIGATIONS OF ANY KIND WHATSOEVER ATTACHED THERETO.

Only the men and women who order one or more copies of this book, and who thereby become members of the group which will comprise our world-wide audience of 200,000,000 people (known as "Mankind United")—or those to whom a direct invitation is extended by The International Registration Bureau will be allowed to receive our 30-day program, or be permitted to vote upon the various measures pertaining to the formation of The Universal Service Corporation described herein.

The world's intelligent clear-thinking people are fully aware of the fact that there is no justifiable reason for further "poverty or wars," and that there are more than enough agricultural and industrial leaders, efficient executives, highly trained and willing workers; more than enough machinery and mechanical inventions—(together with millions upon millions of years of "unused resources")—ready to be co-ordinated for the limitless use of all mankind,—and it is well known that all of these advantages are available just as soon as a sufficient number of "independent," "clear-thinking," "courageous" men and women, "simultaneously demand" that such resources immediately be used for the equal benefit of all. YOUR PURCHASE OF A NUMBER OF COPIES OF THIS BOOK—FOR CIRCULATION AMONG YOUR MANY FRIENDS AND ACQUAINTANCES—WILL CONSTITUTE AN EXPRESSION OF "YOUR" RECOGNITION OF THIS FACT.

Those who co-operate with us towards the fulfillment of this program, will have the satisfaction of having helped to bring to pass a result more vital, more important, and more lasting than the economic accomplishments of any individual or group of individuals—heretofore known—throughout all of human history. Although it may seem to be but a "very little thing" that you are doing, in aiding this volume to circulate through the hands of the world's clear-thinking people, nevertheless the cumulative effect of many millions of men and women granting such cooperation, will inevitably result in the complete fulfillment of each and every one of the promises of freedom described herein.

Men and women who may feel that they have had but little opportunity to render any service which might stand as "a lasting monument" to their memories, or be of permanent value to the human race,—or men and women who may feel that they are so far along in years that they have now very nearly "lived their lives"—and therefore that there is but little they could do to aid such an ambitious program as ours—should bear in mind the fact that no human being is "actually" of less importance than another. They should remember that if each "little drop of water" were to depreciate its importance and "linger in the sky"—instead of dropping upon our earth—all of human life would soon perish from our planet;—and so likewise (only to an "infinitely" greater extent) is the value of each of the earth's inhabitants in his or her relative importance to the progress and welfare of the human race.

No adult is either "too young" or "too old," to do his full share of making it possible for us to develop an audience large enough to warrant the release of our research department's discoveries, proclamations and recommendations.

When 200,000,000 people have each read and purchased a copy of this book, or other publications of The International Registration Bureau,—(as an indication to our research department of not only the interest but also the preparedness of public thought for the discoveries and information which they propose at that time to release to the human race,)—then, "and only then," can the promises described herein be brought to fulfillment by The International Institute of Universal Research and Administration; for only then will there be sufficient "unity of purpose"—evidenced by the world's right-thinking men and women—to warrant the release of our research department's indescribably important discoveries and recommendations.

THE INTERNATIONAL 4-4-8-3-4 CLUB

When you have purchased five (5) or more copies of this book—and have placed four of them in circulation through the Branch Registration Bureau which first brought our program to your attention, and have established your own bureau—you will be invited to form a branch of our International 4-4-8-3-4 Club. To those who are familiar with our program, this name will be an instant reminder of the goal towards which we are striving, and the benefits—which are partly described herein—relative to the immediate availability of a universal labor schedule of only (4) hours per day, (4) days per week, (8) months each year, with a (3) day per week and (4) months per year vacation period,—to which the numerals, "4-4-8-3-4," appearing in the Club's name, refer.

It will be necessary for us to form not less than eight million (8,000,000) of these Clubs, as avenues of direct contact with those who read and become interested in promulgating the message "Mankind United" contains. These "4-4-8-3-4 Clubs," will also provide an opportunity for men and women of similar interests, desires, and aspirations, to meet on the common ground of their "mutual desire" to aid our program, and to bring about the early formation of our requisite world-wide audience.

When you form a branch of The International 4-4-8-3-4 Club, your membership will consist of the men and women who not only have read one of the copies of "Mankind United" which you may have purchased and personally put into circulation, but who also have purchased copies of said book from you, in order that they might thereby assist in the further promulgation of our message. No one will be eligible for membership in your branch of this Club, until he has complied with this qualification by purchasing at least one copy of said "Explanatory" bulletin through you, and has thoroughly studied the contents thereof.

ALTHOUGH YOU WILL NOT BE PERMITTED TO CHARGE EITHER INITIATION FEES OR DUES, NEVERTHELESS THE FORMATION OF ONE OF THESE CLUBS WILL NOT ONLY PROVIDE AN OPPORTUNITY FOR INTERESTING STUDY AND DISCUSSIONS RELATIVE TO OUR PROGRAM, BUT IT WILL ALSO PROVIDE SUITABLE FINANCIAL REMUNERATION IN EXCHANGE FOR YOUR EFFORTS, IF YOU SO DESIRE.

FULL INFORMATION PERTAINING TO THE FORMATION OF A BRANCH OF OUR INTERNATIONAL 4-4-8-3-4 CLUB WILL BE FORWARDED TO YOU WITH YOUR FIRST PURCHASE OF A COPY OF "MANKIND UNITED."

NOT A MAD DREAM

BURGLARS do not enter the homes of people who are sitting at their doors and windows with loaded shotguns!!! It is quite possible that the widespread circulation of the warnings contained in this book, will cause many of the world's "wolves"—who are well camouflaged in their costumes of "Sheep's Clothing"—to comb some of the tangles out of their more or less worn-out coverings, and to even "appear" to take steps through the League of Nations—and other similar avenues—to not only outlaw war, but also to bring about the establishment of facilities which may "seem" capable of ending the depression;—they may even start placing large numbers of the unemployed back into "apparently" perma-nent positions. Our widespread public warnings may also cause them to somewhat alter their preparations for the next world war. However, unless a medium of currency other than "Gold or Silver" (as described herein) is universally adopted—and a lifetime "written guarantee" of not less than three thousand dollars ($3,000.00) per year is placed in the hands of every man and woman in every civilized nation on this earth—"any other steps" which our political leaders may offer to take, and any promises that they may make, will not deceive those who have carefully studied and who fully understand the contents of this volume,—any more than such moves have —throughout the past few years—deceived the carefully-trained and well-informed investigators of our Research Bureau.

The world's subversive forces—(and many honest leaders and other well-intentioned people who are thoroughly mesmerized by their influence)—will no doubt make numerous "libelous" attacks on the character and motives of Our Sponsors, and will accuse them of fostering everything from a "money-making scheme," up to and including a plan for the overthrow of the world's major governments.

We cannot expect the co-operation of either "biased" or "bigoted" mentalities, but it is with the belief that there are two hundred million (200,000,000) right-thinking and intelligent men and women, (who will base their opinion of our movement upon the "ideals" we have herein described, and will withhold any judgment as to the "practicability" of our program, until they have received—during a continuous 30-day period—

sufficient information with which to form a just opinion,)—that we have published "Mankind United."

THE TRUTH OF THE STATEMENT THAT "WHERE THERE IS NO VISION THE PEOPLE PERISH," HAS THROUGHOUT TENS OF THOUSANDS OF YEARS BEEN FULLY VERIFIED BY THE FACT THAT EVERY CIVILIZATION THROUGHOUT ALL OF HUMAN HISTORY HAS BEEN "SELF-DESTROYED;" DESTROYED BY QUALITIES OF JEALOUSY, ENVY, PRIDE, GREED, SELFISHNESS, BIGOTRY AND SELF-GLORIFICATION. THE WORLD'S INHABITANTS DID NOT, DURING THOSE PERIODS, HAVE SUFFICIENT "VISION" TO ESTABLISH AN ECONOMIC SYSTEM BASED UPON THE "SPIRIT" AS WELL AS THE "LETTER" OF "THE GOLDEN RULE," YET IT HAS BEEN PROVEN—CENTURY AFTER CENTURY—THAT ONLY BY ADOPTING AN ECONOMIC SYSTEM WHICH WILL PROVIDE NEITHER FINANCIAL REWARD NOR ANY OTHER FORM OF GAIN FOR THOSE TEMPTED OR MOTIVATED BY "SELFISH" OR "CRUEL" CHARACTERISTICS OF THOUGHT, CAN MANKIND EVER EVEN "HOPE" TO FIND PEACE, CONTENTMENT OR HAPPINESS.

It will be stated that the result which The International Institute of Universal Research and Administration has promised to bring to pass is but a "mad dream." In answer to such forms of attack, we might remind our readers that it does not imply any lack of sound substantial value in connection with The Institute's recommendations, merely because its program is an ambitious one, nor because of the fact that it is somewhat of an innovation compared to the generally accepted "poverty-stricken" limitations of generations of "false education." However, as has invariably been the case throughout countless centuries, even the most "advanced thinkers" of each age through which mankind have traveled, have strenuously resisted every recommendation of progress which did not coincide with the erroneous concepts of life which "false education" and "superstition" have—throughout all past centuries—so strongly embedded into the consciousness of man.

Those who find it profitable to prey upon mankind's superstitions, ignorance and poverty, have with an enviable (?) degree of success, perpetuated every form of "fear" and "limitation" which held promise of keeping the human race in mental darkness. Yet, such people know that we live in the midst of "limitless opportunities" for intelligent progress and accomplishment, and that there is nothing capable of delaying mankind's arrival in the promised land of "peace and plenty," other than an educated sense of self-depreciation, fear and limitation; these qualities of false thinking, the world's Hidden Rulers have made it their business to ceaselessly propagate and perpetuate.

The characteristics of thought which hinder mankind's progress, are most fittingly exemplified in a statement described by a prominent lecturer [1] of a few years ago, which was issued through the School Board of Lancaster, Ohio, in the year 1828, through a letter addressed to a debating society of young men; it stated:—

"You are welcome to the use of the school house to debate all proper questions in, but such things as railroads and telegraphs are 'impossible' and rank infidelity. 'There is nothing in the Bible or the word of God about them.' If God had desired that his intelligent creatures should travel at the frightful speed of fifteen miles an hour by steam, He would have clearly foretold such things through His Holy Prophets. It is a device of Satan to lead immortal souls down to hell."

THIS IS ALSO A REMINDER OF THE DECLARATION OF LOMBROSO, THAT:—
"MAN IS BY NATURE THE 'ENEMY' OF INNOVATION."

The lecturer who used the foregoing illustration then continued stating:—
"If this letter, instead of saying in general terms that the railway and telegraph were 'a device of Satan,' had followed the usual custom by specifically uttering a libelous attack on the character and motives of Morse and Stephenson; if it had violated every rule of justice, honor and loving kindness, for the purpose of misrepresenting the intent and the declarations of these discoverers, and had done it in order to discredit them before the world, it would have fittingly shown forth the ever-continuing disposition of the human mind to resist its own progress, and to thrust martyrdom on every one who is first to discern that which is possible of accomplishment."

"What argument or protest would have prevailed with the dense traditional ignorance which constructed that letter? None!! Nothing but 'demonstration' with its persistent assertiveness. Nothing but the dynamics of 'truth,' will suffice to overwhelm and drive such mental perversity into silence and oblivion."

---

[1] EDWARD A. KIMBALL.

"It is fortunate for mankind, that the discoverers and reformers throughout the ages have had the moral courage and mental poise which enabled them to endure the storms of antagonism and persecution, while they persisted in impressing the facts of their discoveries on the world 'in spite of itself.' It is fortunate that these discoverers have known enough to expect that the rude hand of ignorance would strive to thrust back every scientific advance or promise of advance. It is well that they knew that it would be folly to stem the tide of unfriendly bias or to keep pace—by means of 'dispute and recrimination'—with a bewildering flood of utterances which were unjust or benighted. It is well that the great benefactors of the world have known that there is but 'one thing' that will be sufficient to answer all slander and to put to rout all antagonism.— 'THAT ONE THING IS PROOF'!! The one who has discovered a scientific verity and knows that it is demonstrable, may wait in serene calm until demonstration justifies him and his cause. If it were not thus, most of them would falter and go down in heart-broken despair, and humanity would either stagnate or revert to barbarism."

"All the discoveries and inventions which by means of demonstration and proof have forced themselves on a resisting world, must surely serve to show how largely the world is in need. If humanity had rightly heeded these things and the lessons they imply, it would realize that it is barely on the threshold of knowledge, and must progress in every direction for many years yet to come, before it will be justified in contemplating its handiwork with the thought that further progress is neither needed nor possible. ITS MONOTONE OF COMPLAINT AND LAMENTATION; ITS TEARS, POVERTY, AND DISASTER, CONSTITUTE BOTH 'CONFESSION' AND 'TESTIMONY' THAT MANKIND IS IN 'DIRE TROUBLE' AND IN SUPREME NEED OF EARLY DELIVERANCE."

FOR TENS OF THOUSANDS OF YEARS, THE HUMAN RACE HAS FOUGHT THROUGH RELIGIOUS, RACIAL AND CLASS ANTAGONISMS, TO ADVANCE ITSELF AND TO SOLVE ITS PROBLEMS THROUGH THE APPLICATION OF ITS SO-CALLED PRINCIPLE OR LAW OF "THE SURVIVAL OF THE FITTEST." YET, NEVER, THROUGHOUT THESE THOUSANDS OF YEARS, HAVE WAYS AND MEANS BEEN DISCOVERED BY WHICH IGNORANCE, SUPERSTITION, POVERTY AND WARS MIGHT BE MADE TO CEASE OCCURRING ON THIS PLANET OF OURS. IT HAS TRIED MANY WAYS IN THE DIRECTION OF THIS RULE OF THE SURVIVAL OF THE FITTEST; WAYS WHICH HAVE ONE AND ALL

BEEN MISERABLE FAILURES. "IF THERE BE A WAY WHICH IS EQUAL TO THE NEED, IT MUST SURELY BE SOMEWHAT OR WHOLLY DIFFERENT FROM THE WAYS THAT HAVE FAILED."

INASMUCH AS ALL OF HUMAN SUPERSTITION, POVERTY AND WAR ARE THE EFFECT OF SOME CAUSE, THE ONLY WAY TO ELIMINATE OR TO GET OUT OF THESE TROUBLES, "IS TO UPROOT AND EXTERMINATE THE CAUSE." IS THERE ANY PROMISE OR PROSPECT THAT THIS CAN BE DONE?

The International Institute of Universal Research and Administration, after sixty years of ceaseless investigation, claims that there is a solution and asks only that the substantial, intelligent, clear-thinking people of the world's civilized nations, expend the slight amount of time needed to establish the avenues through which the discoveries of their Research Department may be made available to two hundred million (200,000,000) such people in all parts of our world, in order that these needless causes of human suffering may be attacked simultaneously on a world-wide front. They further state to us—"and stand ready to prove their claims"—that these causes are too widespread and deeply rooted to be exterminated by the efforts of any smaller group, or in an area other than "the entire surface" of our planet in one "over-powering" attack.

"SUPERSTITION," "POVERTY" AND "WAR," BESET THE PEOPLES OF OUR ENTIRE WORLD, AND THESE RELENTLESS ENEMIES TO MANKIND'S FREEDOM—PEACE AND PROGRESS—CAN ONLY BE DESTROYED BY THE "CONCERTED EFFORT" OF "ALL" OF THE WORLD'S ENLIGHTENED THINKERS.

Whenever we of the human race have tired of our bondage to these "age-old" foes, we need only rise up as a body and with "one voice"—"demand our freedom"—in order to gain it. Have we ever had greater opportunities for doing this? more rapid means of transportation or inter-communication, or better avenues of education, than are now available to us?

Our Research Department asks only your invitation to prove that the unemployed of the world can immediately be given profitable and desirable positions,—and through the many avenues of already developed mechanical inventions,—that short working hours and many months of vacations each year "for all" are available—not a thousand years hence—but within less than "one year" after the world accepts its program.

OUR PLANS DO NOT CONFLICT WITH ANY "TRULY" RELIGIOUS OR HUMANITARIAN GROUP, NOR COULD ANY "UNSELFISH" MAN OR WOMAN ON THIS EARTH OBJECT TO OUR RECOMMENDATIONS.

Eight million (8,000,000) combination Branch Registration Bureaus and 4-4-8-3-4 Clubs,—each composed of a membership of not less than twenty-five (25) sincere, intelligent, clear-thinking people,—must be formed throughout the nations of the earth during the following few months, in order that The Institute's program can be readily imparted to those who are capable of acting upon its recommendations, and who are willing to have wars, ignorance and poverty, forever removed from human experience, and are "truly" desirous of helping to accomplish such a result.

These Clubs will literally constitute a group of 8,000,000 "separate research bureaus," whose secretaries and members will have evidenced their willingness to undertake a sincere and careful study of the fundamental causes of poverty and war and to investigate our Research Department's claims that the world's executives, its trained workers, its labor-saving mechanical inventions and its limitless abundance of raw materials, are "more than sufficient" for the immediate eradication of each and every one of the humanly perpetuated and "utterly needless causes" of world-wide illiteracy, poverty and war.

Our plans constitute "an immediately practical solution" to the world's grievous problems of unemployment, poverty, and a rapidly approaching war of self-annihilation;—no worthier invitation to action has ever been offered to intelligent men and women.

It has been rightly stated, that "nothing bigger can come to a human being than to love a great cause more than life itself, and to have the privilege throughout life of working for that cause." Although we ask you to spend but a small part of your life in helping us to establish our program,—your satisfaction and your reward will be permanent—and constantly increasing.

We invite you to participate in the most ambitious and constructive adventure ever undertaken by the people of any age. We invite you to journey with us into a land of "universal unselfishness and generosity;"—a land, the inhabitants of which give "freely" of their individual capabilities and talents for the welfare and happiness of all; and all combine their strength and their talents as a guarantee to one another of security, equal opportunity, freedom, leisure and happiness;—and extend this guarantee to even the least talented of their brethren.

WE INVITE YOU TO HELP US "UNITE MANKIND" UPON THE PLATFORM OF CHRIST JESUS' GOLDEN RULE OF "BROTHERLY LOVE" AND "IMPARTIAL ECONOMIC EQUALITY."

HAVE YOU THE GENEROSITY—THE WISDOM—AND THE COURAGE TO ACCEPT THIS INVITATION???

CHRISTIANS OF THE WORLD! HAVE YOU THE COURAGE TO ACCEPT OUR INVITATION ?

THIS book has been published and copyrighted in the United States of America,—not because there is no other country which grants its people the privilege of free speech or assembly, nor because of the fact that the world's subversive influences are any less aggressive here than in any other liberty-loving nation, nor because the people of America are any more "enlightened" or any less "bigoted" than the citizens of any other country, —but solely because of the fact that, throughout recent genera-tions, millions of people from all of the world's great nations have settled in America. Therefore, our message can be quickly placed in the hands of millions of men and women who not only understand the world's various major languages, but also understand the customs of its many classes of inhabitants, and consequently through them it will quickly spread to all parts of the civilized world.

Here in America, the Sponsors of The International Institute of Universal Research and Administration have found millions of right-thinking, clean-living, high-principled men and women of each of the great nations;—men and women whom they are now inviting to participate in the establishment of an economic system based upon "Practical Idealism," instead of the "Jungle Law" of selfishness and "brute force."

CHRIST JESUS TAUGHT THAT "THE KINGDOM OF HEAVEN"—THE PROMISED LAND—WAS "HERE AT HAND," AND READY TO BE FULLY ENJOYED ANY TIME THAT MEN WERE WILLING TO LIVE IN OBEDIENCE TO HIS TEACHINGS AND PRECEPTS. "CHRISTIANS OF THE WORLD!"—ARE YOU READY TO START "LIVING" AS WELL AS "PREACHING" THOSE PRECEPTS? ARE YOU WILLING "TO LIVE AND TO LET LIVE" AND NOT JUST TALK ABOUT IT???

The Universal Service Corporation—the formation of which will be brought to pass during our Research Department's 30-day program—will constitute a sturdy beginning towards the building of a great and beautiful world-wide estate and universal home for all mankind, with spacious living quarters, delightful gardens, security, opportunity, leisure, smiles, laughter and limitless happiness, to be equally shared and enjoyed in a great and true brotherhood of man: A brotherhood not in name alone, nor as an insidious and subtly planned ensnaring counterfeit—such as is now being offered to the world under the names of "Communism" and "Dictatorships"—but instead, the highest human concept of the divine idea of "the brotherhood of man," a brotherhood built upon the solid foundation of Christ Jesus' "Golden Rule;"—"ABSOLUTE ECONOMIC EQUALITY" IN "FACT" AS WELL AS IN "THEORY."

Again we remind you, that it has been most truly stated:—"There is a principle which is a bar against all information, which is proof against all argument, and which cannot fail to keep man in ever-lasting ignorance; THIS PRINCIPLE IS 'CONTEMPT' PRIOR TO EXAMINATION." [1]

Inasmuch as the only favor we ask of the world's un-bigoted and enlightened men and women, is that they will assist us in forming our audience—(through the circulation of this book)—in order that the Research Department of The International Institute of Universal Research and Administration may safely present its proofs,—and since our requisite audience of 200,000,000 people can readily be formed within a matter of but a few months—(if those of you who constitute the world's "independent," "right-thinking inhabitants" will help us to accomplish this result)—we feel justified in inviting your co-operation.

In order that the oft-repeated statement—"it can't be done"—may be refuted, we have prepared a chart to indicate just how readily—"it could be done"—if each one who hears of our movement, will spend just a few minutes to "pass the word along," by placing as many copies of this book in circulation as his time will permit.

Recognizing the fact that many human beings are largely controlled by habits of apathy and procrastination, we cannot logically expect more than a moderate percentage of the result indicated on said chart, and therefore those of you who have recognized the importance of this movement, must work just so much more zealously if the formation of our audience is to be quickly brought to pass. HOWEVER, THE CHART IRREFUTABLY PROVES THAT "IT CAN BE DONE."

---

[1] Herbert Spencer

The following chart will indicate to you the possible far-reaching effect of your influence provided that—when you have finished reading "Mankind United"—you will then order "four" copies of this book and—within 24 hours after their receipt—invite "four" of your acquaintances to read them, and request that they mail an acknowledgment of having done so—"together with their respective orders for 'four' copies thereof"—in accordance with the instructions on the last page of this volume. If they in turn invite "four" of their acquaintances—within not to exceed "three" days thereafter—to similarly co-operate, and each group does likewise, you will observe from the chart the possible far-reaching effect of the influence of just—"one"—person constructively directed in such a manner:

IF ALL WHO READ THIS BOOK WOULD COOPERATE TO THE EXTENT OF PLACING JUST "FOUR" COPIES THEREOF IN CIRCULATION, NO ONE WOULD NEED TO DO MORE THAN THIS, AND YET A WORLD-WIDE ORGANIZATION SUFFICIENTLY POWERFUL TO ACCOMPLISH THE RESULTS WE HAVE DESCRIBED HEREIN, COULD THEN BE FORMED WITHIN LESS THAN FOUR (4) MONTHS' TIME.

Estimating "one" week for mailing—or other losses of time—to enable each one who reads "Mankind United" to order "four" copies thereof and place them in circulation by lending them to "four" of his acquaintances, we will now assume that "two" weeks have elapsed since you obtained your first four copies and invited four of your acquaintances to do likewise. You will have thereby made it possible for a total of twenty (20) people to read "Mankind United" and to place their orders for copies thereof—within a period of only "two" weeks—as the direct result of the "four" books you generously took time to place in circulation. FROM THIS LOWLY BEGINNING, THE CHART ON THE NEXT PAGE WILL PARTLY ILLUSTRATE THE POSSIBLE INFLUENCE OF YOUR GRACIOUS ACCEPTANCE OF OUR INVITATION UPON THE CUMULATIVE EFFECT OF SUCH "UNSELFISHLY" MOTIVATED "UNITED EFFORT."

**THE CUMULATIVE POWER OF CO-OPERATION **

READ CHART FROM LEFT TO RIGHT

The 1st week's total of | 4 | register 4 | people each or a total of | 16 | people by the end of | the 2nd week

The 2nd week's total of	16 register 4	"	64	"	the 3rd week
The 3rd week's total of	64 register 4	"	256	"	the 4th week
The 4th week's total of	256 register 4	"	1,024	"	the 5th week
The 5th week's total of	1,024 register 4	"	4,096	"	the 6th week
The 6th week's total of	4,096 register 4	"	16,384	"	the 7th week
The 7th week's total of	16,384 register 4	"	65,536	"	the 8th week
The 8th week's total of	65,536 register 4	"	262,144	"	the 9th week
The 9th week's total of	262,144 register 4	"	1,048,576	"	the 10th week
The 10th week's total of	1,048,576 register 4	"	4,194,304	"	the 11th week
The 11th week's total of	4,194,304 register 4	"	16,777,216	"	the 12th week
The 12th week's total of	16,777,216 register 4	"	67,108,864	"	the 13th week
The 13th week's total of	67,108,864 register 4	"	268,435,456	"	the 14th week

The 14th week's total of 268,435,456 added to the rest is a sum total of 357,913,936 people who could—within less than four months' time—be invited to register their willingness to vote on the question of forming a Universal Service Corporation capable of guaranteeing individual as well as collective economic security for the entire human race.

The above figures indicate how readily such a group can be assembled and without undue hardship or sacrifice on the part of anyone.

If you desire, together with the rest of the right-thinking people of this earth, to receive and vote upon the Institute's program, PLEASE DO NOT PROCRASTINATE. REGISTER YOUR INTEREST BY ORDERING FOUR COPIES OF

THIS BOOK TODAY, AND INVITE AT LEAST FOUR OF YOUR FRIENDS TO DO LIKEWISE.

Lincoln most wisely reminded the people of America, of a great Biblical Proverb (Matthew 12:25) when he stated:—

"A HOUSE DIVIDED AGAINST ITSELF
CANNOT STAND"

MANKIND "UNITED"
MEANS
MANKIND FOREVER "UNLIMITED"

Help humanity to unite on the common ground of unselfed service to one another!!!

It can quickly be done after 200 million intelligently industrious people combine their votes
and

DEMAND WORLD-WIDE PEACE AND SECURITY

The following pages describe the vital importance of your immediate co-operation in obtaining these votes.

Although the Communists, Fascists and War Mongers of this age have learned the secret of "undeviating singleness of purpose," the world must still wait for those of us who call ourselves its "Christians and Idealists," to learn the lesson of "courage" and "immovable convictions;"—for at the least sign of danger, opposition, ridicule, or criticism, we quickly withdraw our support from the activities which, (deep down in our hearts) we may have become fully convinced deserve our help. IS IT POSSIBLE THAT THERE IS LESS LOVE OF FREEDOM THAN THERE IS OF SLAVERY, OR THAT THE CHRISTIANS OF THIS AGE HAVE LESS "CHARACTER" AND "COURAGE" THAN ATHEISTS OR HEATHENS?

COMMUNISTS AND FASCISTS WILL DISCIPLINE AND EXERCISE THEIR BODIES—AS WELL AS THEIR MINDS—GIVE UP THEIR LEISURE HOURS, AND EVEN SACRIFICE THEIR "WEDDING RINGS," THAT SWORDS MIGHT THEREBY BE MADE—(WITH WHICH TO MUTILATE THEIR OWN SONS, HUSBANDS,

FATHERS OR BROTHERS)—IN ORDER TO ESTABLISH AND ADVANCE THEIR MOVEMENTS;—BUT DURING THIS GENERATION THE WORLD HAS YET TO SEE THOSE OF US WHO CALL OURSELVES "CHRISTIANS," DO MORE—AS A CLASS OR GROUP—THAN TO SMUGLY SIT BACK WITH FOLDED HANDS AND EXPRESSIONS OF "SANCTIMONIOUS SELF-RIGHTEOUSNESS," WHILE WE WAIT FOR "GOD" TO DO OUR WORK FOR US, AND IN SOME MIRACULOUS MANNER "TO REWARD US FOR THE WORK WE HAVE LEFT UNDONE," AND FOR OUR SELFISHNESS, INDOLENCE, AND MENTAL AND PHYSICAL LAZINESS. GOD HAS NO REWARD FOR "APATHY"!!

THE OLD SAYING THAT "GOD HELPS THOSE WHO HELP THEMSELVES" HAS NEVER BEEN MORE TRUE THAN IT IS TODAY.

If women do not wish to again become just the "property" of men—"as they were for so many thousands of years"—and if free men do not desire the shackles of "physical slavery," as well as their present "mental slavery," they will soon have to not merely "pray" to become better,—(and for God to lay bare a heart which one prophetic woman once wrote—"men already know quite too much about"),—but they must actually "become better," and not just talk about it!!! While we are "praying" for Liberty, and for lives of greater security and a fuller abundance of the good things of this world, we had also better take the time to "work" for that which we claim to want, and to "protect" that which we already possess.

IT HAS LIKEWISE BEEN MOST TRULY STATED, THAT "GOD DOES NOT REWARD MEN FOR EITHER THE WORK THEY LEAVE UNDONE OR FOR THAT WHICH IS POORLY DONE." WE SHUDDER IN HORRIFIED DISGUST AT THE COMMUNISTS' ACCUSATIONS AGAINST THE RELIGIOUS INSTITUTIONS OF OUR DAY, WHEN THEY BLUNTLY STATE THAT "ALL" CHRISTIAN MEN AND WOMEN ARE NOTHING MORE THAN "WHITE-LIVERED-SPINELESS MORONS," WITH NEITHER THE "INTELLIGENCE" NOR THE "COURAGE" TO RECOGNIZE AND "UNITEDLY OPPOSE" THE VAST INCREASE IN STRENGTH AND POWER OF THOSE WHO DESIRE TO DESTROY THE EDUCATIONAL AND RELIGIOUS INSTITUTIONS AND FREE GOVERNMENTS OF THIS EARTH. YET, WHAT HAVE WE DONE—"AS A CLASS"—TO DISPROVE THESE ACCUSATIONS???

IT SHOULD CERTAINLY BE NO LONGER NECESSARY TO PROVE TO ANY WELL-INFORMED MAN OR WOMAN, THAT MANKIND ARE ON THE VERGE OF LOSING NOT ONLY THEIR "RELIGIOUS FREEDOM," BUT EVEN THE

PRIVILEGES OF "FREE SPEECH," AND TO BE GIVEN IN EXCHANGE EVEN LESS THAN THE NEGRO SLAVES OF OLD; FOR WITH THE "MONEY CHANGERS" COMMUNIST AND FASCIST POLITICAL ORGANIZATIONS INCREASING THEIR MEMBERSHIPS THROUGHOUT THE WORLD AT THE RATE OF "TENS OF THOUSANDS OF NEW RECRUITS PER DAY," SUCH A CONDITION SHOULD BE "SELF-EVIDENT" TO EVEN THE MOST "OSTRICH-LIKE" HUMAN BEING;—NO MATTER HOW DEEPLY HE MAY HIDE HIS HEAD IN THE SHIFTING SANDS OF A BIGOTED OR APATHETIC "FALSE SENSE" OF SECURITY.

IS IT POSSIBLE THAT CHRISTIAN MEN AND WOMEN DO NOT REALIZE THAT WITH THE ESTABLISHMENT OF COMMUNISM AND FASCISM THROUGHOUT THE WORLD, THERE WILL NO LONGER BE HOMES—SUCH AS WE NOW ENJOY—NOR CHURCHES, SUNDAY SCHOOLS OR PUBLIC SCHOOLS; NOR IN FACT, EVEN THE PRIVILEGE OF BEING TAUGHT TO "READ AND WRITE" AVAILABLE TO ANY BUT THE RULING ARISTOCRACY—AND THAT THIS RULING CLASS WILL BE COMPOSED OF THE MOST SELFISH AND BRUTAL MEN ON OUR EARTH?? FOR THEY ARE THE ONES WHO WILL EMERGE VICTORIOUS IN THE STRUGGLE TO DESTROY THE FREE INSTITUTIONS AND LIBERTIES OF THIS CIVILIZATION, UNLESS THE INTELLIGENT, CLEAR-THINKING MEN AND WOMEN, "WHO CALL THEMSELVES CHRISTIANS," SHOW AS MUCH AMBITIOUS WILLINGNESS TO "FIGHT"—NOT WITH "SWORDS," BUT WITH "USEFUL AND CONSTRUCTIVE IDEAS"—FOR THEIR RIGHTS, AS ARE THOSE WHO DESIRE TO STEAL THE GOD-GIVEN BIRTH-RIGHT OF FREEDOM FROM HUMANITY.

Where is our much-preached-of love of the Golden Rule? Is there actually any energy, vitality or even "sincerity" in back of our pretended love of its precepts? Do we deserve the right to have even been taught this soul-inspiring definition of a logical and intelligent type of human relationship when, generation after generation, those of us "who call ourselves Christians," sit back—"like inarticulate beasts of the field"—and let hundreds of millions of our brother and sister members of the human family suffer from the nameless fears and superstitions which accompany their complete—yet utterly needless—ignorance and illiteracy?

Where is the proof that we deserve either freedom or security, while no united voice is raised in protest of the fact that five hundred million (500,000,000) men, women, and little children are always hungry—(one out of every four of the earth's inhabitants)—and hundreds of millions are suffering from wholly inexcusable exposure;—homeless, unclothed, unfed, unwanted—"children of God?"—Children who are just as "precious" to Him as any one of the smug well-fed humans who sanctimoniously raises his voice in prayer and thanksgiving for life's blessings;—blessings which God has no intention of letting men continue to enjoy, unless they are shared with all alike, as is even the sunshine, the air, and the songs of birds.

WE FULLY DESERVE THE TITLE OF "SELF-RIGHTEOUS HYPOCRITES," WHEN WE THANK GOD FOR FOOD AND CLOTHES, WHILE WE PLOW UP MILLIONS OF ACRES OF WHEAT AND COTTON CROPS, DESTROY TENS OF MILLIONS OF CATTLE—AND COMMIT SUCH CRIMES—KNOWING FULL WELL THAT THIRTY MILLION (30,000,000) PEOPLE WILL DIE OF STARVATION THIS YEAR. MILLIONS OF HUMAN BEINGS MURDERED EACH MONTH, AFTER SUFFERING MONTHS OR YEARS OF THE SLOW EXCRUCIATING TORTURE OF HUNGER, AND YET THOSE OF US "WHO CALL OURSELVES CHRISTIANS," CANNOT EVEN CLAIM AS AN EXCUSE, THAT WE HAVEN'T, THE TIME TO HARVEST AND DISTRIBUTE THESE NECESSITIES OF LIFE TO OUR NEEDY BROTHERS, FOR RIGHT WHILE THEY ARE DYING OF STARVATION, TENS OF MILLIONS OF OUR OWN PEOPLE ARE IDLE AND ENTIRELY UNEMPLOYED. SINCE WE FEED THE UNEMPLOYED WITH TAXES WE PAY TO THE GOVERNMENT FOR THE DOLES THEY RECEIVE, SURELY WE COULD HIRE THEM WITH THIS TAX MONEY TO HARVEST—INSTEAD OF TO DESTROY—THE FOOD FOR WHICH COUNTLESS MILLIONS OF STARVING HUMAN BEINGS ARE DAILY APPEALING TO US!!!

No, we do not deserve either our liberties or the enjoyment of independence or security, when we are neither willing to fight for such blessings—(through the application of constructive ideas)—nor to share them with others. We no longer have the right to thank God for these blessings, while we are too cowardly or too lazy to protect or to share them; nor any justification for expecting either "progress or happiness" while such qualities of selfishness control our thoughts and our lives: For "God Is Love" and we forfeit the right to commune with Him, when we no longer express this quality. Instead of raising our eyes to Heaven, "like the self-righteous Pharisee," we should bow our heads in shame and grief as did the "Penitent Publican," in the Biblical narrative.

Is it so strange, or any very great wonder, that the "War Mongers" and "Money Changers" of the world have been able to discredit its Christian or so-called enlightened governments; its freedom of speech and freedom of worship;—the home, the benefits of lessons learned at our mothers' knees, and the Sunday schools and Churches which are supposed to teach brotherly love?

Is it any wonder that hundreds of millions of starved, bitter, hate-filled, neglected and unwanted human beings will reach for the bait of "counterfeit brotherhood" offered to them under its many names called "Communism," "Fascism," "Socialism," "Naziism," "White Shirts," "Blue Shirts," "Pink Shirts," "Green Shirts," "Black Shirts," "Gold Shirts," "Silver Shirts," and shirts with all colors of the rainbow;—or that such people are easily deceived into believing that they will find a "mountain of gold" either just around the corner—or at the end of the shirt?

IS IT ANY WONDER THAT THEY GRASP AT SUCH STRAWS OF HOPE—"AS THE 'TALE' OF A SHIRT"—WHEN THE CHRISTIAN PEOPLE OF THE WORLD TO WHOM THEY HAVE THOUGHT THEY COULD APPEAL, HAVE TURNED BACKS OF SCORN AND CONTEMPT UPON THEM, AND HAVE DESTROYED THE FOOD WHICH THEY SO SORELY NEEDED?

IS IT ANY WONDER THAT MILLIONS UPON MILLIONS OF THOSE WHO ONCE LOVED THE TEACHINGS OF THE GENTLE MASTER, AND WHO LOOKED TO THE WORLD'S CHRISTIAN PEOPLE AS CIVILIZATION'S "ONE HOPE" OF SALVATION, HAVE LOST CONFIDENCE IN THOSE WHO CALL THEMSELVES CHRISTIANS?—THOSE WHO STAND IDLY BY "PRATTLING" ABOUT "A GOLDEN RULE," WHILE WITH ONE HAND THEY DESTROY THE WORLD'S RESOURCES OF FOOD, AND WITH THE OTHER HAND PUSH AWAY THOSE WHO WOULD NEED LITTLE MORE THAN A CRUST OF BREAD OR A HANDFUL OF MEAL TO STILL THE TORTURES OF THEIR STARVED PAIN-RACKED LITTLE BODIES!!!

No, it is not enough just to pray, to preach, or to sing, for unless the Christians of the world are willing to unite into one great "International Body," that they may thereby acquire the influence with which to take "concerted action" for the immediate relief of human suffering,—(instead of—as is so often the case—expending their energies and satisfying their emotions with psalm singing,)—they will soon no longer be given even the opportunity to sing. Unless they have sufficient vision to "quickly" awaken and make use of their privileges of "free speech," and the right to assemble and unite their efforts in behalf of worthy activities, their voices will soon be raised with those of the rest of the world's starved, hopeless human beings, while they lie crushed under the heels of the world's "Money Changers."

THIS "EXPLANATORY" BULLETIN—FROM THE RESEARCH DEPARTMENT OF THE INTERNATIONAL INSTITUTE OF UNIVERSAL RESEARCH AND ADMINISTRATION—PRESENTS AN APPEAL IN BEHALF OF INTELLIGENTLY CO-ORDINATED "WORLD-WIDE" ACTION.

CHRISTIANS OF THE WORLD!!! HAVE YOU THE "WISDOM"—THE "VISION"— AND THE "COURAGE" TO ACT UPON OUR INVITATION???

In answer to those who may believe that it would take years to form a world-wide organization two hundred million (200,000,000) strong, we beg to call their attention to the fact that with present day methods of intercommunication — rapid transportation — telephones — radios — automobiles — airmail, etc., etc., such an organization could readily be formed within less than "four months'" time, — and yet not even "one" of the 200,000,000 people we seek, would be required to place more than four (4) copies of this book in circulation, nor spend more than a few hours of time in order to accomplish such a result, — provided that "each" of those who read "Mankind United," will make it his or her business to immediately obtain not less than "four (4) copies" thereof, and place them in circulation. (See chart on page 183).

In fact, when only eight million (8,000,000) of the world's right-thinking inhabitants have each formed a Branch of our International 4-4-8-3-4 Club, (previously described,) it will require less than "one month" thereafter, to complete our audience of 200,000,000 people. Within thirty days from the date that this result has been brought to pass, The Universal Service Corporation can be formed, and within less than one month from that date, the world's unemployed men and women will be going back to work at the rate of over two million (2,000,000) people per week!!!

IF YOU BELIEVE THAT THE CHRISTIAN INHABITANTS OF OUR EARTH HAVE AS MUCH INTELLIGENCE AS THE COMMUNISTS AND FASCISTS,—(OR AS MUCH INTELLIGENCE AS THEIR ATHEISTIC FINANCIAL BACKERS—"THE MONEY CHANGERS" AND "WAR LORDS")—WE SUGGEST THAT YOU HELP US TO PROVE IT; FOR AFTER "SIXTY YEARS" OF CEASELESS RESEARCH, WE HAVE YET TO FIND EVEN "ONE" MAJOR RELIGIOUS GROUP—(WHICH CLAIMS TO BE FOLLOWING IN THE FOOTSTEPS OF "OUR MASTER")—

WHICH EITHER "IS WILLING," OR "HAS THE COURAGE," TO PUT CHRIST JESUS' "GOLDEN RULE" OF "ECONOMIC EQUALITY" TO A WORLDWIDE TEST IN THE PRACTICAL EVERY-DAY BUSINESS AFFAIRS OF HUMAN LIFE. NO, NOT EVEN "ONE" MAJOR RELIGIOUS GROUP WILLING TO SPONSOR THE PRODUCTION AND DISTRIBUTION OF OUR EARTH'S RESOURCES FROM THE STANDPOINT THAT THEIR INEXHAUSTIBLE ABUNDANCE BELONGS AS MUCH TO ONE AS TO ANOTHER! HAVE YOU THE COURAGE AND THE UNSELFISHNESS TO RAISE "YOUR VOICE" IN BEHALF OF THE "PRACTICAL APPLICATION" OF CHRIST JESUS' PRECEPTS TO WORLD ECONOMICS—"EQUAL OPPORTUNITIES"—"EQUAL FREEDOM"—AND "EQUAL INCOME" FOR ALL???

There is no other way on this earth of preventing the spread of the atheistic teachings of Fascism and Communism! For they are winning new recruits at the rate of tens of thousands "per day," and it will not be long before they will be thoroughly capable of overpowering the democracies of the world by "brute force" and "weight of numbers alone;" nor are there any other means of preventing the "Money Changers'" planned civilization-destroying war than by the immediate "United Action" of those of us who call ourselves "Christians." We must forget our personal antagonisms and theological differences of opinion at least long enough to practically apply Christ Jesus' "Golden Rule" to the every-day task of producing and distributing the necessities and luxuries of human life, as well as man's spiritual requirements. OUR "DIVINELY WISE" MASTER MOST CERTAINLY TAUGHT A "GOLDEN RULE" WHICH IS NOT MERELY TO BE "PREACHED ABOUT"—BUT ONE WHICH IS ALSO TO BE "THOUGHT ABOUT," AND TO BE "LIVED"!!!

UNLESS WE ARE WILLING TO ESTABLISH AN ECONOMIC SYSTEM WHICH WILL BE CAPABLE OF "IMMEDIATELY" PROVIDING A UNIVERSAL STANDARD OF ECONOMIC EQUALITY FAR SURPASSING EVEN "THE PROMISES" OF THE COMMUNISTS, (WHOSE POISONOUS BAIT IS NOW BEING SWALLOWED "HOOK, LINE AND SINKER," BY HUNDREDS OF MILLIONS OF OUR WORLD'S "HOMELESS AND HOPELESS" INHABITANTS), WE NO LONGER DESERVE THE RIGHTS OF EITHER "LIFE, LIBERTY, OR THE PURSUIT OF HAPPINESS." AND THEY SHOULD—"AS THEY INEVITABLY WILL"—BE TAKEN FROM US, UNLESS WE HAVE SUFFICIENT "LOVE" OF THESE RIGHTS TO MEASURE UP TO THE PRIVILEGES OF PROGRESS AND "UNIVERSAL WELFARE" WHICH THEY PROVIDE, AND UNLESS WE ARE WILLING TO START DOING UNTO OTHERS

"AS WE WOULD THAT THEY SHOULD DO UNTO US:"—AND NOT JUST "PREACH" AND "SING PSALMS" ABOUT IT!!!

A CALL TO ARMS! AND A BRIEF SUMMARY OF THE INSTITUTE'S PROGRAM WHAT YOU CAN DO TO HELP

ALL that has been said in this "explanatory" bulletin regarding the program of The International Institute of Universal Research and Administration, would be of no avail were it not "acted upon."

Unless those who have read our proclamation decide to "personally cooperate" in the promulgation of this message, they might just as well have not read it at all. Words "without actions" are like rooms without lights—they may be "veritable treasure houses"—and yet if no hand were reached out to make use of the treasures—(by turning on the lights and discovering their true value)—in other words, by acting upon the knowledge of the "availability" of such treasures as our words have described,—there would be no reason for having written them.

Were it not that the "actions" we recommend for the formation of an organization large enough to accomplish the result we have herein described, would require but little more energy than that which you might use in reaching out your hand and pressing an electric light button in some "treasure room" into which you had been led, there might be some slight justification for hesitancy or procrastination. However, the only steps you are asked to take, consist in placing four (4) or more copies of this "Explanatory" bulletin in circulation by lending them to your many friends and acquaintances.

Only such action on the part of many millions of men and women—"and without delay"—can possibly bring about the formation of a group of people sufficiently large to combat the ceaselessly growing menace—not only of Communism—but also that of another great world war; a war, the successful consummation of which will bring about the establishment of a type of human slavery so terrifying that words cannot even start to describe it.

The responsibility of preventing the fulfillment of the plans of our world's incalculably wealthy Hidden Rulers, belongs as much to one as to another, and yet—(if the world's "right-thinking" inhabitants are willing to act as a body and do as did the Children of Israel—in their march around the walls of Jericho—and they will—with "one voice"—demand that these subversive forces be forever uprooted, and that an economic system be founded upon the "Literal Signification" as well as the "Spiritual Principle" of Christ Jesus' Golden Rule)—such a result can be quickly brought to pass,—and with but little individual effort.

If you value the safety and happiness of your loved ones—as well as your own security—you will not only "act" upon the recommendations contained on the last page of this book, but you will do it "Today," while this subject is fresh in your thought, and before numerous responsibilities or demands upon your time cause you to postpone such "needed" action.

WE STILL HAVE THE PRIVILEGES OF "FREE SPEECH" AND "THE RIGHTS OF ASSEMBLY" IN BUT A FEW OF THE WORLD'S GREAT NATIONS. HOW LONG IT WILL BE BEFORE THE RIGHT TO SAY WHAT WE THINK, AND THE PRIVILEGE OF MEETING WITH OUR FELLOW BEINGS FOR THE PURPOSE OF RIGHTING ANY WRONGS UNDER WHICH WE MAY BE SUFFERING, WILL STILL BE GRANTED TO US—IN VIEW OF THE GROWTH OF COMMUNISM AND DICTATORSHIPS—NO ONE KNOWS. BUT "TODAY" IS YOURS!—AND AT "THIS MINUTE"—"NOW!"—WHILE YOU ARE READING THIS BOOK, YOU STILL HAVE THOSE PRIVILEGES. DO NOT DEPRECIATE THEIR IMPORTANCE, NOR BE DECEIVED INTO THINKING THAT THEY WILL ENDURE IN SPITE OF THE UNDERMINING INFLUENCE OF THE "ATHEISTIC TERMITES" OF COMMUNISM AND FASCISM—SELFISHNESS—GREED—BRUTALITY—AND THE MAD AMBITION OF THE FABULOUSLY WEALTHY "MORAL IDIOTS" WHO NOW CONTROL THE WORLD'S MAJOR FINANCIAL AND POLITICAL STRUCTURES! DO NOT BE DECEIVED INTO BELIEVING THAT SUCH RIGHTS WILL EXIST WITHOUT "YOUR HELP" AND THE WEIGHT OF "YOUR INFLUENCE," (EVEN THOUGH IT MAY SEEM TO BE EVER SO SLIGHT IN YOUR OWN EYES.) FOR SUCH IS NOT THE CASE! ALREADY THESE RIGHTS HAVE BEEN LARGELY LOST!!!

THERE ARE BUT FEW PILLARS UPHOLDING THE LIBERTIES OF FREE MEN, THAT HAVE NOT ALREADY BEEN GNAWED THROUGH—OR ROTTED OUT AT THEIR VERY CORES—BY THE POISONOUS ATHEISTIC TEACHINGS OF THE WORLD'S TENS OF MILLIONS OF COMMUNISTS AND FASCISTS;—ATHEISTS

WHO TEACH "THE BROTHERHOOD OF MAN" WHEN THEY SEEK NEW RECRUITS FOR THEIR RANKS, YET WHOSE LEADERS LIVE THE LIVES OF "RAVENOUS WOLVES," AND PRACTICE THE BRUTALITIES OF THE DARK AGES, AS SOON AS THEY HAVE PLACED THEIR VICTIMS COMPLETELY UNDER THEIR DESPOTIC CONTROL.

Only "your help"—combined with millions of other clear-thinking men and women—can prevent civilization's final overthrow by these forces!!! Only the establishment of an economic system based upon the irrevocable principle of "Universal Economic Equality,"—as preached—not by the Communists and Fascists—but by "Christ Jesus"—(when He promised us that the Kingdom of Heaven was "at hand," and its limitless joys available for our happiness whenever we would practice His Golden Rule, and "equally share" the world's bounty with our fellowmen)—can ever destroy the "humanly planned" and "humanly perpetuated" causes of world-wide illiteracy, poverty, and war.

It is imperative that you raise your voice—"now"—in behalf of the establishment of such an economic system, while you are still allowed to speak your thoughts and to meet with your brother-man for discussions regarding them. Your help is greatly needed if we are to maintain—and perpetually retain—such rights. You possess these rights today, but no one on this earth can promise that you will still be granted them tomorrow. We therefore feel fully justified in appealing to you for your co-operation, and in warning you against procrastinating. We not only invite you to act upon the recommendations contained herein, but it would not be possible for us to "too strongly" impress upon your thought, the urgency of acting "today!"

[1]"There is a principle, which is a bar against all information, which is proof against all argument, and which cannot fail to keep man in everlasting ignorance."—AGAIN WE REMIND YOU THAT THIS PRINCIPLE IS—"CONTEMPT PRIOR TO EXAMINATION."

INASMUCH AS OUR WORLD-WIDE PROGRAM WILL BE FREE TO THOSE WHO HAVE PURCHASED AND CAREFULLY STUDIED A COPY OF THIS BOOK, OUR SPONSORS REQUEST THAT YOU POSTPONE ANY ATTEMPT TO JUDGE THE MANY ASPECTS RELATIVE TO THE PRACTICAL OPERATION OF SAID

---

[1] Herbert Spencer

PROGRAM, OR THE UNIVERSAL SERVICE CORPORATION, UNTIL THE CONCLUSION OF OUR RESEARCH DEPARTMENT'S 30-DAY RELEASE OF ITS DISCOVERIES AND RECOMMENDATIONS. THIS REQUEST IS JUSTIFIED—(AS WE HAVE PREVIOUSLY STATED HEREIN)—BY THE FACT THAT NOT EVEN THE WORLD'S MOST BRILLIANT ECONOMISTS COULD AT THIS STAGE IN OUR PROGRAM, WITH ANY DEGREE OF FAIRNESS EITHER TO THEMSELVES OR TO US, PASS JUDGMENT THEREON.

ALL WE ARE ASKING YOU TO DO AT THIS TIME, IS TO HELP US FORM AN AUDIENCE LARGE ENOUGH TO WARRANT THE RELEASE OF OUR RESEARCH DEPARTMENT'S PAST SIXTY YEARS OF DISCOVERIES, AND A FULL AND COMPLETE DESCRIPTION OF ITS RECOMMENDATIONS; BUT WE DO ASK THAT YOU HELP US TO FORM THIS AUDIENCE AND THAT YOU GRANT US YOUR CO-OPERATION IN ITS FORMATION, "WITHOUT DELAY!"

I—If you believe that the world has enough efficient executives, highly trained workers and mechanical inventions, and that it has sufficient undeveloped resources with which to end both poverty and war;—if—(knowing that the world has over one hundred (100) times more agricultural land than has ever been intensively cultivated)—you are willing to permit such undeveloped lands to be made use of to produce the food with which to feed "the entire human race;"

II—If you do not object to voting in favor of granting five hundred million (500,000,000) of the present "unemployed" inhabitants of our earth the right to keep from "starving to death," and if you do not object to allowing them to exchange their labor for food, by creating and maintaining tens of thousands of miles of broad tree-lined highways—constructing greatly needed flood control facilities—canals and harbors—building air ports—draining the swamps and taking water into the deserts—designing and developing thousands of gloriously beautiful parks—playgrounds and athletic fields,—and to thereby turn our world into the garden spot it was intended to be;

III—If you are willing to permit the world's hundreds of millions of intelligent, talented, and highly capable unemployed men and women to regain their morale, and to earn their financial independence by turning our earth into a literal paradise of beauty and security for the entire human race;

IV—If you do not object to having the talents and efforts of such people directed not only for the accomplishment of the above described results, but also combined with the rest of the world's trained workers to provide a beautiful, substantial, and well-furnished home—(set in beautifully landscaped grounds)—for every family on our earth—"within less than ten years"—irrespective of race, religion, class, color or vocation,—and subject only to the willingness of the Corporation's "co-owner" employees to learn how to use—enjoy—and protect such possessions as are made available to them;

V—If you are willing that mankind should receive—through the avenues of more efficient methods of production and distribution—an immediate saving of approximately twenty-five (25c) cents out of the average dollar now spent for merchandise, and that all men and women in every nation should be granted the le lowing described benefits:—

1st.—Guaranteed immediate employment and an international labor schedule of 4 hours per day, 4 days a week, 8 months each year;

2nd.—An assured vacation period (with pay) for all workers, of 3 days per week, and 4 entire months each year;

3rd.—A minimum of $3,000.00 per year ($250.00 per month)—salary or income, for all adults—"both men and women"—irrespective of race, creed, color, class, profession or vocation;

4th.—A pension of not less than $3,000.00 per year for all men and women over 40 years of age, (who desire to have their full time for their own use,)—provided they have worked a total of not less than eleven thousand (11,000) hours for the internationally owned world-wide corporation,—(approximately 20 years of work at 4 hours per day, 4 days per week, 8 months each year, or 10 years of work at 8 hours per day, 4 days per week, 8 months each year);

5th.—A pension of $3,000.00 per year—(without any restrictions as to length of employment)—for all incapacitated men or women, and for all persons over 60 years of age, who desire to have their full time for their own use;

VI—If you are willing to have a great universal service corporation immediately established, which will be "equally owned" and "equally controlled" by those who approve of its formation, and which will be capable of bringing to pass the above described results without bloodshed or resort to "brute force" of any kind, and without "confiscating"—"destroying"—or "acquiring"—anyone's properties or assets,—until just compensation has first been allowed,"—but which will be powerful, influential, and wealthy enough to "fully reimburse," not only those whom it will employ, but also the individuals, groups or companies, whose properties or assets may be required for the successful accomplishment of the results and benefits to which we have herein referred;—a corporation capable of producing enough food, clothes, homes, and educational, cultural and travel facilities, to abundantly meet the demands of every man, woman and child on our planet, and able to make all useful, interesting or beautiful parts of the earth, accessible by adequate highways, harbors and air ports;—a corporation with the facilities for permanently hiring and directing a force of one hundred million (100,000,000) men and women gardeners and landscape architects, exclusively for the purpose of developing and permanently maintaining thousands of parks, gardens, playgrounds, and athletic fields in all nations;—a corporation with the educational facilities for teaching a universal auxiliary language, and thereby rapidly overcoming the religious, racial, and class antagonisms which now result in such widespread and destructive hatred;

VII—If you are willing—through the concerted action of the world's educated and religious peoples—to bring about the disbandment of all armies and navies, and the destruction of all munitions and armaments of war in all nations, and to do so "simultaneously" with the establishment of an International Home Guard capable of maintaining peace and order throughout the world;—and if you are willing that there should be no more revolutions, "wars" or "rumors of wars;" no more illiteracy or "maliciously perpetuated" forms of superstition; no more "hungry" or "starving" men, women, or little children, and no more ugliness or poverty in any part of our gloriously beautiful world home;

VIII—If you are willing to have our Research Department's discoveries presented to you during a great world-wide free 30-day program;—(evidence which will—for all time to come—prove that each and every one of the benefits described in this volume, can be brought to pass at any time that two hundred million (200,000,000) "intelligently industrious" and "right-thinking" men and women agree to combine their talents and their strength towards such an accomplishment;)

IX—If—after receiving the above-mentioned program—you would be willing to cast your vote either "for" or "against" each of the one hundred (100) recommendations which will at that time be submitted to you,—(bearing always in mind that you will then be voting with a "full and complete knowledge" of all facts,—"not blindly"); and—(in final conclusion of this resumé of our program)—if you are willing to take into consideration the fact that every minute of hunger and exposure, now being "needlessly experienced" by hundreds of millions of "starving"—"homeless" human beings, seems like "an eternity of torture" to them, and if you are willing to also take into consideration the further and even more greatly important fact—to you and your loved ones—that every hour of delay lessens mankind's ability to safeguard their lives and their liberties against the impending war of planned wholesale extermination;—then we invite you to help us to help you—your loved ones—your friends and your neighbors, to help the right - thinking men and women of this earth to "immediately" meet together in a common cause on the common ground of a common-sense world-wide program of "right ideas," and a final "conclusive attack" upon the "real causes" of mankind's poverty, bloodshed and suffering.

MEANWHILE, LET US SHORTEN THE PERIOD OF HUMANITY'S "UTTERLY NEEDLESS AGONY," AS MUCH AND AS "RAPIDLY" AS POSSIBLE BY "AT ONCE" GOING INTO ACTION TO SPEED THIS PRACTICAL MESSAGE—OF "PEACE ON EARTH AND GOOD WILL TO ALL MANKIND"—QUICKLY UPON ITS WAY!!!

IN HELPING TO BUILD OUR GREATLY NEEDED NEW ECONOMIC SYSTEM YOU WILL BE STARTING WITH US UPON THE MOST GLORIOUS ADVENTURE EVER EXPERIENCED BY THE MEN OR WOMEN OF ANY AGE; AN ADVENTURE TRULY WORTHY OF INTELLIGENT CREATURES,—FOR YOUR REWARD WILL BE A WORLD OF "BROTHERLY LOVE" AND "UNIVERSAL HAPPINESS";—A WORLD IN WHICH THERE WILL BE NEITHER "WAR" NOR "POVERTY." BEFORE MANY MONTHS HAVE PASSED ALONG THEIR WAY, THOSE WHO ARE NOW THE WORLD'S SUFFERING, HOPELESS, HELPLESS MILLIONS, WILL ENRICH YOUR LIFE WITH THEIR MANY EXPRESSIONS OF GRATEFUL APPRECIATION FOR THE BLESSINGS OF SECURITY AND HAPPINESS WHICH YOUR GENEROUS ASSISTANCE WILL HAVE HELPED TO PROVIDE FOR THEM.

ANTICIPATING YOUR GRACIOUS ACCEPTANCE OF THIS INVITATION, THE INTERNATIONAL REGISTRATION BUREAU—PUBLISHERS OF "MANKIND UNITED"—TOGETHER WITH THE INTERNATIONAL LEGION OF VIGILANTES AND OUR ARMY OF LOYAL, DEVOTED ASSOCIATE WORKERS SINCERELY THANK YOU, AND JOIN IN WELCOMING YOU AS A MEMBER OF "MANKIND UNITED." WHEN, IN THE NOT FAR-DISTANT FUTURE, IT BECOMES YOUR PRIVILEGE TO HAVE "FREELY" REVEALED TO YOU, "THE PROOFS" WHICH WILL CONSTITUTE "A COMPLETE GUARANTEE" OF PERSONAL AS WELL AS INTERNATIONAL SECURITY AND FREEDOM, YOU WILL THEN FULLY RECOGNIZE THIS ACTION—(WHICH DEEP DOWN IN YOUR HEART WE FEEL THAT YOU KNOW IT IS RIGHT FOR YOU TO TAKE)—AS HAVING BEEN THE MOST IMPORTANT ACT OF YOUR ENTIRE LIFE.

NO ACT OF DUTY AT THIS MOMENT "COULD BE" MORE IMPORTANT THAN THAT OF TURNING TO THE LAST TWO PAGES OF THIS VOLUME AND FOLLOWING THE INSTRUCTIONS YOU WILL FIND PRINTED THEREON.

The following solicitation appears at the end of the original book. It is reproduced for completeness. Please be advised that this organization is long defunct—JBH.

WHAT YOU CAN DO TO HELP

FIRST:. . . Order as many copies of "Mankind United" as you can put into circulation among your relatives, friends, acquaintances and neighbors. (If you desire to do so, these books may be sold by you in order to thereby defray the cost of new copies for additional circulation.)

SECOND:. . . You can help to put reliable unemployed friends or relatives into remunerative employment (either part or full time) by having them read "Mankind United," and then arrange to join the force of workers now assisting us in the world-wide circulation of this book.

(Applicants please communicate with local branch registration bureau at address noted on next page hereof. Further information regarding the honorary pension awards herein described—(See pages #161 to #169 inclusive) and details regarding the method by which our co-workers are enabled to qualify for one of these lifetime pensions, will be sent with the answer to said applications).

THIRD:. . . You can organize a branch—or branches—of the International 4-4-8-3-4 Study Club. (See page #170.) Further information relative thereto and instructions for forming branches thereof, should you so desire, will be forwarded to you after you have purchased your first copy of "Mankind United."

FOURTH:. . . You can act as a supervisor or as a lecturer for a branch of the International Registration Bureau, provided you possess the requisite executive experience, organizing ability and qualifications demanded by such a position.

PLEASE NOTE

AFTER YOU HAVE PURCHASED YOUR FIRST COPY OF THIS VOLUME—(AND HAVE THEREBY INDICATED AN "ACTIVE" INTEREST IN OUR PROGRAM)—YOU WILL BE INVITED TO ATTEND ANY MEETINGS WHICH MAY BE HELD BY YOUR LOCAL BRANCH OF THE INTERNATIONAL 4-4-8-3-4 CLUB, AT WHICH TIME—SHOULD YOU WISH FURTHER INFORMATION—A PERSONAL APPOINTMENT WILL BE ARRANGED FOR YOU—AT YOUR CONVENIENCE—BY THE CLUB'S SECRETARY.

INSTRUCTIONS AND MAILING ADDRESS

PRICE AND POSTAGE:. . . The retail selling price of "Mankind United" is $2.50 per copy, plus a postage and mailing charge of 15c per copy within the United States and Canada, and 25c per copy elsewhere. (Terms: . . . Cash with order.)

WHEN PLACING YOUR ORDER:. . . State number of copies wanted and the total amount of the payment you are enclosing. (Your remittance should be sent either by bank draft, post office money order or personal check drawn in favor of the branch registration bureau noted at the bottom of this page. PLEASE DO NOT SEND EITHER CURRENCY OR POSTAGE STAMPS UNLESS YOU REGISTER YOUR LETTER).

LEGIBILITY MOST IMPORTANT:. . . TO AVOID CLERICAL ERRORS PRINT OR WRITE LEGIBLY. BE SURE AND STATE YOUR NAME "IN FULL" (SPECIFY MR., MRS. OR MISS) AND YOUR ADDRESS—POST OFFICE BOX NUMBER—STREET NUMBER (ALSO APARTMENT NUMBER IF ANY)—CITY—STATE—NATION. (In order that your invitation to our 30-day program may be correctly prepared and classified according to your "vocation" or "profession", please state the nature thereof when sending in your order.)

WHERE TO ADDRESS US: . . . Send all orders or other communications to your local branch registration bureau, using the name and bureau number shown at the bottom of this page.

PLEASE NOTE:. . . To protect our representatives against the numerous demands upon their time—which would invariably occur if an address at which people could call "in person " were specified—the International Registration Bureau has recommended that its branch registration bureaus, and its 4-4-8-3-4 Clubs and representatives, (whenever their local post office facilities enable them to do so), use a "post office box number" for their mailing address. In many instances this will, of course, not be possible: We therefore request that if an office or street address is noted at the bottom of this page (as our local representatives' address) that you extend the courtesy of writing for a definite appointment before calling in person. Your gracious compliance with this request will indeed be most deeply appreciated.

ALL ORDERS OR OTHER COMMUNICATIONS SHOULD BE SENT TO THE FOLLOWING ADDRESS:

THE NEW ERA BUREAU
2808 SCHOOL STREET
OAKLAND, CALIFORNIA

Branch # AA-12884 01 The International Registration Bureau

If an acknowledgment of your registration is not received from The International Registration Bureau within 30 days—it is important that you write to the manager of the above bureau for an investigation of the delay. (See Chapter XVII.)

www.ingramcontent.com/pod-product-compliance
Lightning Source LLC
Chambersburg PA
CBHW051545010526
44118CB00022B/2589